BBC
Bitesize

Bitesize
Pearson Edexcel GCSE (9-1)

FRENCH

REVISION WORKBOOK

Series Consultant:
Harry Smith

Author:
Liz Fotheringham

Contents

☑ Tick off each topic as you go.

🕑 Each bite-sized chunk has a **timer** to indicate how long it will take. Use them to plan your revision sessions.

Scan the **QR codes** to visit the BBC Bitesize website. They will link straight through to revision resources on that subject.

Scan the **audio QR codes** for the listening activities. You can also access these by visiting www.pearsonschools.co.uk/BBCBitesizeLinks.

Numbers

② Quick quiz

Draw lines to match up the pairs.

une trentaine	the twelfth
le douzième	75
vingt pour cent	250
deux-cent-cinquante	about thirty
soixante-quinze	20%

> Ordinal numbers in French, such as 2nd and 3rd, are formed by adding **–ième** to the number. Watch out for *1st*, which is **premier** and also has a feminine form **première**.

⑩ Writing out numbers — Grades 1–5

1. Traduis les phrases suivantes **en français**.

(a) There are three hundred and thirty-two rooms in the hotel. **[2 marks]**

🚩 Il y a trois-cent ....

(b) The restaurant is on the twentieth floor. **[2 marks]**

....

(c) A single room costs between seventy-six and eighty-eight euros a night. **[2 marks]**

....

(d) Two and a half thousand people work in hotels in this town. **[2 marks]**

....

> **Vocabulary** A–Z
> **Étage (m)** means *floor*.

> **Vocabulary** A–Z
> **Quatre-vingts** means *eighty*. Drop the **s** for 81–99.

> *Two and a half thousand* can be expressed as *two thousand, five hundred*.

⑦ Understanding tourism statistics — Grades 3–5

2. You hear this report about tourism statistics in France.

Listen to the recording and answer the following questions **in English**.

(a) How many foreign visitors came to France in 2015? **[1 mark]**

....

(b) What is the reason for the difference in visitor numbers in 2016 compared with 2015? **[1 mark]**

....

(c) How has this affected the number of Japanese visitors to Paris? **[1 mark]**

....

(d) How much do Chinese visitors spend on average when shopping in France? **[1 mark]**

....

> Read through the questions carefully and note down the words you need to listen out for.

> Dates can be tricky. If dates are given in the questions, try thinking of what they are in French *before* you listen to the recording. Then you can listen out for the dates, and the relevant answer, more easily.

Exam focus
Listen to the whole extract before reaching your conclusions. Use common sense and context to predict possible answers.

☑ **Made a start** ☑ **Feeling confident** ☑ **Exam ready**

1

The French alphabet

② Quick quiz

Draw lines to match up each letter with its phonetic pronunciation.

C	E	G	I	J	K	Q	Y

ee	euh	ee-grek	jhay	jhee	kah	kuh	say

⑤ Spelling out a name and email address · Grades 1–5

1. Read the following questions and answers. Listen to the recording of the questions and answers. Listen again and say your own answers to the questions.

(a) Quel est votre nom?

Charpentier

(b) Comment ça s'écrit?

C – H – A – R – P – E – N – T – I – E – R

(c) Et votre prénom?

Béatrice

(d) Comment est-ce que vous épelez ça?

B – E (accent aigu) – A – T – R – I – C – E

(e) Et votre adresse courriel?

B (tiret bas) C – H – A – R – P (arrobase) F – R (point) N – E – T

(B_Charp@fr.net)

> **Exam focus**
> Make sure you know how to spell your first name, surname and email address using the French alphabet. You might need to do this in the role play.

⑩ Understanding a telephone message · Grades 1–3

2. You are doing work experience in a hotel and have to take down phone messages.

Listen to the recording and complete the sentences by putting a cross ☒ in the correct box for each question.

Example: The reservation is for...

☐	**A** one person
☒	**B** two people
☐	**C** a family group
☐	**D** a school group

(a) The surname of the person making the reservation is...

☐	**A** Leclerk
☐	**B** Laclair
☐	**C** Leclerc
☐	**D** Lacroix

[1 mark]

(b) The person's first name is...

☐	**A** Jérard
☐	**B** Gérard
☐	**C** Gèrard
☐	**D** Jèrard

[1 mark]

(c) The person also spells out...

☐	**A** the town where he lives
☐	**B** the name of his house
☐	**C** the road he lives in
☐	**D** his email address

[1 mark]

> **Exam focus**
> Try to look at the questions and options before the audio plays, so that you know what you are listening out for.

☑ **Made a start**   ☑ **Feeling confident**   ☑ **Exam ready**

Dates

② Quick quiz

Translate the following phrases **into French**.

1. in February ....
2. on Thursday evenings ....
3. next Wednesday ....
4. last August ....

⑩ Cultural events: important dates Grades 1–5

1. While flying to France, you read about four different French events in the in-flight magazine.

> Au musée d'Orsay, il y aura une exposition des portraits de Cézanne du treize juin au vingt-quatre septembre.

> Pour fêter ses 500 ans, la ville du Havre, en Normandie, offre un programme de découverte de la ville sous le titre *Un Été au Havre*, du vingt-sept mai au cinq novembre.

> En 2016, le premier jour du festival international de cerf-volant de Dieppe était le dix septembre. Le prochain festival sera le huit septembre.

> La fête annuelle de la nature vous offre, du dix-sept au vingt-et-un mai, la possibilité de participer à des événements et des sorties pour mieux apprécier la nature.

Complete the gap in each sentence using a phrase from the box below. There are more words than gaps.

17th May	21st May	27th May	13th June
~~8th September~~	24th September	5th November	10th December

Example: The first day of the next international kite festival is ....8th September...........................

(a) The last day of the 500th anniversary festival in Le Havre is .... **[1 mark]**

(b) The opening date of the art exhibition is .... **[1 mark]**

(c) The last day of the Festival of Nature is .... **[1 mark]**

> If you don't know a word, use other words you do know to help you identify the right part of the text.

⑩ Understanding an audio guide Grades 4–9

2. You hear this information on an audio guide at the Centre Pompidou in Paris.
Listen to the recording and answer the following questions **in English**.

(a) What was announced in 1971? **[1 mark]**

....

(b) On what date did the centre open to the public? **[1 mark]**

....

(c) What needed to be undertaken because of the popularity of the building? **[1 mark]**

....

(d) In which year was there the highest number of visitors for a single exhibition? **[1 mark]**

....

Telling the time

② Quick quiz

Write the following times in **figures**.

1. Il est treize heures. ....

2. Il est midi et demi. ....

3. À huit heures moins le quart. ....

4. Il est onze heures cinquante-cinq. ....

5. Il est sept heures et quart. ....

6. À trois heures moins vingt. ....

⑩ Noting the times you need   Grades 1–5

1. During a school exchange to France, you hear the French teacher give some instructions about an excursion the following day.

   Listen to the recording and answer the following questions **in English**.

   Example: When does the coach depart from school? 7.30 am ....

   (a) How long will the coach stop for during the journey?   **[1 mark]**

   ....

   (b) At what time will the students be free to have lunch?   **[1 mark]**

   ....

   (c) Where must the students be at 3.30 pm and why?   **[2 marks]**

   ....

> **Exam focus**
> Read the questions carefully and listen to the whole extract before writing your answers. Make sure you listen out for the correct information and don't just write down the first thing you hear.

⑩ Arranging to meet up   Grades 1–5

2. Read the following messages that your French friend has shown you. Answer the following questions **in English**.

Laure:	Salut, on a rendez-vous à quelle heure demain? Dix-huit heures trente?
Paul:	Désolé, ça ne va plus parce que j'ai mon entraînement pour le match de rugby jusqu'à dix-neuf heures quinze. Ensuite, je rentre chez moi pour prendre une douche. Il vaut mieux une demi-heure plus tard.
Laure:	D'accord, mais ce sera trop tard pour aller au cinéma. C'est dommage, car je voulais voir ce film. Qu'est-ce qu'on va faire à la place?
Paul:	Est-ce que le bowling t'intéresse? Et puis, on pourrait aller au cinéma le week-end. Disons vingt heures quinze samedi soir?

(a) What time had Paul and Laure originally planned to meet tomorrow?   **[1 mark]**

....

(b) Why can't Paul keep to this time?   **[1 mark]**

....

(c) What time does he suggest they meet instead?   **[1 mark]**

....

(d) Why is Laure disappointed by the change of plan?   **[1 mark]**

....

(e) What is Paul suggesting for Saturday evening and at what time?   **[2 marks]**

....

> **Exam focus**
> Use the number of marks allocated to a question as a guide to how much information to include in your answer. You don't have to write in full sentences.

☑ **Made a start**   ☑ **Feeling confident**   ☑ **Exam ready**

Greetings

② Quick quiz

Should you use **tu** or **vous** in the following situations? Write **tu** or **vous** in the box.

1	talking to more than one person	
2	talking to an adult who is not a member of your family	
3	talking to someone younger than you	
4	talking to someone you do not know well	
5	talking to your grandmother	

⑩ A birthday message   Grades 4–6

1. Traduis le passage suivant **en français**.   **[12 marks]**

> Dear Christine,
>
> Happy birthday! I hope you are having a good day. What presents did you get? I am sorry, I can't come to your place for dinner with your family this evening, but I will see you next weekend and we will celebrate then. See you on Saturday.
>
> Bye
>
> Annette

Chère Christine, ...

Joyeux anniversaire! J'espère ....

....

....

....

....

....

....

Annette ....

Exam focus

Look at the context to decide whether you should use **tu** or **vous**. Then make sure you are consistent with your verb endings and agreement of possessives **ton / ta / tes** or **votre / vos**.

Use the verb **passer** (*to spend time*) to translate *having* (*a good day*).

Use **chez** to talk about someone's home.

As Annette is a girl, the adjective *sorry* must agree.

Use the immediate future (*going to* – **aller** + infinitive) to translate *I will…* and *we will…* .

⑩ Understanding language for specific situations   Grades 4–5

2. While in France you overhear several conversations. Who is speaking to whom? Listen to the recording and put a cross ☒ in each one of the **three** correct boxes.   **[3 marks]**

Example	Teacher to a class of pupils	☒
A	Cinema attendant to a group of people	☐
B	Grandmother to grandson	☐
C	Journalist to people in the street	☐
D	Father to child	☐
E	Pilot to passengers on board an aircraft	☐
F	Shop assistant to someone buying glasses	☐
G	Policeman to a crowd of people	☐

Exam focus

Before you listen, try to predict what words you might hear.

✓ **Made a start**   ✓ **Feeling confident**   ✓ **Exam ready**   5

Opinions

② Quick quiz

Translate the following phrases **into English**.

1. en revanche ....
2. pourtant ....
3. à mon avis..........................
4. ça m'énerve........................
5. ça me plaît ....

⑩ Give your opinions — Grades 1–9

1. You should be able to give your opinions in your speaking exam. Practise by answering these questions aloud. Use this space to make some notes to help you.

(a) Que penses-tu du football?

▸ J'adore / Je n'aime pas du tout le football parce que
....
....

Exam focus

Vary your responses. Use a different phrase to introduce your answer each time.

(b) Comment tu trouves la musique classique?

▸ À mon avis,
....
....

Always give a reason for your answer, using conjunctions such as **parce que** or **car**.

(c) Quels sont les avantages d'Internet?
....
....
....

Aiming higher

Develop and extend your answer in the general conversation by giving the opposite viewpoint, or the opinion of your family or friends as well.

⑩ A film review — Grades 4–9

2. Read the following email from your French friend, Fabien.

Which **three** statements are **true**? **[3 marks]**

Put a cross ☒ in each one of the **three** correct boxes.

Example	Fabien saw the film last Saturday.	☒
A	All the reviews of the film have been critical.	☐
B	Fabien's friends were enthusiastic about the film.	☐
C	Fabien has the same opinion of the film as his friends.	☐
D	Fabien doesn't have anything good to say about the film.	☐
E	Fabien enjoyed the film.	☐
F	Fabien's girlfriend thought the film was good, except for the ending.	☐
G	Fabien likes other films that Omar Sy has starred in.	☐

✉ **Sujet:** le cinéma

Samedi dernier, je suis allé voir un film avec Omar Sy dans le rôle principal. Selon les critiques, c'est un film très réussi et tous mes copains m'ont dit qu'il fallait absolument aller le voir. Cependant, j'ai été vraiment déçu car l'histoire était débile et je n'ai pas aimé le personnage de Sy. En fait, je n'ai rien aimé du film. Par contre, ma petite amie, qui a vu le film avec moi, a trouvé l'histoire émouvante et la fin super bien. Comme moi, elle est fan de Sy et j'ai trouvé ses autres films très bons, surtout *Intouchables*.

Exam focus

Read the text carefully. Pay attention to whose opinions are talked about.

✓ **Made a start**   ✓ **Feeling confident**   ✓ **Exam ready**

Asking questions

⏱ ② Quick quiz

Draw lines to match up the questions and answers.

Est-ce qu'il y a un supermarché près d'ici?	Avec ma famille.
Quand est-ce que le film commence?	Sur la table.
Avec qui vas-tu en France?	Oui, en face du parking.
Pourquoi as-tu choisi ce livre?	Le printemps.
Quelle saison est-ce que tu préfères?	À dix-neuf heures trente.
Où est-ce que tu as mis le livre?	Parce qu'il est intéressant.

⏱ ⑩ Some questions to ask   Grades 1–5

1. Traduis les questions suivantes **en français**.

(a) How do you find French food? (to a group of friends)

🚩 Comment est-ce que ....

(b) What do you want to do this evening? (to your brother)

🚩 Qu'est-ce que ....

(c) Have you got some water? (to a shopkeeper)

🚩 Avez- ....

(d) What kind of music do you like? (to your French pen pal)

🚩 Quel genre ....

(e) Are there any toilets near here?

🚩 Est-ce qu'il y a ....

(f) Where can we buy a sandwich?

🚩 Où est-ce ....

Vocabulary 📖 A–Z
Use **on** to translate *we* in question 1f.

Exam focus 📌
Be aware of the context and use **tu** or **vous** where appropriate.

⏱ ⑩ Asking questions in role play   Grades 1–9

2. Look at the following question prompts from a role play. What questions could you ask? Write some possible questions **in French**.

(a) | • ? Recommandation – activité | Context: tourist office ....

(b) | • ? Exercice | Context: talking to a friend ....

(c) | • ? Heure d'ouverture | Context: planning a visit to a museum ....

(d) | • ? Bien manger – où | Context: arranging to go out ....

(e) | • ? Action – protection de l'environnement | ....

(f) | • ? Concert – opinion | Context: talking to a friend ....

✓ **Made a start**   ✓ **Feeling confident**   ✓ **Exam ready**   7

Describing people

---

② Quick quiz

Translate the following sentences **into French**.

1. I am sixteen years old. ....

2. I was born in 2002. ....

3. I am slim and of medium height. ....

4. I wear glasses. ....

---

⑩ Personality traits   Grades 1–5

1. Félix, a student at a French school, is talking about himself. What does he say?

Listen to the recording and complete these statements by putting a cross ☒ in the correct box for each question.

Example: Félix is looking for a pen pal who speaks...

☐	**A**	Italian
☐	**B**	German
☐	**C**	Spanish
☒	**D**	English

> Listen to the whole extract first. Be wary of words that you hear in the extract and see in the possible answers. Negation and adjectives can easily give a sentence the opposite meaning.

> Don't worry if you don't understand every word. Concentrate on the words you need to understand to answer questions. You may need to infer meaning from what is said and the context of the sentence.

(a) When interacting with others, Félix describes his personality as...

☐	**A**	intelligent
☐	**B**	outgoing
☐	**C**	shy
☐	**D**	thoughtful

[1 mark]

(b) Félix's attitude to trying new food is...

☐	**A**	adventurous
☐	**B**	enthusiastic
☐	**C**	cautious
☐	**D**	inquisitive

[1 mark]

---

⑩ Comparing two sisters   Grades 3–5

2. You are going to France next week and have received the following email from a member of your host family.

Put a cross ☒ in the correct box.

Example: Élise is...

☐	**A**	thanking you for having her to stay
☐	**B**	looking forward to visiting you
☒	**C**	looking forward to your visit
☐	**D**	thanking you for your visit

(a) Élise's sister is...

☐	**A**	14
☐	**B**	16
☐	**C**	18
☐	**D**	22

[1 mark]

(b) Élise says she and her mother...

☐	**A**	have similar personalities
☐	**B**	have similar hair
☐	**C**	are the same size
☐	**D**	have similar attitudes

[1 mark]

(c) Élise says she is...

☐	**A**	more tense than her sister
☐	**B**	as relaxed as her mother
☐	**C**	less laid back than her mother
☐	**D**	more relaxed than her mother

[1 mark]

✉ Sujet: Bonjour!

Salut, je m'appelle Élise. Je suis ravie que tu loges chez nous. Tu me vois sur la photo ci-jointe. J'ai l'air d'avoir vingt-deux ans, mais en fait, je n'ai que seize ans. Par contre, ma sœur Hélène, qui a deux ans de plus que moi, a l'air plus jeune! On dit que je ressemble à ma mère, car nous avons toutes les deux les cheveux longs et bruns. Cependant, je dirais que ma personnalité est plutôt comme celle d'Hélène, car ma mère est parfois un peu tendue, tandis qu'Hélène et moi sommes très décontractées et aimons rire des mêmes choses.

Élise

✓ **Made a start**   ✓ **Feeling confident**   ✓ **Exam ready**

Family

Translate the following sentences **into English**.

1. Mon frère aîné est célibataire.

....

2. J'ai une sœur cadette.

....

3. Les enfants de mon beau-père sont jumeaux.

....

4. Mon demi-frère est plus jeune que moi.

....

⑩ Describing someone's family life — Grades 1–5

1. Traduis le passage suivant **en français**. **[12 marks]**

> I am an only daughter. There are four of us in the house because my grandmother lives with us. I think it's great because she is kind and we like to watch television together. At the weekend, we always go for a walk. Yesterday, we went to a restaurant to celebrate my stepfather's birthday.

My must agree with *grandmother*.

Just use the definite article to translate *at the* (weekend). You don't need an extra word for *at*.

Vocabulary A–Z
Use **à** to translate *in* (the house).

Vocabulary A–Z
Use **faire une promenade** to translate *go for a walk*.

Vocabulary A–Z
Translate *my stepfather's birthday* by saying *the birthday of my stepfather* (**beau-père (m)**).

Je suis fille unique ....

....

....

⑩ Family relationships — Grades 4–9

2. You hear two listeners speaking about their experience of large families on a radio phone-in programme.

Listen to the recording and answer the following questions **in English**.

(a) What does Fabien feel about being a member of a large family? **[1 mark]**

....

(b) What does he say about the relationship between siblings in his family? **[2 marks]**

....

....

(c) At what time of day does Laure like being a member of a large family? **[1 mark]**

....

(d) In what way does she say it is difficult to get some privacy? **[1 mark]**

....

☑ **Made a start**   ☑ **Feeling confident**   ☑ **Exam ready**

Friends and relationships

2 Quick quiz

Are the following descriptions of people positive, negative or both? Write **P**, **N** or **P / N** in the box.

1	Il est toujours très paresseux et ne fait absolument rien pour aider à la maison.	
2	Parfois, ma mère est de mauvaise humeur, mais elle peut aussi être très rigolote.	
3	Ma copine est très sympa et elle est toujours là pour moi.	
4	Ma petite sœur est très égoïste parce que mes parents la gâtent trop.	
5	Il est énergique et travailleur.	

10 Friends and parents   Grades 1–9

1. You could be asked questions about relationships in your speaking exam. Practise by answering these questions aloud. Use this space to make some notes to help you.

   (a) À propos de quoi est-ce que tu te disputes avec tes amis?

   ☞ Normalement, on ne se dispute pas, mais parfois

   ....

   ....

   (b) Comment sont les rapports entre toi et les autres élèves de ta classe?

   ☞ Je m'entends bien avec ...., surtout ....,

   mais ....

   (c) Quand est-ce que tu te disputes avec tes parents?

   ☞ Quand je me dispute avec mes parents, c'est normalement au sujet

   de ....

> **(a)** means *What do you argue about with your friends?* Use frequency adverbs such as **normalement** (*normally*), **quelquefois** (*sometimes*), **de temps en temps** (*from time to time*) or a negative, **ne ... jamais** (*never*), to give an extended answer.

> You could say what you argue about, how you feel or what happens afterwards.

> **Exam focus**
> Repeating part of the question in your answer gives you time to think about how you will respond to the question.

15 Writing about relationships   Grades 4–6

2. Ton ami(e) français(e) t'a envoyé un mail. Il / Elle te pose des questions au sujet de ta famille et de tes amis.
   Écris une réponse. Tu **dois** faire référence aux points suivants:

   - les rapports familiaux chez toi
   - ton opinion au sujet des disputes
   - la résolution d'une dispute récente
   - ton ami(e) idéal(e).

   Écris 80–90 mots environ **en français**.   **[20 marks]**

   ....

   ....

   ....

   ....

   ....

   ....

   ....

Made a start   Feeling confident   Exam ready

When I was younger

⏱ 5 Quick quiz

Translate the following phrases **into French**.

1. I used to play ....

2. I didn't use to like ....

3. I was quite shy ....

4. I wanted to be ....

5. He didn't have many friends ....

....

⏱ 10 A footballer's early years   Grades 4–7 🎧

1. A footballer, Patrice Levry, is talking on the radio about his early life.

Listen to the recording and complete these statements by putting a cross ☒ in the correct box for each question.

Example: Patrice comes from...

☐	**A**	Europe
☐	**B**	Asia
☐	**C**	America
☒	**D**	Africa

(a) In Abidjan he used to play football...

☐	**A**	for a club
☐	**B**	at school
☐	**C**	in the street
☐	**D**	in a park

[1 mark]

(b) He used to play without...

☐	**A**	shin pads
☐	**B**	boots
☐	**C**	club shorts
☐	**D**	a club jersey

[1 mark]

(c) His parents were...

☐	**A**	hard-working
☐	**B**	unemployed
☐	**C**	quite rich
☐	**D**	quite poor

[1 mark]

(d) His skills were first recognised by...

☐	**A**	his parents
☐	**B**	his uncle
☐	**C**	a club in France
☐	**D**	a professional trainer

[1 mark]

(e) His career began in earnest...

☐	**A**	at a youth club
☐	**B**	at the age of ten
☐	**C**	at the age of seven
☐	**D**	on the Ivory Coast

[1 mark]

Exam focus
Use the reading time in the exam before the recording is played to jot down words that you need to listen out for.

⏱ 15 In my youth   Grades 5–9 ✏️

2. Traduis le passage suivant **en français**.   **[12 marks]**

When I was younger my parents had a farm and I used to help them with the animals at the weekend. In the mornings I had to get up early in order to get to school on time. I couldn't spend time with my friends after school because I had to catch the bus home.

....

....

....

....

....

Exam focus
Remember to check your work carefully and make sure you haven't missed anything out.

✓ **Made a start**   ✓ **Feeling confident**   ✓ **Exam ready**

Food

② Quick quiz

For each of the following categories of food and drink items, circle the one that does **not** belong.

1. Boissons:	thé	sucre	café	lait	eau
2. Légumes:	haricots verts	pommes de terre	chou	fraise	épinards
3. Féculents:	beurre	pain	riz	céréales	farine
4. Produits laitiers:	fromage	œufs	beurre	lait	yaourt

⑩ Food trends in France   Grades 4–9

1. You hear this report about food preferences in France.
Listen to the recording and put a cross ☒ in the correct box for each question.

Example: What does the report say about *bœuf bourgignon*?

☐	**A**	It is the most popular dish among the French.
☒	**B**	It is less popular than it used to be.
☐	**C**	It is more popular than a dish from the south-west of France.
☐	**D**	It is more popular than a cheese dish.

(a) What does the report say is a common feature of food preferences in France?

☐	**A**	Choucroute is more popular than pancakes.
☐	**B**	Food from the east and west of France is very popular.
☐	**C**	The French prefer their local specialities.
☐	**D**	Pancakes are the most popular food.

[1 mark]

(b) What is a surprising statistic about French food habits?

☐	**A**	Only a small proportion of French people eat the recommended amount of fruit and vegetables.
☐	**B**	Onions are not very popular.
☐	**C**	They eat more fruit and vegetables than any other type of food.
☐	**D**	They eat more vegetables than meat.

[1 mark]

Exam focus

Think about how phrases might be expressed in a different way from what is given in the answer.

You may hear all the food items mentioned, but listen carefully for specific details, such as how popular a particular item is and where.

⑩ Healthy eating   Grades 4–9

2. Lis ces commentaires sur un forum.

Céline

J'essaie de maigrir, alors j'évite les féculents autant que possible. C'est difficile quand mes copines m'offrent toujours des sucreries, mais j'y arrive! Je dirais que je mange sainement car je prends au moins six portions de fruits et de légumes chaque jour, alors une portion de plus que ce qui est recommandé. Je les achète normalement au supermarché parce que je pense qu'on y vend des produits de bonne qualité.

Henri

Je sais que les cochonneries sont mauvaises pour la santé, mais elles sont vraiment délicieuses et je ne peux pas y résister. Quant aux fruits et légumes, normalement, je mange la quantité recommandée chaque jour, mais parfois je ne peux pas aller au marché où les produits sont bon marché, alors je n'en ai pas assez. À mon avis, les produits du supermarché sont moins frais que ceux du marché.

C'est quelle personne? Choisis entre: **Céline** et **Henri**. Chacun des noms peut être utilisé plusieurs fois.

Exemple: ....Henri........... achète des produits de qualité qui ne sont pas chers.

(a) .... n'achète pas de fruits et légumes au supermarché.   **[1 mark]**

(b) .... suit actuellement un régime.   **[1 mark]**

(c) .... ne mange pas d'aliments qui ne sont pas bons pour la santé.   **[1 mark]**

(d) .... mange cinq portions de fruits et de légumes chaque jour.   **[1 mark]**

   ☑ **Made a start**   ☑ **Feeling confident**   ☑ **Exam ready**

Meals

② Quick quiz

Translate the following sentences **into French**.

1. I have breakfast at 7.30am.

....

2. I had soup for lunch.

....

3. I drink tea at tea time.

....

4. We eat fish for dinner.

....

⑩ Mealtimes are changing   Grades 4–9

1. Lis ce rapport sur les habitudes alimentaires des Français.

> Selon une étude récente, les habitudes alimentaires des Français sont en train de changer. La tradition de s'asseoir à table dans la salle à manger pour prendre les repas n'est plus la norme, car seulement 42% des gens sondés le font. 26% mangent quand même toujours à table mais dans la cuisine. Un Français sur trois mange dans une autre pièce de la maison. Parmi eux, 11% mangent devant la télévision, 8% utilisent la table basse du salon et 5% mangent devant l'ordinateur.
>
> L'étude a aussi révélé que les plats à emporter sont devenus plus populaires. 25% des gens sondés mangent des plats livrés à domicile quand ils veulent regarder un film ou un match. Parmi les jeunes, ce chiffre monte à 54%.

Mets une croix ☒ dans les **trois** cases correctes.   **[3 marks]**

Exemple	Traditionnellement, les Français mangent dans la salle à manger.	☒
A	La majorité des Français prennent leurs repas assis à table.	☐
B	La façon dont les Français prennent leurs repas reste toujours la même.	☐
C	Moins de gens mangent dans la cuisine que dans la salle à manger.	☐
D	Un tiers des Français mangent assis à table.	☐
E	Manger pendant qu'on travaille sur l'ordinateur est plus fréquent que manger devant la télévision.	☐
F	Les Français mangent de moins en moins de plats cuisinés.	☐
G	Plus de la moitié des jeunes Français mangent à la maison des plats qu'ils n'ont pas préparés.	☐

Exam focus

Read the text and the statements carefully before answering. Eliminate any you know are false first.

Look carefully at the figures quoted in the text.

Vocabulary   A–Z

Moins de gens (mpl) means *fewer people*. **Livrés** means *delivered*.

⑩ Talking about food and meals   Grades 1–9

2. You could be asked about meals in your speaking exam. Practise by answering the following questions aloud. Use this space to make some notes to help you.

(a) Est-ce qu'il est important de manger les repas en famille, à ton avis?

....

(b) Quand est-ce qu'on mange un repas spécial chez toi?

....

....

(c) Comment tu trouves les plats épicés?

....

....

Aiming higher

Extend your answers where possible by using a different tense to the first part of your answer (e.g. you could describe a recent special family meal or a recent spicy meal).

✓ Made a start	✓ Feeling confident	✓ Exam ready	**13**

Shopping

② Quick quiz

Draw lines to match up the French and English sentences.

French	English
Je veux me faire rembourser.	I would like to try on this jumper.
Je voudrais échanger ce pull.	I haven't got my receipt any more.
Je n'ai plus mon ticket de caisse.	I want a refund.
Je voudrais essayer ce pull.	I don't want to spend too much money.
Je ne veux pas dépenser trop d'argent.	I would like to exchange this jumper.

⑩ Buying a present — Grades 4–9

1. You could be given a role play about shopping in your speaking exam. Practise speaking aloud, using the following prompts. Use this space to make some notes to help you.

Instructions to candidates: You are in a clothes shop in France. The teacher will play the role of the salesperson and will speak first. You must address the salesperson as *vous*. **[10 marks]**

Vous êtes dans une boutique de vêtements. Vous parlez avec le vendeur / la vendeuse.

1. Vêtement désiré + couleur

   Je cherche ....

   For the first point, you must say what item of clothing you want to buy (*scarf* – **une écharpe**, *hat* – **un chapeau**, etc.) and the colour.

2. Ce magasin – raison

   Les vêtements ....

   For the second point, give a reason for choosing this shop.

3. ! (*Qu'est-ce que vous avez déjà acheté en France?*)

   ....

   You must use the perfect tense to answer the unprepared question!

4. ? Prix

   C'est ....

   Ask how much the item costs for the fourth point.

5. ? Taille

   Est-ce que vous avez ....

   Ask about sizes for the fifth point.

⑩ Advantages and disadvantages of online shopping — Grades 4–9

2. Read these comments about online shopping.

> Je crois qu'on peut gaspiller beaucoup de temps en ligne à chercher le meilleur prix ou un article particulier si on ne sait pas exactement ce qu'on cherche. C'est vrai qu'on peut acheter des vêtements pas chers en ligne, mais souvent, il vaut mieux acheter des articles en promotion ou en soldes en magasin car on peut voir exactement ce qu'on achète et on peut s'assurer que la couleur et la taille nous plaisent.
> *Yasmine*

Answer the following questions **in English**.

(a) What does Yasmine think is one big disadvantage of shopping online? **[1 mark]**

....

(b) Name **two** reasons she often feels it is better to buy clothes from shops. **[2 marks]**

....

Social media

② Quick quiz

Fill in the gaps with a suitable word from the box below.

| amis | contact | en ligne | demi-heure | partager | poster | réfléchir | réseaux sociaux | tchatté |

Les **(1)** .... me permettent de rester en **(2)** .... avec mes

(3) .... J'aime bien **(4)** .... mes photos avec eux. Hier,

j'ai mis des photos **(5)** .... et j'ai **(6)** .... pendant une

(7) .... À mon avis, il faut **(8)** .... avant de

(9) .... un commentaire.

⑩ One teenager's use of social media — Grades 4–9

1. Traduis le passage suivant **en français**. **[12 marks]**

> I love social networks and spend several hours a day chatting to friends and uploading photos. My parents would probably say that I am addicted to them, but I don't agree with them. I am never distracted in class and I always do my homework. Yesterday, I organised an evening with my friends on a social network.

J'adore les réseaux sociaux ....

....

....

....

....

....

....

Vocabulary A–Z
Use **passer** for *to spend (time)*.

Vocabulary A–Z
Use the conditional tense **diraient** for *would say*.

Remember that **ne ... jamais** (*never*) goes either side of the verb.

Use the pronoun **y** in front of the verb to translate *them* in the phrase *addicted to them*.

Vocabulary A–Z
Use **une soirée avec mes amis** to say *an evening with my friends*.

⑩ Opinions about social media — Grades 1–5

2. You hear two people talking about social media for a street survey.

Listen to the recording and answer the following questions **in English**.

(a) How does Chloé like to use social media? **[1 mark]**

....

(b) What does she see as a problem? **[1 mark]**

....

(c) What is a big advantage of social media according to Léo? **[1 mark]**

....

(d) What reason does he give for avoiding social networks? **[1 mark]**

....

☑ **Made a start**   ☑ **Feeling confident**   ☑ **Exam ready**

Mobile technology

② Quick quiz

Translate the following **into French**.

1. to download music ....

2. to call my friends ....

3. to get information ....

4. to send texts ....

⑩ Mobile phones in the classroom   Grades 4–9

1. While in France, you hear a French radio show about a teacher and the use of mobile phones in his classroom. Listen to the recording and answer the following questions **in English**.

(a) What rules does Philippe Leroy have in his classroom? Give **two** details.   **[2 marks]**

🚩 Students are not allowed to use social media and
....

(b) Why does he rarely have problems with students breaking his rules? Give **two** details.   **[2 marks]**

....

(c) How do his students use their mobile phones to help them learn? Give **two** examples.   **[2 marks]**

....

(d) According to his colleagues, how have mobile phones had a positive effect and why?   **[2 marks]**

....

⑩ Using the internet   Grades 4–9

2. Lis ces commentaires dans un forum sur l'utilisation d'Internet.

> Je trouve ça utile quand je veux faire des achats en ligne. Cependant, j'ai peur que mes données personnelles soient volées, et je ne suis pas toujours très prudente en ligne.
> **Christelle**

> Je sais qu'on peut utiliser Internet pour télécharger de la musique et des films, mais je ne le fais jamais. Pour moi, le plus grand avantage est de pouvoir s'informer sur ce qui se passe dans le monde.
> **Didier**

> J'aime bien utiliser Internet, surtout pour faire des recherches pour mes projets scolaires et pour télécharger des films ou émissions de télé.
> **Maya**

> Ce qui m'inquiète, ce sont les individus qui entrent en contact avec des jeunes en ligne avec l'intention de les exploiter.
> **Laurent**

C'est quelle personne? Choisis entre: **Maya**, **Christelle**, **Didier** et **Laurent**.

Chacun des noms peut être utilisé plusieurs fois.

Exemple: ...Maya........... regarde la télé en ligne.

(a) .... achète des produits en ligne.   **[1 mark]**

(b) .... utilise Internet pour s'informer des actualités.   **[1 mark]**

(c) .... ne regarde pas de films sur Internet.   **[1 mark]**

(d) Internet peut être dangereux pour les mineurs selon ....   **[1 mark]**

(e) .... trouve sur Internet des informations utiles pour faire ses devoirs.   **[1 mark]**

☑ **Made a start**   ☑ **Feeling confident**   ☑ **Exam ready**

French customs

BBC

② Quick quiz

Draw lines to match up the pairs.

la messe	Christmas Eve dinner
la fête	church
le cadeau	Mass
le réveillon	party
l'église	gift

⑩ A survey on Christmas customs — Grades 1–5

1. Lis ces résultats d'un sondage sur les Français et Noël.

Une enquête récente sur les fêtes de fin d'année a révélé que:

- 71% des Français préfèrent la fête de Noël au jour de l'An
- pour la plupart des gens (80%), c'est une fête familiale
- 29% mangent du saumon au réveillon et 54% de la bûche. Le champagne reste populaire (62%).
- pour décorer les maisons, on installe le sapin dans 67% des foyers et on sort les décorations (63%). La crèche est toujours une tradition importante pour certains Français (41%), surtout dans le sud. Cependant, seulement 18% vont à la messe de minuit.
- plus de la moitié des gens sondés (56%) ouvrent les cadeaux la veille du 25 décembre, le soir.

Vocabulary A–Z
Fête familiale (f) means *family celebration*.

Vocabulary A–Z
Saumon (m) means *salmon*.

Vocabulary A–Z
The French for *Christmas tree* is **sapin de Noël (m)**.

Complète chaque phrase en utilisant un mot de la case. Il y a des mots que tu n'utiliseras pas.

un arbre	beaucoup	une crèche	dinde	54%	moins
peu	poisson	~~proches~~	plus	29%	voisins

Exemple: Les Français préfèrent passer Noël avec leurs .....proches.......

(a) Comme fête, Noël est .... populaire que le jour de l'an.   **[1 mark]**

(b) 67% des familles apportent .... dans leur maison.   **[1 mark]**

(c) Pour le repas de Noël .... mangent du poisson.   **[1 mark]**

(d) .... de Français vont à l'église à Noël.   **[1 mark]**

⑩ All Saints' Day — Grades 4–9

2. Écoute ce reportage à la radio sur la fête de la Toussaint.

Mets une croix ☒ dans les **deux** cases correctes.   **[2 marks]**

Exemple	La fête des Morts est célébrée au Mexique ainsi qu'en France.	☒
A	En France, la fête des Morts a lieu le deux novembre.	☐
B	La plupart des gens ne travaillent pas le jour de la Toussaint.	☐
C	Le jour de la Toussaint, les Français se souviennent des morts de la Première Guerre mondiale.	☐
D	Aujourd'hui, les Français vont au cimetière pour allumer une bougie.	☐
E	Ils laissent des fleurs au cimetière en souvenir des gens décédés de leurs familles.	☐
F	Les chrysanthèmes n'ont aucune signification.	☐

✓ **Made a start**   ✓ **Feeling confident**   ✓ **Exam ready**

French festivals

② Quick quiz

Translate the following words **into English**.

1. un défilé ....

2. un feu d'artifice ....

3. Pâques ....

4. un jour férié ....

⑩ Festivals and celebrations   Grades 4–9

1. Make some notes for the picture-based task below and practise saying your answers aloud.   **[24 marks]**

> Regarde la photo et prépare des réponses sur les points suivants:
>
> - la description de la photo
> - ton opinion sur l'importance des fêtes
> - une expérience récente d'une fête traditionnelle en France
> - comment tu fêteras Noël ou Pâques
> - ! *(Comment est-ce qu'on célèbre les fêtes dans ta région?)*

🚩 Sur la photo, on voit beaucoup de gens dans la rue qui ....

....

🚩 À mon avis, les fêtes sont importantes parce que ....

....

🚩 Oui, je suis allé(e) / Non, je ne suis jamais allé(e) à une fête traditionnelle

en France, mais ....

....

🚩 Je fêterai Noël ....

....

> Give a reason for the importance of festivals, such as for people *to enjoy themselves* (**s'amuser**).

> If you have never been to a French festival, you could talk about one you would like to experience, for example *Bastille day* (**La Fête nationale**) or *Christmas* (**Noël (m)**) and *New Year* (**Le Nouvel An**) in France.

⑩ Celebrating Candlemas   Grades 4–9

2. Écoute ce podcast. Complète les phrases en choisissant un mot ou des mots dans la case. Il y a des mots que tu n'utiliseras pas.

> **La Chandeleur** (*Candlemas*) is a Christian holiday in February.

assombries	chrétiens	décembre	~~février~~	garder
illuminées	mois	ranger	Romains	saison

Exemple: La Chandeleur a lieu au mois de *février* ....

(a) C'est une fête célébrée par les ....   **[1 mark]**

(b) Traditionnellement on doit .... la crèche jusqu'à cette date.   **[1 mark]**

(c) Le soir les maisons sont ....   **[1 mark]**

(d) Les crêpes symbolisent le changement de ....   **[1 mark]**

✓ **Made a start**   ✓ **Feeling confident**   ✓ **Exam ready**

Reading

Quick quiz ⏱5

Translate the following sentences **into French**.

1. Normally I read in the evening.

....

2. I like downloading romantic novels.

....

Opinions about reading ⏱10 — Grades 4–7 👓

1. Read the comments.

> **Pour vous, est-ce que la lecture est importante?**
>
> **Élodie:** Quand j'étais petite je trouvais la lecture difficile et je ne lisais que des livres illustrés. Heureusement, un professeur m'a beaucoup encouragée et maintenant j'adore lire toutes sortes de livres, surtout les romans historiques et classiques. Je pense même écrire un roman un jour.
>
> **Hugo:** Au collège mon professeur m'a forcé à lire des livres, surtout des romans classiques qui ne m'intéressaient pas du tout. Maintenant je lis, bien sûr, mais ce sont plutôt les blogs et les articles en ligne que je préfère. De cette façon je me tiens au courant.
>
> **Félix:** Depuis mon enfance les livres jouent un rôle énorme dans ma vie. Mes parents m'ont encouragé à lire en lisant beaucoup eux-mêmes et en allant à la bibliothèque quand j'étais tout petit. Maintenant la lecture est un moyen d'échapper au stress de la vie quotidienne.

Answer the questions **in English**. You do not need to write in full sentences.

(a) Who finds that reading is a form of relaxation? **[1 mark]**

📍 Félix

....

(b) Who had a bad experience with reading at school? **[1 mark]**

....

(c) To whom does Félix attribute his love of reading? **[1 mark]**

....

(d) What is Hugo's main purpose for reading now? **[1 mark]**

....

(e) What might Élodie like to do in the future? **[1 mark]**

....

Exam focus 📌
Read through all the texts completely before making your choices.

Talking about your reading habits ⏱10 — Grades 1–9 💬

2. You could be asked about reading in your speaking exam. Practise by answering these questions aloud. Use this space to make some notes to help you.

(a) Qu'est-ce que tu aimes lire?

....

(b) Que penses-tu des livres électroniques?

....

(c) Est-ce que tes habitudes de lecture ont changé depuis ton enfance?

....

(d) Parle-moi d'un livre que tu as lu récemment.

....

Give reasons for your opinions, such as 'it is practical when you travel' for the question about digital books.

Exam focus 📌
Remember that what you say doesn't need to be strictly true. Use words and phrases that you know, but be prepared to answer a follow-up question for anything you say.

Music

② Quick quiz

Translate the following **into French**.

> Use **jouer + de** to talk about what instrument you play.

1. I've been playing the piano for two years.

....

2. I used to play the guitar.

....

3. When I was younger, I liked classical music.

....

4. My favourite genre of music is rock.

....

⑩ Musical tastes

Grades 4–9

1. Translate this passage **into English**.

[7 marks]

> Quand j'étais jeune, je ne comprenais pas pourquoi ma grand-mère adorait la musique classique. Cependant, je joue du violon dans un orchestre depuis trois ans et j'ai appris à apprécier ce genre de musique. En ce moment, nous avons des répétitions pour un concert qui aura lieu à la fin du mois.

When I was young, ...

....

....

....

....

....

....

Exam focus

Read the text carefully before you start to translate. Think about the tense of the verb you are translating.

> Use the context to translate **répétition (f)** accurately. *Rehearsal* is a more appropriate translation than *repetition*.

Vocabulary

A–Z

Present tense + **depuis** + *length of time* is translated as *have been (do)ing for (length of time)*.

> **Aura lieu** is the future tense of **avoir lieu**, meaning *to take place*.

⑩ Opinions about music

Grades 4–9

2. A radio listener is giving her opinion about Stromae's new album. What does she say?

Listen to the recording and complete the sentences by putting a cross ☒ in the correct box for each question.

(a) The speaker's opinion of Stromae's new album is...

☐	**A**	totally negative
☐	**B**	mainly negative
☐	**C**	totally positive
☐	**D**	mainly positive

[1 mark]

(b) She says the music is...

☐	**A**	memorable
☐	**B**	catchy
☐	**C**	forgettable
☐	**D**	dull

[1 mark]

☑ **Made a start**   ☑ **Feeling confident**   ☑ **Exam ready**

Sport

⏱ ② Quick quiz

For each of the following categories of sports, circle the one that does **not** belong.

1. Un sport d'équipe:	le basket	le rugby	le surf	le cricket
2. Un sport individuel:	le volleyball	l'escrime	l'athlétisme	le golf
3. Un sport nautique:	la voile	l'équitation	la planche à voile	le ski nautique
4. Un sport d'hiver:	le patinage	le snowboarding	l'escalade	le ski

⏱ ⑩ Interview with a sportsman — Grades 4–9 🎧

1. You hear an interview with Noah, a French sportsman.

Listen to the interview and put a cross ☒ in the correct box for each question.

Example: What did Noah do regularly in the past?

☒	**A** played football
☐	**B** went to football matches
☐	**C** swam
☐	**D** played tennis

(a) What does Noah like about his current sport?

☐	**A** It's good for developing communication skills.
☐	**B** He doesn't have to rely on others for success.
☐	**C** It helps contribute to the success of the team.
☐	**D** The social aspect.

[1 mark]

> Listen to the whole extract before answering. Listen out for important little words like **mais** (*but*), **cependant** (*however*) and **pourtant** (*however*) that can change the meaning.

(b) What does he see as the main benefit of sport generally?

☐	**A** keeping physically active
☐	**B** a reduction in cases of obesity
☐	**C** the development of fewer cases of diabetes
☐	**D** greater mental agility

[1 mark]

> Listen out for tenses used in the first extract. *Regularly* can be expressed as *a number of times per week*. The French for *to swim* is **nager**, and *swimming* is **la natation**.

(c) What does he think trainers should **not** focus on?

☐	**A** the effort put in by the sportsmen and women
☐	**B** the participation by players
☐	**C** points, results and the competition
☐	**D** the best athletes

[1 mark]

> The French for words like *communication*, *success* and *contribute* are cognates but are pronounced differently in English. Sound them out in your head before listening to the extract.

⏱ ⑮ Your sporting activities — Grades 4–6 ✏

2. Ton ami(e) français(e) veut savoir ce que tu penses du sport.

Écris un mail à ton ami(e) français(e). Tu **dois** faire référence aux points suivants:

- les sports que tu fais à l'école
- ta participation à un événement sportif récent
- pourquoi le sport est important
- une activité sportive que tu vas faire dans l'avenir.

Écris 80–90 mots environ **en français**. **[20 marks]**

....

....

....

....

....

Cinema

② Quick quiz

Translate the following **into English**.

1. un écran ....

2. effrayant ....

3. se dérouler ....

4. la vedette ....

⑩ Film preferences and opinions

Grades 1–9

1. Write down some possible answers to the following questions and practise saying them aloud.

   (a) Préfères-tu regarder un film à la télévision ou au cinéma?

   📍 Je préfère regarder un film ....

   ....

   (b) Quel genre de films n'aimes-tu pas regarder?

   📍 Je n'aime pas les films ....

   ....

   (c) Parle-moi d'un film que tu as vu récemment.

   📍 La semaine dernière je suis allé(e) voir ....

   ....

Exam focus 📌

Listen carefully to the question and make sure your reason matches. You need to talk about a film genre you **don't** like for question 2.

Give a reason for your answer. For **(a)**, you could talk about the size of the screen (**l'écran (m)**), the comfort of an armchair (**un fauteuil**) or a sofa (**un canapé**), the cost of seeing a film (**le prix**) or the ease of downloading a film (**télécharger**).

Exam focus 📌

Be prepared to give an opinion on different types of films.

Remember to vary the way in which you introduce your opinion. You can extend your answer to **(c)** by giving your opinion about another type of film or by saying something about a film you have seen.

⑩ Reactions to a film

Grades 5–7

2. Lis ces commentaires sur un film récent dans un forum en ligne.

> Certes, les effets visuels créés par l'ordinateur étaient impressionnants mais c'est le drame des deux personnages perdus dans l'espace que j'ai trouvé particulièrement captivant. On pouvait s'identifier aux personnages à travers leurs émotions, eux qui devaient faire face aux désastres qui se déroulaient sur l'écran. Un vrai tour de force!
> **Albert**

> C'est incroyable comment ils ont utilisé la technologie pour créer l'illusion d'être dans l'espace. Je ne comprends pas comment ils ont fait. C'est ça qui a attiré le plus mon attention car l'histoire n'était pas du tout réaliste. En fait, sans ces effets spéciaux, le film n'aurait rien de remarquable.
> **Benoît**

Réponds aux questions **en français**. Il n'est pas nécessaire d'écrire des phrases complètes.

(a) Qui recommanderait ce film sans hésitation?　　　　　　　　　　**[1 mark]**

....

(b) Quel était le meilleur aspect du film pour Benoît?　　　　　　**[1 mark]**

....

(c) Quel aspect du film est-ce qu'Albert a trouvé fascinant?　　　**[1 mark]**

....

✓ **Made a start** ✓ **Feeling confident** ✓ **Exam ready**

Television

② Quick quiz

Draw lines to match up each type of TV programme with the right definition.

un feuilleton	Une émission pour savoir ce qui se passe dans le monde.
un dessin animé	Une émission pour les enfants.
les actualités	Une émission qu'on regarde pour savoir le temps qu'il va faire.
la météo	Une série dramatique qu'on peut regarder plusieurs fois dans la semaine.

⑮ TV programmes: what and when — Grades 4–6

1. Ton ami(e) français(e) t'a envoyé un mail au sujet de la télévision. Écris une réponse. Tu **dois** faire référence aux points suivants:

- tes habitudes et préférences
- une émission récente
- tes habitudes dans l'avenir
- les publicités – ton opinion.

Écris 80–90 mots environ **en français**.　　　　**[20 marks]**

> Say what your TV viewing habits are during the week (**en semaine**) and at the weekend.

> **Publicités** means *adverts*. You must give your opinion of them.

Exam focus
Remember to check that adjectives agree with what they're describing and that you have used the correct tense of the verb.

J'adore les émissions
....
....
....
....
....
....
....

⑩ TV habits — Grades 1–9

2. You could be asked about television in your speaking exam. Practise by answering these questions aloud. Use this space to make some notes to help you.

(a) Comment tu trouves les émissions de télé-réalité?

....
....
....

(b) Quand est-ce que tu regardes la télé de rattrapage?

....
....
....

Exam focus
Be prepared to answer questions on other types of television programmes, like documentaries or dramas.

Aiming higher
Use the imperfect tense to talk about what you used to watch, and use pronouns to refer to things you have already mentioned:

Avant, je regardais beaucoup d'émissions de télé-réalité. Cependant, maintenant, je les trouve bêtes. *Before, I used to watch a lot of reality TV programmes. However, I find them stupid now.*

Holiday plans and preferences

② Quick quiz

For each of the following holiday categories, circle the word or phrase that does **not** belong.

1. **Logement:**	auberge de jeunesse	camping	hôtel	plage
2. **À la campagne:**	faire de l'escalade	visiter une ferme	visiter un musée	faire des randonnées
3. **Au bord de la mer:**	nager	se bronzer	faire du ski	faire de la voile
4. **En plein air:**	faire du canoë-kayak	faire de l'équitation	faire ses bagages	faire des promenades

⑩ Holidays   Grades 4–9

1. Make some notes for the picture-based task below and practise saying your answers aloud.   **[24 marks]**

> Regarde la photo et prépare des réponses sur les points suivants:
>
> - la description de la photo
> - ton opinion sur les vacances passées dans un camping
> - des vacances récentes
> - où tu logeras en vacances avec tes amis
> - ! (*Pourquoi est-ce que les vacances sont importantes?*)

Sur la photo, on voit des gens qui ....

....

À mon avis, les vacances dans un camping peuvent ......

....

Récemment j'ai passé des vacances ....

....

L'année prochaine, je partirai en vacances avec mes amis. On logera

....

....

Exam focus

Make a note of the vocabulary you might need for this topic.

To describe the photo, you could say how many people there are, where they are (**dans un camping**) and what they are doing (**ils sont assis et font la cuisine / préparent un repas**).

Give your opinion about camping for the second bullet point. Talk about advantages, such as the facilities on the campsite (**les équipements de loisirs (m)**), and disadvantages, such as weather (**le temps**).

Aiming higher

Use conjunctions such as **pourtant**, **cependant** and **d'un autre côté** to introduce different tenses.

⑦ Holiday plans   Grades 4–5

2. You overhear some people talking about their holiday plans. What type of holiday are they planning to go on **this year**?

Listen to the recording and put a cross ☒ in each one of the **three** correct boxes.   **[3 marks]**

Example	activity holiday	☒
A	beach holiday	☐
B	camping holiday	☐
C	skiing holiday	☐
D	cultural sightseeing holiday	☐
E	holiday abroad	☐
F	cruise holiday	☐
G	cycling holiday	☐

✓ **Made a start**   ✓ **Feeling confident**   ✓ **Exam ready**

Holiday experiences

⏱ Quick quiz

Translate the following phrases **into French**.

1. a year ago ....

2. last July ....

3. during my stay ....

4. when it was raining ....

⏱ The ups and downs of an activity holiday

Grades 7–9

1. Lis ce rapport de vacances dans un blog.

En fait, c'était mal parti avec l'annulation de notre vol. Heureusement, on nous a transférés vers une autre compagnie aérienne. Bien sûr, on n'est pas arrivés à l'heure prévue et nous avons manqué le repas du soir. Ce qui m'a plu pendant mes vacances, c'est que chaque jour nous pouvions faire une activité différente. C'était formidable d'être en plein air et d'avoir de nouvelles expériences. Un jour, nous voulions faire du canoë-kayak mais nous ne pouvions pas en faire à cause de la pluie. Ce jour-là, nous sommes restés au centre et on a joué à des jeux d'intérieur.
Lucas

Vocabulary
Compagnie aérienne means *airline* and **vol (m)** means *flight*.
Nous sommes arrivés trop tard means *we arrived too late*.
Ce qui m'a plu means *what I liked*.

Exam focus 📌
When the instructions and questions are in French, you have to answer in French.

Réponds aux questions **en français**. Il n'est pas nécessaire d'écrire des phrases complètes.

(a) Comment est-ce que Lucas a voyagé pendant ses vacances?   **[1 mark]**

🪧 En avion
....

(b) Pourquoi Lucas a-t-il peut-être eu faim le soir de son arrivée sur son lieu de vacances?   **[1 mark]**

....

(c) Quel aspect de ses vacances est-ce qu'il a aimé en particulier?   **[1 mark]**

....

(d) Pourquoi est-ce qu'il a dû quelquefois modifier ses projets pour la journée?   **[1 mark]**

....

⏱ Writing about holiday experiences

Grades 4–9

2. Un magazine français cherche des articles sur les vacances.

Écrivez un article pour intéresser les lecteurs.

Vous **devez** faire référence aux points suivants:

- pourquoi les vacances sont importantes
- vos vacances récentes
- les vacances à l'étranger – avantages et inconvénients
- projets pour des vacances dans l'avenir.

Justifiez vos idées et vos opinions.

Écrivez 130–150 mots environ **en français**.   **[28 marks]**

Aiming higher ⬆
Remember to use past, present and future tenses in your answer.

....
....
....
....
....
....
....
....
....
....

Continue your answer on a separate sheet of paper.

☑ **Made a start**   ☑ **Feeling confident**   ☑ **Exam ready**   25

Travel and transport

② Quick quiz

You might see the following signs while in France. What do they mean?

1.

Salle d'attente

....

3.

Péage d'autoroute

€

....

2.

Guichet

....

4.

Attachez votre ceinture de sécurité

....

⑩ At the station   Grades 4–9

1. You could be given a role play about travel in your speaking exam. Practise using the following prompts. Use this space to make some notes to help you.

Instruction to candidates: You are at a train station in France and wish to buy tickets to go to Marseilles. The teacher will play the role of the employee and will speak first.

You must address the employee as *vous*.

[10 marks]

Vous êtes à la gare. Vous voulez acheter des billets pour aller à Marseille.

1. Billets désirés (**deux** détails)

🚩 Je voudrais deux
....

> You must say what tickets you want to buy: **aller simple (m)** is a *single journey* and **aller-retour (m)** is a *return journey*.

2. Ce moyen de transport – raison

🚩 Parce que c'est
....

> Give a reason for choosing this means of travel, such as *fast* (**rapide**), *practical* (**pratique**) or *comfortable* (**confortable**).

3. **!** (*Qu'est-ce que vous avez déjà fait en France?*)

🚩 Je suis allé(e)
....

> The unprepared question requires an answer using a past tense.

4. **?** Mode de paiement

🚩 Est-ce que je peux
....

> Ask how you can pay or if you can use a particular method of payment.

5. **?** Durée du voyage

🚩 Combien
....

> Ask how long the journey lasts.

⑩ Understanding station announcements   Grades 4–5

2. Écoute ces annonces à la gare.

Complète les phrases suivantes. Mets une croix ☒ dans la case correcte.

(a) Le train de Strasbourg arrivera…

☐	**A**	à l'heure
☐	**B**	en retard
☐	**C**	en avance
☐	**D**	à 14h 30

[1 mark]

(b) Les passagers sur le quai numéro trois…

☐	**A**	peuvent monter dans le prochain train qui arrive
☐	**B**	doivent attendre cinq minutes pour prendre un train
☐	**C**	doivent attendre plus de cinq minutes pour un train
☐	**D**	peuvent franchir la ligne jaune

[1 mark]

☑ **Made a start**   ☑ **Feeling confident**   ☑ **Exam ready**

Accommodation

(2) Quick quiz

Translate the following phrases **into English**.

1. une chambre climatisée

....

2. avec vue sur la mer

....

3. avec coffre-fort

....

4. une chambre familiale

....

(10) Making a hotel reservation   Grades 1–5

1. While doing work experience with a small hotel in France, you are asked to check the voicemail messages.

Listen to the message and answer the following questions **in English**.

(a) What kind of room does the customer want? Give **two** details.   **[2 marks]**

🚩 A room for 2 adults
....

....

(b) What are the dates of the customer's proposed stay?   **[1 mark]**

....

(c) What does the customer want to know?   **[1 mark]**

....

> Try to predict what the speaker might say and work out what words you need to listen out for. For the first question, you could expect to hear the number of people staying in the room or particular facilities, such as a room with a view or with a balcony.

> **Exam focus**
> If you are asked for two pieces of information, but three are mentioned, you won't get any more marks for giving extra answers.

(10) Hotel accommodation   Grades 1–5

2. Tu es en vacances. Tu postes cette photo sur des réseaux sociaux pour tes ami(e)s.

Écris une description de la photo **et** exprime ton opinion sur ton hôtel.

Écris 20–30 mots environ **en français**.   **[12 marks]**

....

....

....

....

....

....

....

....

....

....

> There are 6 marks for communication and content in this task, and 6 for linguistic knowledge and accuracy.

Dealing with problems

5 Quick quiz

For each of the following categories of problem, circle the word or phrase that does **not** belong.

1. A general type of problem:	panne	perte	achat	vol
2. A problem with road travel:	accident	gîte	travaux	embouteillage
3. A problem with rail transport:	délai	annulation	formulaire	grève
4. Exchanging an item:	choix	reçu	échanger	endommagé

10 Role play at a cycle shop — Grades 4–9

1. You could be given a role play about problems in your speaking exam. Practise using the prompts below. Use this space to make some notes to help you.

Instructions to candidates: You are in a bicycle shop in France and want to get your bike repaired. The teacher will play the role of the shop assistant and will speak first.

You must address the shop assistant as *vous*. **[10 marks]**

Vous êtes dans un magasin de vélos. Vous parlez au vendeur / à la vendeuse.

1. Votre vélo – problème

   Mon vélo ....

   > Say your bicycle has broken down, the *brakes* (**freins**) don't work or that you have a *burst tyre* (**pneu crevé**) for the first point.

2. Hébergement

   Je loge à ....

   > Say where you are staying for the second point.

3. **!** (*Où êtes-vous déjà allé(e) pendant votre séjour en France?*)

   Je suis déjà allé(e) ....

4. **?** Durée de réparation

   Combien de temps ....

   > Ask how long the repair will take for the fourth point.

5. **?** Coût de la réparation

   Ça coûte ....

   > Ask how much the repair will cost for the fifth point.

10 Problems during an exchange visit — Grades 4–7

2. Hervé parle de l'échange qu'il vient de faire.

   Complète les phrases en choisissant un mot ou des mots dans la case. Il y a des mots que tu n'utiliseras pas.

un accident	financier	une grève	linguistique	moins
une panne	pièce d'identité	plus	valise	~~un voyage scolaire~~

Exemple: Hervé parle d' *un voyage scolaire* ....

(a) Hervé a eu un problème .... **[1 mark]**

(b) Béatrice avait perdu sa .... **[1 mark]**

(c) Ils ne pouvaient pas voyager en train à cause d' .... **[1 mark]**

(d) Le trajet de l'aéroport à l'école était .... long que prévu. **[1 mark]**

Made a start ☐ Feeling confident ☐ Exam ready ☐

Directions

5 Quick quiz

Draw lines to match up the French and English sentences.

Traversez la place.	Follow the sign.
Allez jusqu'au rond-point.	Go straight ahead at the crossroads.
Suivez le panneau.	Go as far as the roundabout.
De l'autre côté du pont.	Cross the square.
Au carrefour va tout droit.	On the other side of the bridge.

10 Role play in a tourist office · Grades 1–5

1. You could be given a role play about directions in your speaking exam. Practise saying your responses to the prompts below aloud. Use this space to make some notes to help you.

Instructions to candidates: You are working in a tourist information office and are helping a French tourist. The teacher will play the role of the French tourist and will speak first.

You must address the French tourist as *vous*.   **[10 marks]**

Vous êtes à l'office de tourisme. Vous parlez avec un(e) touriste français(e).

1. Poste – situation

   🚩 Elle est ....

   > For the first point, use prepositions such as *next to, opposite, between, to the left of,* etc. to describe location.

2. Monument à visiter – recommandation + raison

   🚩 Il y a un musée. Il ....

   > You can mention any suitable place to visit, such as a museum, castle or church for the second point.

3. ! (*Quand est-ce qu'il est ouvert?*)

   🚩 Il est ....

   > ! is the unprepared question. While you are preparing, think about what it could be.

4. Directions (**deux** détails)

   🚩 Allez ....

   > For the fourth point, use phrases like *go straight ahead, turn left / right* or *take the first / second road.*

5. ? Durée de séjour en Grande-Bretagne

   🚩 Combien de ....

   > You must ask the teacher how long they are spending in Great Britain for the final point.

10 Finding your way around · Grades 3–5

2. Your French friend has sent you a message to help you find your way around during a day trip.

> Pour le vieux quartier, prends la sortie de la gare « rue de Bretagne ». Va tout droit jusqu'au parc. Tu verras le château devant toi. Ne continue pas dans le parc mais tourne à gauche et va tout droit. Tu arriveras au vieux quartier après 500 mètres.
>
> Dans le vieux quartier n'oublie pas de visiter le musée de la ville. Il se trouve sur la place de la République en face de la mairie. Tu trouveras aussi la tour de l'Horloge au coin de la place entre la cathédrale et la poste. Il y a une banque juste en face.

Put a cross ☒ in the correct box.

(a) To get to the old part of town, you must...   **[1 mark]**

☐	**A** go straight ahead and then right
☐	**B** go straight ahead and through the park
☐	**C** go along the Rue de Bretagne and through the park
☐	**D** go straight ahead and turn left

(b) The clock tower is...   **[1 mark]**

☐	**A** opposite the cathedral
☐	**B** next to a bank
☐	**C** on the same square as the town hall
☐	**D** between the post office and the town hall

☐ **Made a start**   ☐ **Feeling confident**   ☐ **Exam ready**

Eating out

② Quick quiz

For each of the following categories, circle the word or phrase that does **not** belong.

1. An item on the menu:	le plat principal	l'addition	le dessert	l'entrée
2. Item of cutlery:	un couteau	une cuillère	une fourchette	un verre
3. Restaurant facility:	une assiette	une terrasse	des toilettes	le wi-fi
4. Description of starter or main course:	épicé	salé	savoureux	content

⑩ Food and eating out   Grades 4–9

1. Make some notes for the picture-based task below and practise saying your answers aloud.   **[24 marks]**

> Regarde la photo et prépare des réponses sur les points suivants:
> - la description de la photo
> - ton opinion sur la cuisine française
> - ton dernier repas au restaurant
> - un futur repas au restaurant
> - ! *(Quel genre de cuisine est-ce que tu aimes le plus?)*

🚩 Sur la photo, il y a cinq ....

   Ils sont au ....

🚩 J'adore la cuisine française parce que ....

   ....

🚩 La dernière fois que je suis allé(e) au restaurant, c'était .....

   ....

🚩 Le week-end prochain nous irons ....

   ....

> Concentrate on using the words you already know to describe the picture.

> Give your opinion and a reason for the second bullet point.

> Use the past tense in response to the third bullet point and the future tense for the fourth bullet point.

> Say what kind of food you like and give a reason to answer the final bullet point.

⑩ Problems in a restaurant   Grades 1–5

2. You hear these conversations in a restaurant.
   Listen to the recording and answer the following questions **in English**.

   Part (a)

   (i) Why do the people complain about their table? Give **two** details.   **[2 marks]**

   ....

   ....

   (ii) What does the waiter offer them? .... **[1 mark]**

   Part (b)

   (i) What had the second group of people ordered for their meal? .... **[1 mark]**

   (ii) What alternative do they choose? .... **[1 mark]**

| ☑ **Made a start** | ☑ **Feeling confident** | ☑ **Exam ready** |

Shopping on holiday

5 Quick quiz

Translate the following sentences **into French**.

1. Is there a cash machine near here? ....

2. I need some stamps. ....

3. Have you got any postcards? ....

10 Buying souvenirs   Grades 4–9

1. Make some notes for the picture-based task below and practise saying
your answers aloud.   **[24 marks]**

> Regarde la photo et prépare des réponses sur les points suivants:
>
> - la description de la photo
> - l'importance des souvenirs – ton opinion
> - des souvenirs que tu as achetés en vacances
> - ce que tu achèteras la prochaine fois
> - ! (*Est-ce que tu préfères acheter des souvenirs ou prendre des photos quand tu es en vacances?*)

Sur la photo
....

....

À mon avis les souvenirs
....

....

Quand j'ai visité
....

....

Je ne sais pas   mais
....

....

> When describing a picture, think about answering the questions *Who? What? When? Where?* and *How?*

> Give a reason for your opinion using **parce que** or **car**.

> **Exam focus**
> You don't have to tell the truth when answering a question. Use words and phrases that you know.

10 Advice for buying souvenirs   Grades 4–9

2. Translate this passage **into English**.

Ramener des souvenirs de vos voyages, c'est normal, mais faites attention si vous voulez éviter des erreurs coûteuses. Vérifiez que vos achats rentrent dans vos bagages et qu'ils ne sont pas trop lourds, sinon vous devrez payer des frais supplémentaires si vous prenez l'avion. Alors, il vaut mieux choisir des petits objets tels que des bijoux, des porte-clés ou des vêtements légers.   **[7 marks]**

....

....

....

....

....

....

✓ **Made a start**   ✓ **Feeling confident**   ✓ **Exam ready**   **31**

Where I live

② Quick quiz

Translate the following phrases **into English**.

1. au rez-de-chaussée ....
2. une maison mitoyenne ....
3. le sous-sol ....
4. le vestibule ....

5. une pièce ....
6. le grenier ....
7. habitation à loyer modéré ....
8. une armoire ....

⑮ Comparing new and old homes — Grades 4–9

1. Traduis le passage suivant **en français**. **[12 marks]**

> A month ago, we moved to a brand new flat in a building in the centre of town. Our old house was bigger, but it was also very old-fashioned. We are on the fifth floor and I have my own room next to my parents' one. We have a balcony, but I would prefer to have a garden.

Il y a un mois,

....
....
....
....
....
....
....
....
....
....

Vocabulary A–Z
Use the verb **déménager** for *to move*.

Vocabulary A–Z
Use **tout** as an intensifier to say *brand* (new).

Vocabulary A–Z
Use the adjective **ancien** in front of a noun to mean *old / former*.

Vocabulary A–Z
Use the adjective **propre** in front of a noun to mean *own*.

Vocabulary A–Z
Use the demonstrative pronoun (**celui / celle**) to say *my parents' one* (literally *that of my parents*).

⑩ Low-cost housing in France — Grades 4–9

2. You hear this report about housing in France.

Listen to the report and answer the following questions **in English**.

(a) What type of housing is being described in the report? **[1 mark]**

....

(b) What does the report say about the people who live in this type of housing? Give **two** details. **[2 marks]**

....

(c) What characterises the majority of people who live in this type of accommodation? **[1 mark]**

....

(d) What is the distinguishing feature of the lowest percentage of people mentioned? **[1 mark]**

....

Made a start   Feeling confident   Exam ready

The neighbourhood

② Quick quiz

Translate the following words **into English**.

1. l'heure de pointe ....
2. les transports en commun ....
3. le jardin zoologique ....
4. le centre commercial ....
5. animé ....
6. le quartier ....

⑩ Your neighbourhood — Grades 4–9

1. Make some notes for the picture-based task below
and practise saying your answers aloud.

[24 marks]

Regarde la photo et prépare des réponses sur les
points suivants:

- la description de la photo
- ce qu'il y a dans ton quartier – ton opinion
- activités récentes dans ton quartier
- un événement qui aura bientôt lieu dans ton quartier
- ! (Qu'est-ce que tu changerais dans ta ville?)

Sur la photo, on voit ....
....

Je trouve que les environs ....
....

Le week-end dernier ....
....

Dans un mois il y aura ....
....
....

To describe the photo, you could say where they are,
what they are doing and what the weather is like.

Say what there is in your neighbourhood and give
your opinion about it for the second bullet point. For
example, **le cinéma**, **le club de jeunes**, **le centre sportif**.

Talk about a festival or event such as **une course de
10 km**, **un défilé**, for the fourth bullet point.

Aiming higher ⬆

Use the imperfect tense to compare where you live now
and have lived previously, or what your town is like now and
was like in the past. **Avant, il y avait beaucoup d'activités
qu'on pouvait faire en ville, mais aujourd'hui, beaucoup
d'endroits ont fermé.** *Before, there used to be lots of things
you could do in town, but now, lots of places have closed.*

⑩ Advantages and disadvantages of living in a village — Grades 4–9

2. You hear Gérard and Safia talking about village life.
Listen to the recording and answer the following questions **in English**.

(a) What is the disadvantage for Gérard of living where he does? **[1 mark]**
....

(b) What is his solution to this problem? Give **two** details. **[2 marks]**
....

(c) What does Safia like about where she lives now? **[1 mark]**
....

(d) In what way could it be improved further? **[1 mark]**
....

✓ **Made a start**   ✓ **Feeling confident**   ✓ **Exam ready**

Town and region

---

2 **Quick quiz**

Translate the following **into French**.

1. field ....
2. hill ....
3. to get around ....

4. in the mountains ....
5. factory ....
6. farm ....

---

10 **A region of France: Provence** **Grades 4–9**

1. A neighbour asks you to help him read part of a letter he has received from a French friend. Translate this passage **into English**. **[7 marks]**

> Je viens de revenir de Provence. Si tu ne connais pas cette région, ça vaut la peine de la visiter pour ses villages pittoresques perchés parmi les montagnes, ainsi que pour ses vignobles qui s'étendent jusqu'aux grands fleuves. Cela m'a vraiment plu, malgré les douleurs dont j'ai souffert après avoir fait le tour de la région à vélo.

I've just come back from
....
....
....
....
....
....

Vocabulary A–Z
Ça vaut la peine means *it's worth the effort.*

Vocabulary A–Z
S'étendre jusqu'aux means *to stretch as far as.*

Vocabulary A–Z
Vignoble (m) means *vineyard.*

Exam focus
Remember to read through your translation and make sure it reads well in English.

If you don't know what **douleur (f)** means, try to work it out from context and the other words in the sentence, such as **souffrir** (*to suffer*).

Perchés is a cognate and it very similar to its English equivalent.

---

15 **Writing about where you live** **Grades 4–6**

2. Ton ami(e) français(e) veut des infos sur ta région.

Écris une réponse à ton ami(e). Tu **dois** faire référence aux points suivants:

- ta région – description + opinion
- les transports dans ta région
- ce que tu as fait récemment dans ta région
- tes projets pour les vacances.

Écris 80–90 mots environ **en français**. **[20 marks]**

Aiming higher
Use superlatives to add weight to your descriptions. **C'est la plus belle vue.** *It's the most beautiful view.*

....
....
....
....
....

✓ **Made a start** ✓ **Feeling confident** ✓ **Exam ready**

Francophone countries

② Quick quiz

Translate the following phrases **into English**.

1. la Côte d'Ivoire ....

2. le Maroc ....

3. francophone ....

4. l'Afrique de l'Ouest ....

5. d'outre-mer ....

6. une île ....

⑩ Primary education in Africa   Grades 4–9

1. While doing research about education in French-speaking countries, you come across the following report.

> **Exam focus**
> Read the whole passage through once to get the overall sense before you try to answer the questions.

Answer the following questions **in English**.

(a) On which countries does the ÉLAN project focus? Give **two** details.   **[2 marks]**

🚩 8 French-speaking countries in ....

(b) Why was primary school difficult for children in these countries in the past? Give **two** details.   **[2 marks]**

....

....

(c) How will the ÉLAN project help these children?   **[1 mark]**

....

LE JOURNAL

En 2007, on a lancé un projet dans huit pays francophones d'Afrique subsaharienne pour aider les enfants à mieux réussir à l'école primaire.
Dans ces pays, qui sont parmi les plus pauvres du monde, le français est la langue officielle et la langue de l'enseignement dans les écoles primaires, tandis que la plupart des enfants dans ces établissements parlent une langue africaine comme langue maternelle. Pour eux, le français est une deuxième langue. Le projet École et langues nationales en Afrique (ÉLAN) offre un enseignement bilingue. De cette façon, les enfants apprennent par le moyen des deux langues. Ils gardent leur langue africaine, une partie importante de leur identité et développent leurs compétences en français.

⑩ Public transport in Dakar   Grades 4–9

2. You hear a report about the *cars rapides* in Dakar.

Put a cross ☒ in each one of the **two** correct boxes for each question.

(a) What does the report say about the *cars rapides*?

Example	The *cars rapides* are a type of minibus.	☒
A	The *cars rapides* will disappear from the streets of Dakar.	☐
B	The *cars rapides* are used to transport animals.	☐
C	There are forty *cars rapides* that carry people around Dakar.	☐
D	The *cars rapides* are all the same colour.	☐
E	It's difficult to recognise the *cars rapides.*	☐

[2 marks]

(b) What does the report say about changes planned for the transport system in Dakar?

A	Buses are going to be introduced that are brightly coloured.	☐
B	The *cars rapides* are better for the environment.	☐
C	The buses come from factories in Asia.	☐
D	The buses will be more popular with people who don't have much money.	☐
E	Travelling in a *car rapide* is cheaper than in one of the new buses.	☐

[2 marks]

✓ **Made a start**   ✓ **Feeling confident**   ✓ **Exam ready**   **35**

Seasons and weather

② Quick quiz

For each of the following categories, circle the word that does **not** belong.

1. The word that does **not** refer to rainfall: mouillé   brouillard   précipitation   averse

2. The word that does **not** refer to cold weather: orageux   glacial   geler   neige

3. The word that is **not** to do with a storm: tonnerre   éclair   orage   soleil

4. The word that is **not** a season: printemps   météo   hiver   été

⑩ Weather forecast   Grades 4–9

1. You hear the weather forecast for France.

Listen to the recording and complete the sentences by putting a cross ☒ in the correct box for each question.

Example: In the west the weather will be...

☐	**A**	sunnier than yesterday
☒	**B**	not as warm as yesterday
☐	**C**	warmer than yesterday
☐	**D**	misty all day

(b) In the east, the weather tomorrow will be... **[1 mark]**

☐	**A**	fine but windy
☐	**B**	wet and foggy
☐	**C**	fine and warm
☐	**D**	cold, windy and wet

(a) In the north, the weather will... **[1 mark]**

☐	**A**	stay the same all day
☐	**B**	get better towards the end of the day
☐	**C**	be better in the first part of the day
☐	**D**	be at its best in the middle of the day

(c) In the south, the sky will... **[1 mark]**

☐	**A**	be overcast all day with the possibility of showers
☐	**B**	become brighter in the second part of the day
☐	**C**	be clear all day
☐	**D**	be clear but will then turn showery again

Exam focus

Listen to the whole extract before you choose your answer. You may hear words from each possible answer in the recorded extract.

⑩ Talking about the seasons   Grades 1–9

2. You could be asked questions about the seasons or weather in your speaking exam. Practise by answering these example questions aloud. Use this space to make some notes to help you.

(a) Quelle est ta saison préférée? Pourquoi?

....

....

....

(b) Qu'est-ce que tu feras l'été prochain?

....

....

....

(c) Comment tu as trouvé l'hiver l'an dernier?

....

....

Exam focus

Listen carefully for the verb tense used in the question. Are you being asked about the past, the present or the future? Make sure that you use the correct tense in your answer.

Aiming higher

Extend your answer by using conjunctions, such as **mais, pourtant** or **d'autre part**, to introduce a different tense.

☑ **Made a start**   ☑ **Feeling confident**   ☑ **Exam ready**

My studies

Quick quiz ②

Translate the following sentences **into French**.

1. My favourite subject is history because it's fascinating.

....

2. I think maths is difficult, but it's a compulsory subject.

....

School subjects ⑩   Grades 1–9

1. You could be asked about your studies in your speaking exam. Practise by answering these questions aloud. Use this space to make some notes to help you.

(a) Quelles matières sont les plus importantes? Pourquoi?

À mon avis, ... sont les matières les

plus importantes parce que ....

Par contre, ...

> Use adjectives such as **utile** (*useful*), **pratique** (*practical*) and **stimulant** (*stimulating*) to justify your answer to question **(a)**. You could extend your answer by saying which subjects you don't think are important.

> Use the perfect tense in your answer to question **(b)**.

(b) Quelle matière as-tu trouvée la plus facile cette année?

Cette année, ...

....

....

> Give a reason for your answer to question **(c)**. Useful vocabulary could be: *he is strict but fair* (**il est strict mais juste**); *she has a good sense of humour* (**un bon sens de l'humour**); *gives clear explanations* (**des explications claires (f)**) and *too much homework* (**trop de devoirs (m)**).

(c) Comment est-ce que tu t'entends avec tes profs?

....

....

Aiming higher ⬆

Phrases like **de plus** (*moreover / besides*) and **néanmoins** (*nevertheless*) are useful when you want to give a more extended answer.

Attitudes to school subjects and teachers ⑩   Grades 4–9

2. Lis ce mail.
Mets une croix ☒ dans les **deux** cases correctes.   **[2 marks]**

● ● ●

✉ **Sujet:** La visite
Envoyer

Salut! J'attends ta visite à notre collège avec impatience. Tu feras bientôt la connaissance de tous mes profs! Le prof de maths est vraiment sérieux mais il enseigne bien et personne n'a de mauvaises notes. La plupart de mes copains s'entendent bien avec le prof d'EPS. Pour ma part, ce n'est pas le cas car il me critique tout le temps. Cependant, je pense que tu aimeras notre prof d'anglais parce qu'elle nous raconte toujours des histoires amusantes. Je viens de recevoir mon bulletin scolaire. Je m'attendais à avoir de mauvaises notes en allemand parce que c'est une langue que je trouve difficile à comprendre et en plus je n'arrive pas à apprendre le vocabulaire. D'autre part, j'avais pensé que j'allais échouer à l'épreuve d'informatique car c'est compliqué comme matière, mais j'ai été agréablement surprise.
Gaëlle

Exemple	Gaëlle écrit au sujet des matières scolaires et de ses professeurs.	☒
A	Elle dit que tout le monde a de bonnes notes en maths.	☐
B	Gaëlle s'entend mieux avec son prof d'EPS qu'avec sa prof d'anglais.	☐
C	Gaëlle espérait recevoir de meilleures notes en allemand.	☐
D	Gaëlle pensait qu'elle allait recevoir de mauvaises notes en informatique.	☐

Your school

BBC

② Quick quiz

Translate the following phrases **into English**.

1. le règlement scolaire ....

3. mal équipé ....

2. les installations scolaires ....

4. les activités extrascolaires ....

⑩ School rules   Grades 4–9

1. You hear these French students talking about their school rules.

Listen to the recording and put a cross ☒ in the correct box for each question.

Example: Julien thinks that the use of mobile phones in lessons...

☐	**A**	should always be allowed
☐	**B**	should very rarely be allowed
☒	**C**	should never be allowed
☐	**D**	should sometimes be allowed

> Read the question and options through carefully before you listen. Then listen to the whole text before answering the questions.

> The example is specifically about mobile phone use in **lessons**.

(a) Recently, Amélie...

☐	**A**	didn't obey any of the rules
☐	**B**	broke one of the rules
☐	**C**	obeyed all the rules
☐	**D**	obeyed all except two of the rules

[1 mark]

> **Règlement (m) intérieur** means *school rules*. Try to predict what might be said.

(b) For Baptiste the worst school rule forbids...

☐	**A**	tattoos
☐	**B**	mobile phones
☐	**C**	head wear
☐	**D**	make-up

[1 mark]

⑩ Life in school   Grades 1–5

2. Traduis les phrases suivantes **en français**.

(a) My school is very big.   **[2 marks]**

....

(b) I think the school day is too long.   **[2 marks]**

....

(c) I don't like the school rules.   **[2 marks]**

....

(d) I wear a uniform every day but the French don't wear a uniform.   **[3 marks]**

....

(e) Yesterday I went to art club after school.   **[3 marks]**

....

School trips, events and exchanges

5 Quick quiz

Translate the following phrases **into English**.

1. participer à un spectacle ....

2. la cérémonie pour la remise des prix ....

3. une répétition d'orchestre ....

4. avoir le mal du pays ....

5. jouer dans une pièce de théâtre ....

6. chanter dans une chorale ....

10 The experience of a school exchange   Grades 4–5

1. Karim parle de l'échange.

Complète les phrases en choisissant un mot ou des mots dans la case. Il y a des mots que tu n'utiliseras pas.

bien	culturelles	deux semaines	difficile	~~en été~~	facile	en hiver
positive	mal	négative	sportives	une semaine		

Exemple: Karim a participé à un échange ..*en été*..........................

(a) L'échange a duré .... **[1 mark]**

(b) Il s'est .... entendu avec la famille d'accueil. **[1 mark]**

(c) Il était .... de comprendre les parents de son correspondant. **[1 mark]**

(d) Pendant l'échange il a fait des activités .... **[1 mark]**

(e) Pour lui l'échange était une expérience .... **[1 mark]**

> Use your knowledge of language and grammar to find the word needed for the each gap. For instance, is it a noun or an adjective, a singular or plural word?

> **Exam focus**
> You are unlikely to hear the exact words in the box in the recording. You will need to infer the meaning from what you hear, so think about how the words in the box might be conveyed differently.

30 School events   Grades 4–9

2. Un site internet cherche des articles sur les événements culturels et sportifs au collège.

Écrivez à ce site internet. Vous **devez** faire référence aux points suivants:

- pourquoi les événements culturels et sportifs sont importants
- un événement culturel récent dans votre collège
- si vous allez participer à de tels événements l'année prochaine
- comment on peut intéresser les jeunes à ces événements.

Justifiez vos idées et vos opinions.

Écrivez 130–150 mots environ **en français**.   **[28 marks]**

....

....

....

....

....

> Continue on a separate sheet of paper if you need more space.

| ☐ Made a start | ☐ Feeling confident | ☐ Exam ready | **39** |

Using languages

⏱5 Quick quiz

Fill in the gaps with a suitable word or phrase from the box. There are some words you do not need.

| améliorer | Belgique | comprendre | couramment | me débrouille |
| écoute | écriture | Espagne | lecture | lentement | prononciation |

Comme j'ai passé beaucoup de temps en **(1)**........................., je parle français

(2)........................ Je **(3)**........................ aussi assez bien en flamand, mais je trouve la

(4)........................ parfois difficile et j'ai du mal à me faire **(5)**........................

⏱10 An email to a language school — Grades 1–5

1. Vous voulez faire un stage linguistique en France. **[16 marks]**

Écrivez un mail au directeur de l'école et donnez les informations suivantes:

- quand vous voulez faire ce stage
- vos compétences linguistiques actuelles
- pourquoi vous désirez faire ce stage
- les activités extrascolaires que vous voulez faire.

Écrivez 40–50 mots **en français.**

Monsieur / Madame,

En juillet prochain, je voudrais

....

....

....

....

Cordialement

> Remember to write in full sentences.

> Say when you want to do the course for the first bullet point.

> Talk about your current linguistic skills for the second bullet point.

> Say why you want to do the course for the third bullet point.

> Mention what extracurricular activities you want to do for the final bullet point.

Exam focus
You should use the **vous** form when addressing the head of the language school.

⏱10 Talking about using languages — Grades 4–9

2. You could be asked questions about using languages in your speaking exam. Practise by answering the following questions aloud.

Use this space to make some notes to help you.

(a) Quelles langues est-ce que tu parles?
....

(b) Est-ce que tu trouves facile d'apprendre une langue étrangère?
....

(c) Est-ce qu'il est important d'apprendre une langue?
....

(d) Est-ce que tu utiliseras tes langues plus tard?
....

Aiming higher
Always extend your answers as fully as possible by giving an opinion and a reason.

Made a start | Feeling confident | Exam ready

Ambitions

② Quick quiz

Translate the following **into French**.

1. I intend to go to university.

....

2. I want to start a family.

....

3. My dream is to buy a car.

....

4. I hope to become a hairdresser.

....

⑩ Three students' future plans   Grades 4–9

1. Des jeunes parlent de leurs ambitions.

Mets une croix ⊠ dans la case correcte.

Exemple: Maintenant, Lucy voudrait...

☐	**A**	travailler dans un théâtre
☐	**B**	une carrière flexible
⊠	**C**	être bien payée
☐	**D**	se marier tout de suite

(a) Après avoir fait son stage, Alice a décidé de...   **[1 mark]**

☐	**A**	changer d'idée à propos de son avenir
☐	**B**	travailler de façon indépendante
☐	**C**	toujours travailler chez elle
☐	**D**	travailler dans un bureau

(b) Ce qui intéresse Guy, c'est...   **[1 mark]**

☐	**A**	de partir en Australie avant d'aller à l'université
☐	**B**	de travailler immédiatement
☐	**C**	une carrière où il peut utiliser ses compétences linguistiques
☐	**D**	de gagner de l'argent aussitôt que possible

Exam focus

Before you listen to the audio, work out what each of the options means.

Listen carefully to what Lucy wants to do *now*. Predict how these options might be referred to using different words, like **acteur (m)** or **comédienne (f)** for **travailler dans un théâtre**.

⑮ Work and ambitions   Grades 4–6

2. Tu contribues à une discussion sur les ambitions sur un site internet français.

Écris à ce site internet. Tu **dois** faire référence aux points suivants:

- tes qualités personnelles
- tes ambitions personnelles pour l'avenir
- tes expériences professionnelles récentes
- l'importance du travail – ton opinion.

Écris 80–90 mots environ **en français**.   **[20 marks]**

Aiming higher

Try to include what other people think of you, so you can use the third person. **On dit que je suis...** or **Mes parents pensent que je...**

....

....

....

....

....

Education post-16

② Quick quiz

Translate the following sentences **into English**.

1. L'année prochaine, nous pourrons laisser tomber plusieurs matières.

....

2. J'ai envie de devenir apprenti parce que je voudrais faire quelque chose de pratique.

....

⑩ A plan for sixth form and beyond   Grades 4–9

1. Traduis le passage suivant **en français**.   **[12 marks]**

> I have decided to go into Year 12 in September and to study for my A levels. I am planning to drop sciences, but will continue with maths and languages because I want a career in business. Some of my friends will be taking a gap year after completing their A levels, but I would like go to university straight away.

Use **le bac** to translate *A levels*. Remember to use the definite article with school subjects.

Vocabulary A–Z
Use **dans le commerce (m)** to translate *in business*.

Vocabulary A–Z
Use the verb **faire** to translate *completing*.

Translate *straight away* as *immediately* or *at once*.

J'ai décidé d'entrer en première ....

....

....

....

....

....

....

....

⑩ Decisions and reasons   Grades 4–5

2. You hear a conversation between two young people talking about their post-16 plans.

Listen to the recording and answer the following questions **in English**.

(a) What are the advantages of an apprenticeship for Adam? Give **two** details.   **[2 marks]**

....

....

....

(b) Why has Lola chosen to do *le bac L*? Give **two** details.   **[2 marks]**

....

....

....

☑ **Made a start**   ☑ **Feeling confident**   ☑ **Exam ready**

Charity and voluntary work

② Quick quiz

What do the following phrases mean **in English**?

1. collecter des fonds ....

2. soutenir quelqu'un ....

3. être solidaire ....

4. avoir plus confiance en soi ....

⑩ Reasons for volunteering   Grades 3–5

1. You hear a radio phone-in programme about volunteering.

   Listen to the recording and put a cross ⊠ in each one of the **three** correct boxes.   **[3 marks]**

		Maurice	Angélique	Paul
Example	I've been volunteering for half a year.	⊠	☐	☐
A	I support a charity that helps deprived people overseas.	☐	☐	☐
B	I want to change the world for the better.	☐	☐	☐
C	I want to do something useful for children in my town.	☐	☐	☐
D	I support an animal rescue charity.	☐	☐	☐
E	I am doing something to help in my neighbourhood.	☐	☐	☐
F	I volunteer in order to find a job.	☐	☐	☐
G	I volunteer at a soup kitchen.	☐	☐	☐

Exam focus

Before listening, jot down the French words that you need to listen out for.

Think about how words might be expressed differently, such as charities for specific animals might be mentioned instead of a general animal rescue charity.

⑮ Writing about volunteering experiences   Grades 4–6

2. Un site internet français pour les jeunes demande ton opinion sur le bénévolat.

   Écris à ce site internet. Tu **dois** faire référence aux points suivants:

   - description de l'association caritative que tu soutiens
   - tes actions récentes comme bénévole
   - l'importance du bénévolat – ton opinion
   - tes projets pour collecter des fonds.

   Écris 80–90 mots environ **en français**.   **[20 marks]**

....

....

....

....

....

....

....

....

✓ **Made a start**	✓ **Feeling confident**	✓ **Exam ready**

Jobs and careers

② Quick quiz

Translate the following sentences **into French**.

1. I would like to be a doctor. ....
2. My father is an engineer. ....
3. I had an interview yesterday. ....

⑩ Jobs and careers   Grades 1–5

1. Make some notes for the picture-based task below
   and practise saying your answers aloud.   **[24 marks]**

   > Regarde la photo et prépare des réponses aux points suivants:
   > - la description de la photo
   > - ce qui est important dans le choix d'un travail – ton opinion
   > - une expérience récente de travail
   > - le métier que tu voudrais faire
   > - un métier que tu ne voudrais pas faire et la raison.

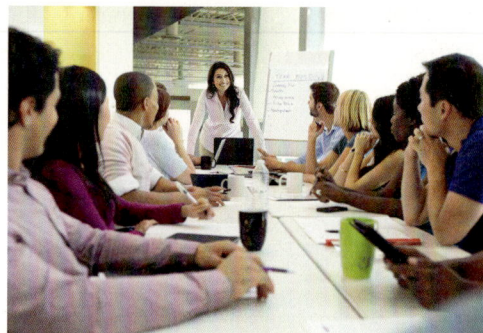

   📍 Sur la photo on voit dix personnes assises autour
   ....
   d'une table dans un bureau.
   ....
   ....

   > Describe the people in the picture and say what they are doing: **être assis autour d'une table** (*to be sitting around a table*), **discuter de quelque chose** (*to discuss something*).

   📍 À mon avis le salaire
   ....
   ....

   > Talk about what is important for you in a job: **le salaire** (*salary*), **les horaires (m) de travail** (*working hours*) or **les collègues** (*colleagues*).

   📍 Pendant l'été, j'ai
   ....
   ....

   > Talk about where you would like to work: **dans un bureau / une banque / un collège** (*in an office / a bank / a school*) and give a reason.

   📍 J'adore les animaux, alors
   ....
   ....

   > Talk about why you wouldn't like to do a particular job: **le salaire n'est pas bon, le travail n'est pas intéressant**.

   📍 Je ne voudrais pas travailler
   ....
   parce que
   ....

⑩ My part-time job   Grades 4–9

2. Translate this passage **into English**.   **[7 marks]**

   > Je viens de trouver un petit boulot dans un restaurant. Ce n'est pas bien payé, cependant le travail me plaît parce que je fais partie d'une équipe et ça me permettra de développer de nouvelles compétences. Il faut bien communiquer avec les clients et être très attentif. Hier, j'ai reçu quatre-vingts euros de pourboires!

....
....
....
....

✓ **Made a start**   ✓ **Feeling confident**   ✓ **Exam ready**

International events

---

⑤ Quick quiz

Translate the following phrases **into English**.

1. réunir des gens ....

2. rapporter de l'argent ....

3. la foule ....

4. attirer des visiteurs ....

5. les prix augmentés ....

6. l'infrastructure améliorée ....

---

⑩ Bringing the world together   Grades 4–9 💬

1. Make some notes for the picture-based task below and practise saying your answers aloud. **[24 marks]**

Regarde la photo et prépare des réponses sur les points suivants:

- la description de la photo
- les jeunes aux festivals de musique – ton opinion
- ton expérience d'un événement international
- un événement international que tu iras voir l'année prochaine
- ! (Est-ce que c'est mieux de regarder un événement sportif / musical à la télé ou en vrai?)

🚩 Sur la photo on voit ....

....

🚩 À mon avis ....

....

🚩 Je ne suis jamais allé(e) ....

....

🚩 L'année prochaine ....

....

> Talk about how it is important to stay safe (**être prudent**), protect oneself from the sun (**se protéger**) and to avoid drugs (**éviter les drogues**) for the second bullet point.

---

⑩ The Eurovision Song Contest   Grades 4–7 🎧

2. You are listening to a radio phone-in programme.

Listen to the recording and answer the following questions **in English**.

(a) What is Hugo's attitude to the Eurovision Song Contest? **[1 mark]**

....

(b) What do he and his friends comment on? Give **two** details. **[2 marks]**

....

(c) What does he find particularly entertaining? **[1 mark]**

....

(d) Why would he perhaps change the voting system? Give **two** details. **[2 marks]**

....

✓ **Made a start**   ✓ **Feeling confident**   ✓ **Exam ready**   **45**

Campaigns and good causes

⑤ Quick quiz

Fill in the gaps with a suitable word or phrase from the box.

| l'argent | améliorer | commerce équitable | pauvres | prix | vie |

Grâce au **(1)** .... les producteurs situés dans les pays **(2)** ....

peuvent obtenir un meilleur **(3)** .... pour leurs produits. Ils reçoivent

aussi de **(4)** .... pour **(5)** .... leurs conditions de

(6) .... dans leur village.

---

⑩ Attitudes to good causes   Grades 4–7 🎧

1. You hear Alice talking about her family's attitude to good causes.

Put a cross ☒ in each of the **two** correct boxes. **[2 marks]**

Example	Her father supports people who are abroad.	☒
A	Everyone in her family writes letters.	☐
B	Her mother does not support the same cause as her father.	☐
C	Her mother is interested in helping children.	☐
D	Her mother makes regular donations of money to a charity.	☐
E	The projects she supports aim to improve the lives of deprived girls in France.	☐

> Listen carefully to the whole extract before drawing your conclusions.

> Listen out for specific details, such as what her mother donates regularly.

---

⑮ Les Restos du Cœur   Grades 8–9 👓

2. Lis cet article.

> **Les Restaurants du Cœur**
>
> Depuis plus de trente ans, l'association caritative 'Les Restos du Cœur' a comme but principal la distribution d'aliments et de repas chauds aux plus démunis, soit les sans-abri mais aussi ceux qui disposent de moyens modestes telles que les personnes âgées dont la pension est très faible et les familles monoparentales.
>
> Lancée par un discours à la radio en 1985, l'association a été l'idée de l'humoriste et acteur Coluche. Il avait été scandalisé par le gaspillage alimentaire et la destruction des surplus agricoles. Il a proposé qu'on organise des soupes populaires à Paris de novembre à mars, montrant l'exemple pour que cette initiative puisse être reprise dans d'autres grandes villes.
>
> L'aide alimentaire n'est plus la seule action de l'association. On aide les gens à se réinsérer dans la société, par exemple en les aidant à trouver un logement et en leur donnant des conseils financiers.

Réponds aux questions **en français**. Il n'est pas nécessaire d'écrire des phrases complètes.

(a) Comment est-ce que les Restos du Cœur aident les personnes défavorisées? **[1 mark]**

....

(b) Qu'est-ce qui a poussé Coluche à fonder les Restos du Cœur? **[1 mark]**

....

(c) Comment est-ce que l'activité des Restos du Cœur a changé au cours des années? **[1 mark]**

....

✓ **Made a start**   ✓ **Feeling confident**   ✓ **Exam ready**

Global issues

② Quick quiz

Complete the following headlines using words from the box.

| déboisement | guerre | incendie | séisme |

1. Des centaines de maisons en ruines à cause d'un ....

2. La violence provoquée par la .... en Syrie persiste.

3. Des milliers d'espèces menacées par le .... en Amérique du Sud.

4. Beaucoup de gens souffrent de brûlures suite à un .... hier.

⑩ Attitudes to global issues   Grades 4–5 🎧

1. You hear this radio programme about attitudes to global issues.

Listen to the recording and answer the following questions **in English**.

(a) What group of people is Laurent talking about?   **[1 mark]**

🚩 People who say that
....

....

(b) How does he feel about their attitude?   **[1 mark]**

....

....

(c) What evidence for the problem does Amina mention? Give **two** details.   **[2 marks]**

🚩 There have been floods in
....

....

....

> Before you listen, write down any French words you know that relate to global issues, for example: **le réchauffement de la Terre** (*global warming*) and **le déboisement** (*deforestation*), **la pauvreté** (*poverty*), **la famine** and **la guerre** (*war*).

> Listen carefully to the whole extract to infer what Laurent's feelings are before you answer question **(1b)**.

⑩ Solving global problems   Grades 4–9 💬

2. You could be asked questions about global issues in your speaking exam. Practise by answering these questions aloud. Use this space to make some notes to help you.

(a) Comment est-ce qu'on pourrait protéger les espèces en voie de disparition?

....

(b) Comment est-ce qu'on peut aider les victimes de catastrophes naturelles?

....

(c) De quelle façon est-ce qu'on contribue au réchauffement de la Terre?

....

The environment

② Quick quiz

Draw lines to match up the sentence halves to make good advice about looking after the environment.

Triez les ordures...	pour économiser de l'énergie.
Fermez le robinet en vous brossant les dents...	pour faciliter le recyclage.
Éteignez les appareils électriques...	pour réduire la pollution de l'atmosphère.
Ne faites pas de petits trajets en voiture...	pour ne pas gaspiller d'eau.

⑩ Environmental choices at home — Grades 4–9

1. Traduis le passage suivant **en français**. **[12 marks]**

Every week, we throw away too many things. Since last year, my family has refused to buy fruit and vegetables wrapped in plastic, and yesterday I re-used a plastic bag when I went shopping. We have reduced our energy use by turning down the central heating. Next year, we hope to protect the environment by installing solar panels on the roof.

⇒ Chaque semaine, on jette ....

....

....

....

....

....

....

Vocabulary A–Z
Use **jeter à la poubelle** to translate *to throw away*.

Vocabulary A–Z
Use **depuis** + present tense to translate *since…*

Use the past participle of the verb **emballer** to translate *wrapped*.

Vocabulary A–Z
Translate *energy use* as *consumption* (**consommation (f)**) *of energy*.

Use **en** + present participle to say *by installing*.

⑩ An environmental problem — Grades 4–9

2. You hear this extract from a radio report about an environmental issue.

Listen to the recording and answer the following questions **in English**.

(a) Which environmental issue is talked about in the report? **[1 mark]**

....

(b) Why is the environmental issue such a problem? Give **one** detail. **[1 mark]**

....

(c) What is the solution to the problem? **[1 mark]**

....

(d) What has helped to bring about a change? **[1 mark]**

....

| Made a start | Feeling confident | Exam ready |

Pronunciation strategies

② Quick quiz

Draw a curved line where you need to make a liaison (‿). A liaison is when you pronounce the last letter, which would normally be silent, because the next word starts with a vowel. Listen to the audio clip to check your answers.

1. Est-ce qu'ils ont une table pour six personnes?

2. Est-ce que vous avez voyagé en avion?

3. Ces assiettes sont assez sales.

4. Ils adorent les oignons.

5. À la fin, on était fatigués mais très heureux.

6. Mes amis n'aiment pas cet acteur.

⑩ Silent consonants   Grades 1–9

1. Underline the consonants that you **do not** pronounce in the following sentences. Practise saying these sentences aloud and then compare with the audio clip.

(a) Il fait assez froid dans le nord et un peu chaud dans le sud du pays en hiver.

(b) Samedi, j'ai été très surpris parce qu'un flashmob a eu lieu devant l'arrêt d'autobus!

(c) Ma sœur vient d'acheter un anorak vert pour son petit ami.

(d) Le chef a préparé le bœuf et les choux de Bruxelles avec des noix d'une façon tout à fait délicieuse.

(e) Après le repas, il avait mal à l'estomac parce qu'il avait trop mangé.

(f) De nos jours, il est impossible de vivre sans portable.

> You should pronounce the final consonant of a word when it is followed by a vowel or silent **h**.

> You usually pronounce the following consonants when they are at the end of a word: **b**, **c**, **f**, **k** and **q**.

> Many French vowel sounds have different spellings but are pronounced the same, for example **–er**, **–ez**, **–é**, **–és**.

⑩ Correct pronunciation   Grades 1–9

2. Practise saying the following sentences aloud so they sound natural. Listen to the audio clip to check your pronunciation.

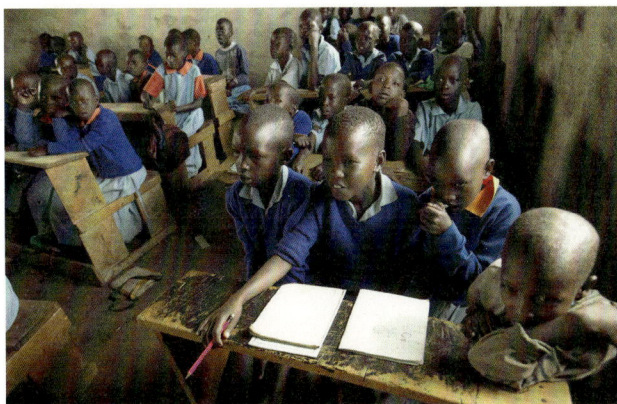

> Sur cette photo, on voit beaucoup d'enfants africains qui sont dans leur salle de classe. Ils portent un uniforme bleu. Il n'y a pas assez de place pour tous les élèves et ils doivent partager un banc. Certains n'ont ni cahier ni crayon. Je pense qu'ils sont assez pauvres.
>
> À mon avis, l'éducation est très importante. Alors, il faut absolument continuer à l'école jusqu'à l'âge de dix-huit ans pour développer ses compétences et avoir de meilleures chances dans la vie.

> Remember that cognates (words that are similar in English) are pronounced differently in French. Take care with words that end with **–ion**, like **préparation (f)** or start with **im–** or **in–**, like **improbable** and **indépendant**.

Exam focus
Understanding the link between sound and spelling will also help in your listening exam.

✓ **Made a start**   ✓ **Feeling confident**   ✓ **Exam ready**   49

Speaking strategies

② Quick quiz

In your speaking exam, you can use these verbal strategies as part of your responses. Match the strategy to the problem.

If you don't know the French word for something…	you could use a filler phrase, such as **eh bien**.
When answering a question…	you could paraphrase or describe the item.
If you need time to think…	you could repeat words and phrases from the question to give yourself time to think.

⑩ Answering questions　　　　Grades 1–9

1. Write notes in French to answer the following questions, and then practise saying your answers aloud.

(a) Quelle saison n'aimes-tu pas?

....

....

....

You could describe the seasons and weather. If you can't remember vocabulary for that, you could change the subject slightly by talking about an activity you like to do in a particular season.

Aiming higher
Extend your answer by comparing two seasons. You could say what you like to do in each season.

(b) Quels sont les problèmes des SDF?

....

....

....

For **(b)**, you could talk about not having any money, (**ne pas avoir d'argent**) having no home, living on the street in winter (**vivre dans la rue en hiver**), and falling sick (**tomber malade**).

If you need time to think while you're answering a question, you can use filler phrases such as **alors** (so) and **c'est-à-dire** (that is to say / what I mean is…)

Exam focus
Focus on what you can say rather than worrying about the words you don't know.

⑩ General conversation questions　　　　Grades 1–9

2. Write notes in French to answer the following questions, and then practise saying your answers aloud.

(a) Quelle est la date la plus importante de l'année pour toi?

....

....

Exam focus
If you need time to think about an answer, you could say: **C'est une question intéressante** or **Laissez-moi réfléchir un instant**.

(b) Comment serait ton copain idéal / ta copine idéale?

....

....

Exam focus
Listen out for the tense used in the question. Make sure you use the correct one in your answer.

(c) Qu'est-ce que tu as fait le week-end dernier?

....

....

Aiming higher
To gain top marks remember to expand on your answer by using adjectives and adverbs to add details, and use a range of tenses. This can be done by making comparisons between different time frames.

✓ **Made a start**　　✓ **Feeling confident**　　✓ **Exam ready**

Asking for clarification strategies

② Quick quiz

You can use the following sentences to ask for clarification in the speaking exam. Translate them **into English**.

1. Pouvez-vous répéter la question, s'il vous plaît?

....

2. Comment dit-on 'playground' en français?

....

3. Qu'est-ce que ça veut dire?

....

⑩ How do you say it?   Grades 1–9

1. Translate the following sentences **into French**.

(a) Can you explain the word 'peluche'?

....

> You can also use the informal form **Peux-tu...?** to translate *Can you…?*

(b) I don't know how to say *to squabble* in French.

....

> **Vocabulary** [A–Z]
> Use **savoir** to translate *know*.

(c) I don't understand the word 'facteur'.

....

> **Vocabulary** [A–Z]
> Use **comprendre** to translate *understand*.

(d) How do you write that?

....

(e) What do you mean when you say...?

....

⑩ Requests for clarification   Grades 1–5

2. While in France you overhear some snippets of conversations.

What is happening in each one?

Listen to the recording and put a cross ☒ in each one of the **three** correct boxes.

Example	Checking understanding by repeating the question	☒
A	Asking for the meaning of a word	☐
B	Asking for repetition because the speaker didn't hear the question	☐
C	Asking for repetition because the speaker didn't understand the question	☐
D	Asking someone to explain what they mean	☐
E	Asking someone to speak more slowly	☐
F	Asking someone to speak more clearly	☐
G	Checking the spelling of a word	☐

[3 marks]

✓ Made a start   ✓ Feeling confident   ✓ Exam ready

General conversation

⑤ Preparation ✎ ☑

1. Before your speaking exam you will have a few minutes to prepare. The general conversation will be on the two themes not covered by the picture stimulus card. Write down a few notes on each theme that you could use for support in your exam.

Theme 1: Identity and culture	Theme 2: Local area, holiday and travel	Theme 3: School	Theme 4: Future aspirations, work and study	Theme 5: International and global dimension

⑩ Getting off to a good start   Grades 1–9 💬 ☑

2. You can talk about the aspect you have chosen for your topic for up to a minute. Use this space to make some notes on the following topics to help you remember what you want to say. Practise giving your presentation aloud.

(a) Les fêtes en famille

....

....

....

(b) Les problèmes environnementaux

....

....

....

> **Exam focus** 📌
> There are 36 marks for general conversation: 12 marks for communication and content, 12 marks for interaction and spontaneity, and 12 marks for linguistic knowledge and accuracy.

> When you prepare for your presentation, write down single words and short phrases as prompts rather than whole sentences.

> When you express an opinion, give a reason using conjunctions such as **parce que** and **car**.

> The teacher may ask you follow-up questions based on what you say. Think about what these might be and plan ahead.

> Listen carefully to the teacher's follow-up questions and use the correct tense – past, present or future – in your answer.

⑩ Ambitions   Grades 1–9 💬 ☑

3. You could be asked about your ambitions in your speaking exam. Practise answering these questions aloud. Use this space to make some notes to help you.

(a) Quel serait ton métier de rêve? Pourquoi?

....

....

(b) Est-ce que c'est une bonne idée de prendre une année sabbatique, à ton avis?

....

....

(c) Quel métier voulais-tu faire quand tu étais jeune?

....

....

Using a picture stimulus

⑩ **Friends and relationships**   Grades 1–5

1. Make some notes for the picture-based task below and
practise saying your answers aloud.   **[24 marks]**

> Regarde la photo et prépare des réponses sur les points
> suivants:
>
> - la description de la photo
> - les qualités d'un bon ami / d'une bonne amie
> - activités récentes avec tes ami(e)s
> - activités avec tes ami(e)s pendant les grandes
>   vacances
> - ton / ta meilleur(e) ami(e).

....

....

....

....

....

....

To answer the second bullet point, say what you think
makes a good friend and why.

Use the past tense to answer the third bullet point.

Exam focus

The teacher may say **autre chose?** if they want you to add
more detail to your description of the photo.

---

⑩ **Holidays and travel**   Grades 4–9

2. Make some notes for the picture-based task below and
practise saying your answers aloud.   **[24 marks]**

> Regarde la photo et prépare des réponses sur les points
> suivants:
>
> - la description de la photo
> - genre de vacances préféré – ton opinion
> - activités faites en vacances cette année
> - projets pour les vacances l'an prochain
> - ! (*Comment seraient tes vacances idéales?*)

....

....

....

....

....

....

Role play (Foundation)

⏱ A travel agency

Grades 1–5

1. Practise using the following role play, saying your responses aloud. Use this space to make some notes to help you.

[10 marks]

Instructions to candidates: You are at a travel agency in France to book a holiday. The teacher will play the role of the agency employee and will speak first.

You must address the employee as *vous*.

> *Vous êtes dans une agence de voyages en France. Vous parlez avec l'employé(e).*
>
> 1. Vacances désirées – destination
> 2. Logement préféré
> 3. **!** (*Vous voulez passer combien de temps en vacances?*)
> 4. Activités en vacances
> 5. **?** Départ – heure

> Say where you want to go for the first point.

> Say where you want to stay (**hôtel, camping**) for the second point.

> **!** is the unpredictable question. Think about what this might be while you prepare.

> Say what you like doing on holiday for the fourth point.

> You must ask what time you leave to go on holiday for the final point.

....
....
....
....
....

⏱ Using technology

Grades 1–5

2. Practise using the following role play, saying your responses aloud. Use this space to make some notes to help you.

[10 marks]

Instructions to candidates: You are talking to a French friend about technology. The teacher will play the role of the French friend and will speak first.

You must address your French friend as *tu*.

> *Tu es chez ton ami(e) français(e). Tu parles de technologie avec lui / elle.*
>
> 1. Portable – utilisation
> 2. Internet – avantage
> 3. **!** (*Combien de temps est-ce que tu passes en ligne chaque jour?*)
> 4. Jeux vidéo – opinion
> 5. **?** Réseaux sociaux préférés

> Keep your language simple, as you can gain full marks in the role play by successfully communicating each point. Don't try to be too ambitious – focus on accurately and clearly conveying the message. Remember that pronunciation is important and can affect whether the message has been clearly communicated or not.

....
....
....
....
....

✓ **Made a start**   ✓ **Feeling confident**   ✓ **Exam ready**

Role play (Higher)

(10) **Travel arrangements**   Grades 4–9

1. Practise using the following role play, saying your responses aloud. Use this space to make some notes to help you. **[10 marks]**

Instructions to candidates: You are at a travel agency in France to book a holiday. The teacher will play the role of the agency employee and will speak first.

You must address the employee as *vous*.

> ***Vous êtes dans une agence de voyages en France. Vous parlez avec l'employé(e).***
>
> 1. Vacances – quand?
> 2. Mode de transport + raison
> 3. **!** (*Quel pays avez-vous déjà visité?*)
> 4. **?** Logement – où
> 5. **?** Activités à destination

> Say when you would like to go on holiday for the first point.

> Say how you would like to travel and give a reason for the second point.

> **? Logement – où** means you must ask where you can stay.

> **? Activités à destination** means you must ask what you can do at your holiday destination.

Exam focus

! is the unprepared question. You must answer it using the past tense.

....

....

....

....

....

(10) **Sport**   Grades 4–9

2. Practise using the following role play, saying your responses aloud. Use this space to make some notes to help you. **[10 marks]**

Instructions to candidates: You are talking to a French friend about sports. The teacher will play the role of your French friend and will speak first.

You must address your French friend as *tu*.

> ***Tu es chez ton ami(e) français(e). Tu parles de sport avec lui / elle.***
>
> 1. Sport – combien de fois
> 2. Activités après le sport + raison
> 3. **!** (*Quelles autres activités sportives as-tu faites récemment?*)
> 4. **?** Sport – quand
> 5. **?** Sport à la télé – opinion

....

....

....

....

....

....

✓ **Made a start**   ✓ **Feeling confident**   ✓ **Exam ready**

Listening strategies

⑤ Quick quiz

Draw lines to match up the following English headlines with key words that you might hear in a French listening exam.

Strike
Drought
National Day
Road accident
Bullying at school

harcèlement	intimidation	persécuter	menacer
défilé	feu d'artifice	fête nationale	célébration
travail	refuser	grève	manifestation
absence	eau	manquer	sécheresse
collision	mort	blessé	véhicule

⑩ Events in La Réunion   Grades 4–9

1. You hear a podcast about an event on the island of La Réunion.

   Listen to the recording and complete the sentences by putting a cross ☒ in the correct box for each question.

   Example: The Leu Tempo festival...

☐	**A** is a traditional dance festival
☐	**B** was held for the first time in May
☐	**C** lasts for fourteen days
☒	**D** is a well-established festival

   > The report says the festival is **ancien**, but there is no reference to traditional dance. It says that the festival takes place in May, but not that this was the first time.

   > **Exam focus** 📌
   > Read the questions and answers through before you listen so that you know what information you need to find out.

   (a) During the Safiko festival...   **[1 mark]**

☐	**A** only local artists perform
☐	**B** only international artists perform
☐	**C** hotel rooms get booked up quickly
☐	**D** tourists can enjoy a folk music concert

   (b) Le Grand Raid is an event for people who...   **[1 mark]**

☐	**A** are super fit
☐	**B** like cycling up and down hills
☐	**C** enjoy hiking in natural surroundings
☐	**D** want to discover the island by car

⑩ Life at boarding school   Grades 4–5

2. You hear Éloïse and Daniel talking about life at boarding school.

   Listen to the recording and answer the following questions **in English**.

   (a) What aspect of boarding school life does Éloïse like?   **[1 mark]**

   ....

   (b) What aspect of boarding life would she like to change perhaps? Give **two** details.   **[2 marks]**

   ....

   ....

   (c) What does Daniel describe as a positive aspect of boarding?   **[1 mark]**

   ....

   (d) What does he dislike?   **[1 mark]**

   ....

   > You know this exercise is about boarding school, so you can work out that **la pension** and **les pensionnaires** will be false friends.

   > **Exam focus** 📌
   > Before you listen, think about the positives and negatives of boarding school and the related words you know in French.

✓ **Made a start**   ✓ **Feeling confident**   ✓ **Exam ready**

Listening 1

5 Preparing to answer in French

1. Section B of the listening paper has questions **in French** that you need to answer **in French**.

Complete the following sentences.

(a) Before you listen, you should ....read... all the questions carefully.

(b) Try to .... what you need to listen out for, based on the headings you are given.

> You might need to listen for a specific detail or draw a conclusion from the whole text.

> Think about the French vocabulary you know for that topic.

10 Young people's problems   Grades 4–9

2. Ariane, Raoul et Fatima parlent de leurs problèmes.

Complète les phrases en choisissant un mot ou des mots dans la case. Il y a des mots que tu n'utiliseras pas.

amies	d'alcool	~~bonnes~~	de drogues	financiers
de logement	parents	mauvaises	n'accepte pas	
responsabilités	ne savent pas	temps libre		

Exemple: Autrefois, Ariane n'avait pas de ...bonnes............... notes.

(a) Maintenant, Ariane a des problèmes avec ses .... **[1 mark]**

(b) Les parents de Raoul .... qu'il fume. **[1 mark]**

(c) Raoul ne consomme pas .... **[1 mark]**

(d) Fatima a beaucoup de .... chez elle. **[1 mark]**

(e) La famille de Fatima avait des problèmes .... **[1 mark]**

> **Exam focus**
> Use your knowledge of grammar to help you work out what kind of word is needed for each gap.

7 A tourist guide   Grades 3–5

3. Écoute ce guide qui parle de sa ville.

Comment sont les monuments? Choisis entre: **cher, vieux, intéressant** et **ouvert**.

Chacun des mots peut être utilisé plusieurs fois.

Exemple: Le vieux quartier est ...intéressant.................................... .

(a) Le musée n'est pas .... **[1 mark]**

(b) L'hôtel de ville n'est pas .... **[1 mark]**

(c) Le château est .... **[1 mark]**

(d) Le parc est .... **[1 mark]**

(e) Le pont est .... **[1 mark]**

> Before listening, think about how the adjectives might be differently expressed, for example by using a phrase that conveys the same meaning. Watch out for negatives in both the questions and the audio.

✓ **Made a start**   ✓ **Feeling confident**   ✓ **Exam ready**   57

Listening 2

5 **Preparing to answer in English** 🎧 ☑

1. In Section A of the listening paper, you will be given questions **in English**. You need to answer them **in English**.

Practise predicting the words that you might hear below. The topic is the environment.

Problem	Solution
pollution of rivers (la pollution des rivières)	
air pollution (la pollution de l'air)	
disappearance of species (la disparition des espèces)	
pollution of the oceans	réduire le plastique, les risques pour la vie marine…

10 **Jobs: advantages and disadvantages** | Grades 4–9 | 🎧 ☑

2. At a careers fair you hear two people, Riley and Céline, talking about their jobs.
Listen to the recording and answer the following questions **in English**.

   (a) What kind of people would be interested in the job that Riley does? **[1 mark]**

   ....

   (b) What does he like about his job? Give **one** detail. **[1 mark]**

   ....

   (c) What is **one** disadvantage? **[1 mark]**

   ....

   (d) What are **two** positive aspects of a career in the sciences, according to Céline? **[2 marks]**

   ....

   (e) What is one of the drawbacks of this career? **[1 mark]**

   ....

> Consider the French vocabulary you know for this theme. Listen out for these words, but remember to write your answers **in English**.

> Riley describes his work as **travail indépendant**, which means the same as *freelance*.

> Generally, speakers will sound positive when talking about the advantages of something, and negative when they speak about disadvantages. This isn't always the case though.

10 **Understanding problems** | Grades 4–5 | 🎧 ☑

3. While on a French exchange, you hear a boy in your French friend's class, Loïc, explaining why he arrived late to school. Answer the following questions **in English**.

> Each question is only worth one mark, so you just need to give a simple answer for each one.

   (a) What was the **main** reason why Loïc was late to school? **[1 mark]**

   ....

   (b) How was this situation made worse? **[1 mark]**

   ....

☑ **Made a start** ☑ **Feeling confident** ☑ **Exam ready**

Reading strategies

⑤ Quick quiz

1. Decode the spelling patterns. Translate the following words **into English**.

(a) hâte ....   **(b)** plâtre ....   **(c)** honnête ....   **(d)** intérêt ....

(e) épice ....   **(f)** étrange ....   **(g)** étable ....   **(h)** hôpital ....

2. What are the English equivalents of the following French suffixes in bold?

(a) prim**aire** ....   **(b)** universi**té** ....   **(c)** act**if** ....

⑩ Using vocabulary and grammar to work out meaning   Grades 4–9

1. Translate the following passage **into English**.

> Pendant mon stage en France, j'ai eu la chance de passer une journée au siège d'une chaîne de librairies, situé sur la côte. On y est allés en car et le chef d'entreprise nous a accueillis quand nous sommes arrivés. J'avais pensé que cette visite ne serait pas intéressante mais en fait, je l'ai trouvée absolument fascinante.

....

....

....

....

You might not know the word accueillis, but from the context you should be able to work out that it means *welcomed* or *received*.

Make sure that you use the correct tenses in your translation.

Work out whether a word is a verb, noun or adjective from its position in a sentence, or the endings.

Exam focus

Watch out for *false friends:* words that look like English words, but have a different meaning in French, like **attendre** *to wait* and **journée (f)** *day*.

⑩ A restaurant review   Grades 4–9

2. You are looking online for somewhere to eat and come across the following review.

> Une grande déception après plusieurs visites agréables. Normalement, l'accueil est chaleureux et le service attentif et efficace. Cette fois, que de problèmes! Malgré notre réservation, il a fallu attendre au moins un quart d'heure lors de notre arrivée. La table qu'on nous a donnée n'était pas près de la fenêtre avec vue sur la plage comme nous l'avions demandé, mais dans un coin à côté des toilettes où nous avons été dérangés toute la soirée. À un moment donné, le patron a hurlé après les serveurs devant les clients, de sorte que tout le monde a arrêté de parler. On ne peut pas dire que c'était une soirée tranquille.

Answer the following questions **in English**.

(a) How did the reviewer feel about their visit on **this** occasion?   **[1 mark]**

....

(b) How did this compare to previous occasions? Give **two** details.   **[2 marks]**

....

(c) What was the particular problem with their table? Give **two** details.   **[2 marks]**

....

(d) What happened during the evening for the reviewer to make their final comment?   **[1 mark]**

....

✓ Made a start   ✓ Feeling confident   ✓ Exam ready   **59**

Reading 1

(5) **Section A: Answering in English**

In Section A of the reading paper, you will need to answer questions **in English**.

1. You receive the following text message from your French friend Marc.

> Que la vie est injuste! Ma sœur est forte dans toutes les matières au collège et tout ce qu'elle fait est toujours parfait. Mes parents lui donnent une récompense chaque fois qu'elle a de bons résultats aux examens. D'un autre côté, moi, je ne reçois jamais rien!

(a) What does Marc think about his sister?

....

(b) Give a reason for this reaction.

....

(10) **Restaurant review**   Grades 4–5

2. You and your friends are looking for somewhere to eat and come across this online review of a restaurant.

> Jeudi soir, nous avons dîné en famille au restaurant *La Petite Auberge*. Nous avons choisi cet établissement parce que mes amis me l'avaient recommandé, en disant que les prix étaient raisonnables. Comme j'ai été déçue! On n'a jamais autant payé pour un repas si ordinaire. La soupe que j'ai choisie était trop salée et le cassoulet manquait de goût. Pourtant, j'aurais pu manger deux portions de mon dessert, une mousse au chocolat! Il est vrai qu'il y avait une bonne ambiance dans ce restaurant et que le personnel était attentif mais je ne pense pas qu'on y retournera.
> **Gaëlle**

What does the review tell us?

Put a cross ☒ next to each of the **two** correct boxes.   **[2 marks]**

Example	Gaëlle visited the restaurant on a weekday evening.	☒
A	Gaëlle's friends recommended the restaurant.	☐
B	Gaëlle thought the meal was good value for money.	☐
C	Gaëlle thought that the service could be improved.	☐
D	Gaëlle thought that one course of her meal was particularly good.	☐
E	Gaëlle would like to go back to the restaurant on another occasion.	☐

Exam focus

Read the whole passage before you decide on your answers.

J'aurais pu manger means *I could have eaten*.

The adjective **attentif** refers to the staff.

(5) **Television viewing habits**   Grades 5–7

3. You are interested in the television opinions of young French people and have found the following post on an online forum.

> Mes parents me critiquent chaque fois que je regarde une émission de télé-réalité en disant que c'est une perte de temps. Ils ne comprennent pas que de telles émissions sont divertissantes et m'aident à me détendre car je suis tellement stressé par mon travail scolaire. De toute façon, j'ai rarement le temps de regarder les émissions à l'heure à laquelle elles sont diffusées. Heureusement, j'ai ma tablette. D'autre part, mes parents préfèrent regarder les informations chaque soir à une heure précise sur le grand écran du salon, tandis que je suis l'actualité sur les réseaux sociaux.
> **Gérard**

Answer the following questions **in English**.

(a) What do Gérard's parents think about reality TV shows?   **[1 mark]**

....

(b) What is Gérard's attitude to reality TV?   **[1 mark]**

....

(c) How does the way in which he and his parents find out about the news differ? Give **two** details.   **[2 marks]**

....

For one or two marks, you only need to give short answers.

☑ **Made a start**   ☑ **Feeling confident**   ☑ **Exam ready**

Reading 2

⑤ Section B: Answering in French

In Section B of the reading paper, you will have to answer questions **in French**.

1. Voici des titres de la première page des journaux dans un kiosque en France. Il s'agit d'un reportage au sujet de quoi?
Écris la lettre dans la case correcte.

A	Des milliers de maisons en ruines, dix-mille personnes sans domicile
B	Deux morts, trois blessés sur le boulevard périphérique
C	État d'urgence déclaré suite à des précipitations prolongées
D	Installation de panneaux solaires sur le toit de la mairie

1	accident de la route	
2	initiative verte	
3	inondations	
4	séisme	

⑩ Conseils pour un entretien Grades 4–5

2. Lis ces conseils pour te préparer à un entretien d'embauche.

- Faites attention à la manière dont vous vous habillez car on vous jugera sur votre apparence. Évitez donc les vêtements trop à la mode, portez de préférence des vêtements noirs, blancs ou bleu foncé.
- Il faut absolument que vous arriviez à l'heure. Renseignez-vous sur les modes de transport de sorte que vous ne soyez pas en retard et que vous évitiez le stress de dernière minute.

Couleurs vives means *bright colours*.

Exam focus
Read both the text and the question very carefully before choosing an answer. Be wary of answers that use the exact same words as the text.

Mets une croix ☒ dans la case correcte.

(a) Pour un entretien, il faut… **[1 mark]**

☐	**A** s'habiller uniquement en noir
☐	**B** porter un uniforme
☐	**C** porter des vêtements à la mode
☐	**D** éviter les vêtements de couleurs très vives

(b) Pour aller à l'entretien, il vaut mieux… **[1 mark]**

☐	**A** bien savoir comment vous irez au rendez-vous
☐	**B** décider au dernier moment comment vous y voyagez
☐	**C** se déplacer en transports en commun
☐	**D** éviter les transports en commun

⑩ My friends Grades 4–5

3. Lis ce mail de ton ami français, Albert.

Quand tu vas venir chez moi, tu vas rencontrer mes amis. Raoul raconte toujours des histoires drôles. Lui, c'est la personne avec qui je m'entends le mieux. Je passe aussi beaucoup de temps avec Didier car nous sommes tous les deux membres de l'équipe de foot. Marcel est le plus bavard d'entre nous et il a souvent des ennuis avec les professeurs au collège.

C'est quelle personne? Choisis entre: **Raoul**, **Didier** et **Marcel**.

Chacun des noms peut être utilisé plusieurs fois.

Exemple: Albert dit que Raoul.. est amusant.

(a) Il dit que .... parle trop. **[1 mark]**

(b) Son ami .... est sportif. **[1 mark]**

(c) Son meilleur ami est .... **[1 mark]**

(d) .... a probablement un mauvais bulletin scolaire. **[1 mark]**

☑ **Made a start** ☑ **Feeling confident** ☑ **Exam ready**

Reading 3

(10) A Maupassant short story | Grades 4–9

1. Read the short extract from Guy de Maupassant's *Une Vie*.

> *Julien avait cessé de se raser, de sorte que sa barbe longue, mal coupée, l'enlaidissait incroyablement. Ses mains n'étaient plus soignées; et il buvait, après chaque repas, quatre ou cinq petits verres de cognac.*

> Read the questions to see if they help you work out the meaning of an unfamiliar word.

Answer the following questions **in English**.

(a) What does the first sentence tell you about how Julien looks after his appearance? **[1 mark]**

....

(b) What possible explanation is there for the way he looks? **[1 mark]**

....

Exam focus
Use your knowledge of prefixes and suffixes to work out the meaning of words: **–ment** is the ending for an adverb and often corresponds to *–ly* in English.

> Look for familiar short words you know, like **laid** (*ugly*) inside a longer word, like **enlaidir** (*to make something ugly*). Part of the verb **croire** (*to believe*) is in the word **incroyablement** (*unbelievably*).

Exam focus
You could use highlighters to mark words that you know.

(10) Une Vie | Grades 4–9

2. Read this further extract from Guy de Maupassant's *Une Vie*.

> *Pour Jeanne, les relations avec Julien avaient changé complètement. Il semblait tout autre depuis le retour de leur voyage de noces, comme un acteur qui a fini son rôle et reprend sa figure ordinaire. C'est à peine s'il s'occupait d'elle, s'il lui parlait même; toute trace d'amour avait subitement disparu; et les nuits étaient rares où il pénétrait dans sa chambre.*
>
> *Elle avait pris son parti* de ces changements d'une façon qui l'étonnait elle-même. Il était devenu un étranger pour elle, un étranger dont l'âme et le cœur lui restaient fermés. Elle y songeait souvent, se demandant d'où venait qu'après s'être rencontrés ainsi, aimés, épousés dans un élan de tendresse, ils se retrouvaient tout à coup presque aussi inconnus l'un à l'autre que s'ils n'avaient pas dormi côte à côte.*
>
> ***prendre son parti** – to go along with

Put a cross ☒ in each one of the **three** correct boxes. **[3 marks]**

Example	Jeanne noticed that Julien's personality had changed since they got married.	☒
A	Jeanne and Julien are a happy couple now.	☐
B	Jeanne no longer recognises the man she married.	☐
C	Julien was more tender towards Jeanne before their honeymoon.	☐
D	Julien ignores his wife now.	☐
E	Julien and Jeanne always spend the night together now.	☐
F	Julien works as an actor.	☐
G	Julien is always very kind to Jeanne.	☐

Made a start | Feeling confident | Exam ready

Reading 4

1. Read the extract from the novel by Antoine de Saint-Exupéry. The pilot meets *le petit prince*.

> *J'ai ainsi vécu seul, sans personne avec qui parler véritablement, jusqu'à une panne dans le désert du Sahara, il y a six ans. Quelque chose s'était cassé dans mon moteur, et comme je n'avais avec moi ni mécanicien, ni passagers, je me préparai à essayer de réussir, tout seul, une réparation difficile. C'était pour moi une question de vie ou de mort. J'avais à peine de l'eau à boire pour huit jours.*
>
> *Le premier soir je me suis donc endormi sur le sable à mille milles de toute terre habitée. J'étais bien plus isolé qu'un naufragé sur un radeau au milieu de l'océan. Alors vous imaginez ma surprise, au lever du jour, quand une drôle de petite voix m'a réveillé. Elle disait:*
>
> *– S'il vous plaît... dessine-moi un mouton!*

Answer the following questions **in English**. You do not need to write in full sentences.

(a) Where was the pilot when he met *le petit prince* and what had happened to him? **[2 marks]**

....

(b) Why was it urgent that he find a solution to his problem? **[1 mark]**

....

(c) How did he feel when he went to sleep on that first evening? **[1 mark]**

....

(d) What happened the following morning? **[2 marks]**

....

> **Mouton** is similar to the English word 'mutton' and means 'sheep'.

2. Lis cet extrait du *Grand Meaulnes* d'Alain Fournier. Augustin Meaulnes décrit une visite à Paris.

> *Aujourd'hui, dès mon arrivée à Paris, je suis allé devant la maison indiquée. Je n'ai rien vu. Il n'y avait personne. Il n'y aura jamais personne. La maison que disait Frantz est un petit hôtel à un étage. La chambre de Mlle de Galais doit être au premier. Les fenêtres du haut sont les plus cachées par les arbres. Mais en passant sur le trottoir on les voit très bien. Tous les rideaux sont fermés et il faudrait être fou pour espérer qu'un jour, entre ces rideaux tirés, le visage d'Yvonne de Galais puisse apparaître.*
>
> *La nuit est venue. Les fenêtres se sont allumées un peu partout mais non dans cette maison. Il n'y a certainement personne.*
>
> *Au moment où j'allais partir une jeune fille, ou une jeune femme – je ne sais – est venue s'asseoir sur un des bancs mouillés de pluie. Elle était habillée en noir. Lorsque je suis parti, elle était encore là, immobile malgré le froid du soir, à attendre je ne sais quoi, je ne sais qui. Tu vois que Paris est plein de fous comme moi.*

Réponds aux questions **en français**. Il n'est pas nécessaire d'écrire des phrases complètes.

(a) Pourquoi Augustin est-il allé à Paris? **[1 mark]**

....

....

(b) Pourquoi était-il difficile de voir quelqu'un à la fenêtre de l'hôtel? **Deux** détails. **[2 marks]**

....

....

(c) Comment Augustin savait-il qu'il n'y avait personne dans le bâtiment qu'il observait? **[1 mark]**

....

....

(d) Quel temps faisait-il ce jour-là? **[2 marks]**

....

....

✓ **Made a start**　✓ **Feeling confident**　✓ **Exam ready**

Translation into English

⑤ Short translations

1. Translate the following **into English**.

(a) la petite amie de mon frère ....

(b) chez mes grands-parents ....

(c) Il travaille comme professeur depuis deux ans. ....

(d) Je viens de rentrer de France. ....

⑩ An email about jogging   Grades 4–9

2. Your French friend has sent you an email. Translate it **into English**.   **[7 marks]**

> Je fais du jogging régulièrement depuis deux ans. Actuellement je m'entraîne pour participer à une course de dix kilomètres qui aura lieu le week-end prochain. Aujourd'hui, il faisait un peu froid mais après avoir couru pendant une demi-heure, j'avais chaud. Mon prof de sport vient de me dire que de telles conditions sont bonnes pour une course.

In the first sentence, translate the verb using a past tense in English – *have been …ing*. Use *for* to translate **depuis** here (to show a length of time).

Actuellement is a false friend. It means *at the moment*.

Aura lieu is the future tense of **avoir lieu** *(to take place)*.

Don't miss little words like **un peu**.

Translate **vient de** with *has just*.

Exam focus
Read your translation through to make sure it sounds like natural English.

....
....
....
....
....
....
....

⑩ A description of an evening with friends   Grades 4–9

3. Translate this passage **into English**.   **[7 marks]**

> Hier soir, quelques-uns de mes camarades de classe sont venus chez moi pour voir un film que j'avais téléchargé. Après avoir regardé le film, nous avions faim et nous sommes allés dans la cuisine pour chercher un casse-croûte. Mes parents disent que je ne devrais pas grignoter entre les repas puisqu'ils ont peur que je grossisse, mais cela m'est égal!

....
....
....
....

☑ **Made a start**   ☑ **Feeling confident**   ☑ **Exam ready**

Writing strategies

---

⑤ Quick quiz

Correct the mistakes in the following sentences. Rewrite the sentences. The number of errors in each one is given in brackets.

1. [ATTENTION: ERREURS!] Ma sœur et gentil mais pas tres travailleure. Elle ne fais rien a la maison. (6)

....

2. [ATTENTION: ERREURS!] Ils ont cherche une blanc chemise au magasin grand. (4)

....

---

⑮ A shopping trip | Grades 1–9

1. You are writing your response to the following bullet points on a writing task.

- Faire des achats – où?
- Achats récents

Read the response. Rewrite it using the following suggestions:

- Use a conjunction to link the first two sentences.
- Extend **Je vais faire les magasins** by adding a time phrase and saying who you will go with.
- Replace **j'achète** with the **nous** or **il(s) / elle(s)** form.
- Link the sentence **J'ai acheté un pull...** to the previous sentence by using **mais** and a time phrase.
- Link the final sentence to the previous sentence by using **qui** to refer back to **un pull**, and add an adjective to **chaussettes**.

> J'aime faire des achats. C'est amusant. Je vais faire les magasins dans ma ville. Normalement, j'achète des magazines et des bonbons. J'ai acheté un pull et des chaussettes. Le pull n'était pas cher.

....

....

....

....

---

⑮ Writing about school | Grades 4–6

2. Ton ami(e) français(e) te demande des renseignements sur ton collège.

Écris un mail. Tu **dois** faire référence aux points suivants:

- une journée ordinaire dans ton collège
- les matières – tes préférences
- une activité extrascolaire récente
- ce que tu vas faire l'année prochaine – études.

Écris 80–90 mots environ **en français**.   **[20 marks]**

Exam focus
Remember to use three tenses, adjectives, opinions and time phrases.

Aiming higher
Read through your answer a couple of times. Look out for any mistakes you make regularly, such as agreements, verb endings and word order.

....

....

....

....

✓ **Made a start**   ✓ **Feeling confident**   ✓ **Exam ready**   **65**

Translation into French (Foundation)

(10) Translating sentences   Grades 1–5

1. Traduis les phrases suivantes **en français**.

(a) My mother is tall and has blue eyes.   **[2 marks]**

....

....

(b) We live in a small house in the country.   **[2 marks]**

....

....

(c) At the weekend I go cycling with my father.   **[2 marks]**

....

....

(d) I don't like swimming in the sea.   **[2 marks]**

....

....

(e) Last month I went to France with my friends.   **[2 marks]**

....

....

> **Exam focus**
> Check you have the correct verb endings and agreements on verbs and adjectives.

> Make sure *tall* agrees with *mother*.

> Make sure *small* agrees with *house* **(f)**.

> Use either **faire du cyclisme** or **faire du vélo** for *to go cycling*.

> Use **aimer** followed by an infinitive. **Ne** and **pas** must go around the first verb.

(10) Translating sentences   Grades 1–5

2. Traduis les phrases suivantes **en français**.

(a) My sister is shy but hard-working.   **[2 marks]**

....

(b) On Sundays, we have lunch at my grandparents.   **[2 marks]**

....

(c) There is a swimming pool next to the cinema.   **[2 marks]**

....

(d) I like doing exercise in the morning.   **[2 marks]**

....

(e) In summer, I played tennis.   **[2 marks]**

....

Translation into French (Higher)

Translating a passage

(10)

Grades 4–9

1. Traduis le passage suivant **en français**.

[12 marks]

> I get on well with everyone in my family, except my younger sister who is lazy and never helps at home. Last weekend, I had to go shopping and make dinner. We had chicken with vegetables, and afterwards there was cheese and fruit. I think it's important to eat healthily, but junk food sometimes tastes better.

Lazy (**paresseux**) must agree with *younger sister*.

Use either **nous** or **on** to translate *we*.

Use the correct form of **du**, **de la** and **des** with food items.

....

....

....

....

....

....

....

....

....

....

Translating a passage

(10)

Grades 4–9

2. Traduis le passage suivant **en français**.

[12 marks]

> My elder brother and I volunteer with a charity that supports refugees. I think it would be very difficult to leave my family and friends and go to a new country. There are a lot of refugees in my town and some of them live on the streets. Last week, we raised some money by selling cakes.

....

....

....

....

....

....

....

....

....

....

✓ **Made a start**   ✓ **Feeling confident**   ✓ **Exam ready**

Writing (Foundation)

⑩ Confirming holiday arrangements — Grades 1–5 ✓

1. Vous allez passer des vacances dans une chambre d'hôte en France.

Écrivez un mail au propriétaire avec les informations suivantes:

- détails de votre arrivée
- votre moyen de transport
- le petit déjeuner – vos préférences
- pourquoi vous voulez visiter cette région.

Il faut écrire des phrases complètes.

Écrivez 40–50 mots environ **en français**. **[16 marks]**

....

....

....

....

....

> Give the date and time of your arrival for the first bullet point.

> Say how you are travelling for the second bullet point.

> **Exam focus** 📌
> Remember to use the formal words for *you* and *your* (**vous** / **votre** / **vos**).

> **Exam focus** 📌
> Remember to write in complete sentences.

⑩ Describing a photo — Grades 1–5 ✓

2. Tu vas en vacances. Tu postes cette photo sur des réseaux sociaux pour tes amis.

Écris une description de la photo **et** exprime ton opinion sur les transports.

Écris 20–30 mots environ **en français**. **[12 marks]**

....

....

....

....

✓ **Made a start** ✓ **Feeling confident** ✓ **Exam ready**

Writing (Higher)

⏱ 40 Complaining about a hotel stay — Grades 4–9

1. Vous écrivez un mail pour vous plaindre au directeur de l'hôtel où vous avez passé vos vacances.

Vous **devez** faire référence aux points suivants:

- détails de votre séjour
- pourquoi vous écrivez – les problèmes
- votre opinion de l'hôtel
- vos suggestions pour améliorer la situation.

Justifiez vos idées et vos opinions.

Écrivez 130–150 mots environ **en français**.   **[28 marks]**

....
....
....
....
....
....

> Write to a hotel manager about problems during your stay. For example, *the staff* (**le personnel**) were *rude* (**impoli**) or not *welcoming* (**accueillant**), or the *lift* (**l'ascenseur (m)**), television or *shower* (**la douche**) was not *working* (**fonctionner**). Problems in the room could relate to the *view* (**la vue**), the size, the *heating* (**le chauffage**) or amenities, such as WiFi.

> You must make suggestions to the manager as to how to improve the situation. You could use the conditional (**vous devriez** – *you should*, **vous pourriez** – *you could*).

Aiming higher
Justify your opinions using different phrases: **parce que / car** (*because*); **pour** + infinitive (*in order to*); **afin de** + infinitive (*in order to*); **alors, par contre, mais, puisque**. Include higher level language and structures: pluperfect tense, perfect infinitive (**après avoir / être** + past participle). Use the conditional to write about what you would or could do in the future.

> Use **Monsieur / Madame**, **vous** and **votre** for formal communication. **Salutations distinguées** is used for a formal ending.

⏱ 40 Writing about a school exchange — Grades 4–9

2. Vous écrivez un article sur votre visite à votre école partenaire en France pour un magazine.

Vous **devez** faire référence aux points suivants:

- vos activités et impressions pendant votre séjour
- le meilleur aspect de l'échange
- l'importance des échanges scolaires – votre opinion
- projets pour une autre visite à l'étranger.

Justifiez vos idées et vos opinions.

Écrivez 130–150 mots environ **en français**.   **[28 marks]**

....
....
....
....
....
....
....

✓ **Made a start**   ✓ **Feeling confident**   ✓ **Exam ready**

Articles

⑤ Quick quiz

Translate the following sentences **into English**. Underline the articles that you do not need to translate into English.

1. Le Portugal est plus petit que l'Espagne. ....

2. Il est journaliste. ....

3. J'apprends le français depuis trois ans. ....

4. Elle habite une jolie maison dans un petit village. ....

⑩ Using the definite and indefinite article   Grades 1–5

1. Translate the following sentences **into French**.

(a) At the weekend, I like watching football on television.

    week-end, ...

> Use the definite article in front of *week-end*.

(b) There is a swimming pool and a sports centre in my town.

    Il y a   piscine ....

(c) Geography, history and art are my favourite subjects.

    géographie ....

> Check the gender of nouns when deciding which article to use. Use the definite article before school subjects and country names.

(d) He is learning German.

    Il apprend ....

(e) Switzerland is a small country.

    Suisse est ....

⑩ Translating short sentences   Grades 1–5

2. Translate the following sentences **into French**.

(a) My stepmother is a doctor.

....

> You don't need the indefinite article (**un / une**) when talking about people's jobs.

(b) She has fair hair and brown eyes.

....

(c) She has a good job in a big hospital.

....

(d) On Sundays we have lunch at one o'clock.

....

(e) I love fruit but I hate vegetables.

....

☑ **Made a start**   ☑ **Feeling confident**   ☑ **Exam ready**

Prepositions

⑤ Quick quiz

Draw lines to match up the pairs.

(a)

après	between
dans	on
derrière	after
entre	under
sous	behind
sur	in

(b)

malgré	except
parmi	under
à travers	according to
sauf	in spite of
sous	across
selon	among

⑩ Prepositions to fill the gaps · Grades 4–5

1. Fill in the gaps with the correct preposition from the box. You can use the prepositions more than once.

pendant	pour	en	malgré	dans	pour	chez	depuis

(a) *En* ..... juin, nous allons .... Italie .... avion.

(b) .... la pluie, nous sommes sortis pour faire une promenade .... les champs.

(c) Mon frère a travaillé *dans* ...... une colonie de vacances .... deux mois.

(d) .... l'été, nous irons *en* ..... Espagne .... une semaine.

(e) Nous allons passer Noël .... mes grands-parents.

(f) J'ai laissé mon pull .... coton .... haut.

(g) J'apprends le français .... quatre ans.

> **En** means *to* or *in* with feminine countries, *in* when used with months and seasons and *by* which means of transport.

> Use **pour** to translate *for* when referring to a length of time in the future and use **pendant** for a length of time in the past.

> Use **chez** when you want to say *at someone's house*.

⑩ Translating prepositions · Grades 4–9

2. Translate this passage **into French**.

> I would like to live near my cousin, who lives in Scotland, in a valley between two mountains. In front of her house, there is a lake where she goes swimming before breakfast. During the day, she usually goes for a walk with her dog, except when it snows. In winter, she wears a lot of woollen clothes and leather boots.

....

....

....

....

....

....

☐ **Made a start**   ☐ **Feeling confident**   ☐ **Exam ready**

The preposition à

⑤ Quick quiz

1. Fill in the gap with the correct form of the preposition **à**: **à**, **au**, **à la**, **à l'** or **aux**.

(a) On se retrouve .... théâtre.

(b) Je vais aller .... Champs-Élysées .... Paris.

(c) Il a mal .... estomac.

(d) Demain, on va .... piscine.

2. The preposition **à** has different meanings in different contexts. What does it mean in these sentences?

(a) Mon appartement est <u>au</u> premier étage.   **(b)** Je te verrai <u>au</u> théâtre.   **(c)** Je vais <u>à</u> Marseille.

....

⑩ Les jeux de boules

1. Translate this passage **into English**. Pay attention to the circled words.

(Au) printemps, j'ai passé mes vacances dans le sud de la France. J'ai logé dans un appartement (à) deux-cents mètres du vieux port de Marseille. Chaque jour, j'ai fait une promenade (à) cheval ou j'ai joué (aux) boules avec une vieille femme (aux) cheveux gris. Dans le sud, on appelle ça jouer (à la) pétanque. On se retrouvait (à) 16h (au) port et on passait deux heures (à) jouer. Mais un jour, j'avais mal (au) dos, alors elle m'a invité (au) café. J'ai commandé un sandwich (au) fromage et une glace (à la) fraise.

> The preposition **à** can be translated by *in, at, on, to, by* or *with,* depending on the context. Sometimes you don't translate it at all: **jouer au football** (m) means *to play football*.

🪧 In spring, I spent my holidays in

....

....

....

....

....

....

⑩ Shopping for food   Grades 1–5

2. You have been given a picture-based task as part of your writing exam and want to write these four sentences. Translate them **into French**.

(a) On the photo, there are four people who are at home.

....

(b) The girl on the left is smiling.

....

(c) They are playing a card game.

....

(d) The blonde woman in the middle has four cards.

....

☑ **Made a start**   ☑ **Feeling confident**   ☑ **Exam ready**

Partitives and preposition *de*

Quick quiz

Choose the correct form of **de** to fill each gap.

de	d'	du	de la	des	de l'

1. Il vient .... États-Unis.

2. La poste est à côté .... cinéma.

3. J'ai fini .... regarder le film.

4. Je n'ai pas .... frères.

5. La voiture .... ma mère est rouge.

6. Il y a .... poulet et .... frites.

Using *de* in all kinds of sentences — Grades 4–5

1. Translate the following sentences **into French**.

(a) The car park is to the left of the hotel and next to the park.

⚐ Le parking
....

(b) I must borrow my friend's phone.

⚐ Je dois
....

(c) I would like some soup with some bread and butter.

⚐ Je voudrais
....

(d) There are some pretty houses opposite the cathedral.

⚐ Il y a
....

(e) He has come back from Japan and China.

⚐ Il est
....

(f) She has a kilo of potatoes but she hasn't got any onions.

⚐ Elle a un kilo
....

Vocabulary A–Z

À gauche de means *to the left*, à côté de means *next to*.

Translate *my friend's phone* as *the phone* (**le portable**) *of my friend*.

Just use **de** when a plural adjective (**jolies**) comes before a noun.

In negative sentences just use **de** or **d'**.

Describing where you would like to live — Grades 1–5

2. Translate this passage **into French**.

> I have invited some friends of my parents to dinner, but I haven't got any food in the house. I will have to go to the supermarket opposite the museum to buy some fish, some vegetables and some ice cream. I don't need any coffee. I've already bought some mineral water in the shop next to the post office.

....
....
....
....
....
....

```

# Nouns

## ⑤ Quick quiz

Masculine or feminine? Tick either **M** or **F**. Then write two **French** examples.

|  | M | F | Examples |
|---|---|---|---|
| Continents are |  |  |  |
| Days, months and seasons are |  |  |  |
| Weights and measures are |  |  |  |
| Most countries and rivers are |  |  |  |
| Most shops are |  |  |  |

## ⑩ Masculine and feminine job names

1. For each of the following nouns, write the gender, the equivalent noun in the opposite gender, and the meaning.

(a) informaticien *M, informaticienne F, – IT technician*

(b) infirmier .....................................

(c) pharmacienne .....................................

(d) chanteur .....................................

(e) chercheuse .....................................

(f) ouvrier .....................................

(g) directrice .....................................

(h) employée.....................................

(i) étudiant .....................................

(j) électricien .....................................

Many jobs and occupations have different endings depending on whether they refer to a man or a woman. **–ier**, **–eur**, **–ant**, **–teur** and **–ien** are masculine endings. **–ière**, **–euse**, **–ante**, **–trice** and **–ienne** are feminine endings.

## ⑩ Using nouns to describe a photo                     Grades 1–5

2. You have been given a picture-based task to prepare and want to say the following sentences. Translate them **into French**.

(a) A group of friends are sitting outside on chairs around a table.

..............................................................

..............................................................

(b) They are in a garden and it is very sunny.

..............................................................

(c) One of the girls is wearing a red dress and another girl is wearing a hat.

..............................................................

..............................................................

(d) They are eating salad and drinking lemonade.

..........................................................................................................................

(e) The girl in the red dress has long hair.

..........................................................................................................................

☑ **Made a start**   ☑ **Feeling confident**   ☑ **Exam ready**
```

Adjectives

⑤ Quick quiz

Use the letters and words in the box to fill in the gaps.

e	s	agrees	feminine	gender	in front of	singular	after

In French, an adjective changes its form so that it .... with the word it is describing. It must match the .... (masculine or ....) of the noun and whether it is .... or plural. Most adjectives add an .... in the feminine form and an .... in the plural and go .... the noun. Adjectives such as **beau**, **gros**, **bon**, **joli**, **grand** and **petit** go .... the noun.

⑩ Meanings of adjectives   Grades 1–5 👓

1. Underline the adjective(s) in each of the following sentences and translate the sentences **into English**.

(a) Avez-vous les mains <u>propres</u>? *Have you got* ....

(b) Il porte un pantalon bleu foncé et une veste gris clair. ....
....

(c) On peut visiter les ruines de l'ancien château dans le grand parc.
....

(d) Les réponses aux questions étaient fausses. ....
....

(e) J'ai un portable neuf. Il était assez cher. ....
....

(f) Nous habitons une belle maison dans une vieille ville. ....
....

Vocabulary 🔤 A–Z

Propre means *clean* when used after the noun, and *own* when used before.

Foncé used with a colour means *dark*.

Clair means *light*.

Ancien means *ancient* when used after the noun, and *former* when used before.

> Adjectives must agree with the noun even if they are not directly in front or after them.

> **Belle** and **vieille** are feminine forms of the adjectives **beau** and **vieux**.

⑩ Translating adjectives   Grades 4–9 ✏️

2. Translate the sentences below **into French**.

(a) Last Saturday I went for a long walk in a beautiful park.
....

(b) I will visit an interesting museum next week.
....

(c) There are a lot of beautiful plates and some old costumes.
....

(d) Where is the Italian bakery?
....

☑ **Made a start**   ☑ **Feeling confident**   ☑ **Exam ready**

Comparatives and superlatives

(3) Quick quiz

Read the following facts about France. Circle the option so that each statement is correct.

1. La France est **plus / moins / aussi** grande que la Suisse.

2. La Seine (776 km) est **plus / moins / aussi** longue que la Loire (1013 km).

3. La tour Eiffel est le monument le plus **petit / court / haut** de Paris.

4. Le Mont Blanc (4808 m) est **plus / moins / aussi** haut que le Puy de Sancy (1885 m).

5. La Réunion est **le plus grand / la plus grande** département d'outre-mer de France.

(10) Comparing twins · Grades 4–5

1. Translate this passage **into English**.

> Frédéric et Liliane sont des jumeaux. Liliane est plus intelligente que son frère et elle a toujours les meilleures notes. Cependant, il est moins timide qu'elle et il est plus heureux de parler avec des gens qu'il ne connaît pas. Ils aiment tous les deux regarder la télé mais Frédéric pense que les émissions de télé-réalité sont pires que les jeux télévisés.

> **Meilleur(e / s)** means *better / best* and is used for the comparative and superlative for **bon(ne / s)**.

> **Pire(s)** means *worse / worst* and is used for the comparative and superlative for **mauvais(e / s)**.

Frédéric and Liliane are twins.
....
....
....
....
....

(10) Making comparisons · Grades 4–5

2. Translate the following sentences **into French**.

(a) The best song won the competition.
....

(b) This is the worst hotel.
....

(c) She is as active as her mother.
....

(d) He is not as strong as his father.
....

(e) Belgium is smaller than Switzerland.
....

Made a start ☑   Feeling confident ☑   Exam ready ☑

Possessive and demonstrative adjectives

(5) Quick quiz

Translate the following sentences **into English**.

1. Cet hôtel est près de notre maison. ....

2. Mes cousins passent leurs vacances chez moi. ....

3. Pierre et sa sœur ont visité ce musée. ....

4. J'ai acheté ces légumes au marché. ....

5. Avez-vous fait vos devoirs cette semaine? ....

6. Ma sœur va sortir avec ses copines ce soir. ....

(10) Possessives and demonstrative adjectives

1. Fill in the gaps with the correct form of the adjective shown in brackets.

(a) Thomas parle avec .... sœur. (his)

(b) Où sont .... papiers? (your)

(c) Laure cherche .... père. (her)

(d) Ils sont chez .... grands-parents. (their)

(e) J'ai perdu .... montre. (my)

(f) .... train est arrivé en retard. (our)

(g) .... plat est délicieux. (this)

(h) .... arbre est très vieux. (this)

(i) .... chaussures sont chères. (these)

(j) Je ne l'ai pas vu .... fois. (this)

> *His* or *her* must agree with the noun it goes before, not the subject of the verb. **Sa sœur** means *his sister*, if the subject is male.

> The adjective must agree with the gender and number of the noun it precedes. Use a dictionary to help you.

(10) Plans for the weekend — Grades 1–5

2. You are writing a response to the following bullet point in a writing task.

• Projets pour ce week-end

Translate this passage **into French**.

> This weekend, we are going to visit our cousins. Their father is my mother's brother, and his wife is our favourite aunt. On this occasion, my cousin Robert wants to show me his new bike, and his sister, my cousin Susanne, plans to try out this new recipe for biscuits.

....

....

....

....

....

....

....

Indefinite and interrogative adjectives

⑤ Quick quiz

1. Fill in the table with all four forms of **tout**, meaning *all*.

masculine singular	feminine singular	masculine plural	feminine plural

2. Fill in the table with all four forms of **quel**, meaning *which*.

masculine singular	feminine singular	masculine plural	feminine plural

⑩ Using the right form of *tout* and *quel*

1. Fill in the gap with the correct form of the word in brackets. Then write the meaning of each phrase.

(a) .... mes amies (tout) all my friends ....

(b) .... fromage voulez-vous? (quel) ....

(c) Quelle .... horreur! (quel) ....

(d) .... les professeurs (tout) ....

(e) .... l'année (tout) ....

(f) .... est ta chanson préférée? (quel) ....

> Make sure that the adjective agrees with the noun that follows it:
> **amies (fpl)**, **fromage (m)**, **horreur (f)**, **professeurs (mpl)**, **année (f)** and **chanson (f)**.

⑩ Translating sentences using *tout*, *quel*, *chaque* and *quelque*   Grades 1–5

2. Translate the following sentences **into French**.

(a) Which film do you want to see? ....

(b) Every month, I buy a few magazines. ....

(c) Which colour do you prefer? ....

(d) All the tickets are expensive. ....

(e) I lost all my money. ....

(f) I've put all my things in the suitcase. ....

(g) Each person must buy a ticket. ....

(h) A few months ago, I went to France. ....

	Made a start		Feeling confident		Exam ready

Adverbs

---

⑤ Quick quiz

Rewrite the following adjectives as adverbs.

1. exacte

....

2. absolu

....

3. clair

....

4. entier

....

5. générale

....

6. récent

....

7. courageux

....

8. total

....

9. parfait

....

10. précis

....

11. doux

....

12. abondant

....

---

⑩ All types of adverbs 👓

1. Fill in the gaps with the correct adverb from the box.

bien	demain	constamment	couramment	facilement
hier	mieux	rapidement	régulièrement	

> Check that you know what the adverbs in the box mean. **Mieux** is the comparative of **bien** and means *better*.

🚩 **(a)** Hier .... , je suis allé au théâtre.

(b) Quand je suis en France, je peux communiquer .... car je parle français ....

(c) Je joue du piano .... , c'est-à-dire quatre fois par semaine.

> **Quatre fois par semaine** (f) means *four times a week*. You need an adverb of frequency with a similar meaning.

(d) Mon ami français a parlé très .... , alors je n'ai rien compris.

(e) Les enfants bavardaient .... , sans arrêt!

(f) Il a joué vraiment .... car il a marqué trois buts.

> **Vocabulary** 📘 A–Z
> **Sans arrêt** (m) means *without stopping*.
> **Il a marqué trois buts** (m) means *he scored three goals*.

(g) L'autre équipe a gagné car elle a .... joué que nous.

> **Nous irons** is the future tense. Use an adverb of time that refers to the future.

(h) .... , nous irons voir un film.

---

⑩ Describing work as a volunteer   Grades 4–9 ✏️

2. Translate this passage **into French**.

> From time to time, I do volunteer work in a museum, usually on a Saturday, but sometimes on Sunday. Recently, I had to speak politely to some visitors who were behaving badly and talking too loudly. Normally, I never have to speak severely with visitors, but I am constantly surprised that parents don't always supervise their children.

....

....

....

....

....

Quantifiers and intensifiers

5 Quick quiz

Draw lines to match up the pairs.

(a)

beaucoup de	very
très	a little
assez	a lot of
trop	quite
un peu	too
tout à fait	utterly

(b)

vraiment	lots of
tellement	more and more
tant de	really
plein de	fewer and fewer
de plus en plus	so much / many
de moins en moins	so

10 Understanding quantifiers and intensifiers — Grades 4–9

1. Underline the quantifier and / or intensifier in the following and translate the sentence **into English**.

(a) <u>Tant</u> de pays en Afrique sont très pauvres. *So many countries* ....

> The first sentence has both an intensifier (an adverb used to give emphasis) and a quantifier (a noun that shows an amount).

(b) Il y avait trop de soleil sur la terrasse.

....

(c) Il avait juste assez d'argent pour acheter une tranche de pain.

....

> **Vocabulary** A–Z
> **Incroyablement** comes from the verb **croire**, meaning *to believe*.

(d) L'examen était incroyablement dur!

....

(e) Après avoir couru un marathon, elle était complètement épuisée.

....

> **Vocabulary** A–Z
> **Couru** comes from the verb **courir**, *to run*. **Epuisée** means *exhausted*.

5 Using intensifiers and quantifiers — Grades 4–9

2. Translate the following sentences **into French**.

(a) The film was too long and utterly boring.

....

(b) There are fewer and fewer people who don't have access to the internet.

....

(c) I am not at all sure.

....

(d) I have read quite a lot of his books.

....

(e) After so much effort he won the race relatively easily.

....

(f) He began to run faster and faster.

....

| ✓ Made a start | ✓ Feeling confident | ✓ Exam ready |

Subject and object pronouns

Quick quiz

Are the following statements true or false? Tick the correct box.

		True	False
1	You always use **tu** if you are talking to just one person.		
2	**Ils** replaces **mes parents** in the following sentence: **Mes parents sont gentils.**		
3	You use **leur** to say *to them*.		
4	Direct and indirect object pronouns go after the verb.		
5	**Me**, **te**, **le** and **la** change to **m'**, **t'** and **l'** in front of a vowel or silent *h*.		

Replacing nouns with pronouns   Grades 4–9

1. Replace the underlined words with a pronoun.

(a) <u>Mes parents</u> donnent un vélo <u>à mon frère</u>.

🚩 Ils lui donnent un vélo.
....

> Use an indirect object pronoun to replace the noun in phrases that use **à**. The indirect object pronoun replaces both **à** and the noun.

(b) <u>Le professeur, M. Martin,</u> a parlé <u>aux élèves</u>.

....

> The pronoun replacing **le livre** must go in front of the verb **lire**.

(c) <u>Ma sœur</u> est en train de lire <u>le livre</u>.

....

> Use the pronoun *we* for **mon frère et moi**. The object pronoun goes between the modal verb, **voulons** and the infinitive **voir**.

(d) <u>Mon frère et moi</u> voulons voir <u>le film</u>.

....

> The past participle (**acheté** and **montré**) must agree with the direct object pronoun. **Billets** is masculine plural and **photos** is feminine plural.

(e) Je n'ai pas acheté <u>les billets</u>.

....

> In negative sentences, **ne** goes in front of the object pronoun and **pas** goes after the auxiliary verb.

(f) <u>David</u> a montré <u>ses photos</u> <u>à ses parents</u>.

....

Using subject and object pronouns

2. Translate the following sentences **into French**, using the words in brackets to help you choose the correct pronoun.

(a) I am going to buy it (the book) next week.

....

(b) The waiter gave him (my father) the bill.

....

(c) The teacher spoke to us (my classmates and me).

....

(d) I gave it (the address) to her.

....

(e) I downloaded them (photos) from the internet.

....

| ✓ Made a start | ✓ Feeling confident | ✓ Exam ready | **81** |

Stressed and possessive pronouns

⑤ Quick quiz

Translate the following phrases **into French**. They all use stressed pronouns.

1. for him ....
2. behind me ....
3. with them (f pl) ....
4. it's yours (sing) ....

5. without us ....
6. at yours (pl) (your home) ....
7. not them (m pl) ....
8. it's her ....

⑩ Understanding possessive pronouns   Grades 4–9 👓

1. Underline the possessive pronoun in the following sentences. Then translate the sentences **into English**.

(a) Leur maison est plus petite que la nôtre.

    Their house is smaller than
    ....

> A possessive pronoun is a word like *mine, yours, his, hers, ours* and *theirs*.

(b) J'ai mon passeport, mais mon frère ne trouve pas le sien.

    ....

(c) Elle avait oublié son parapluie, alors elle a emprunté le mien.

    ....

> Sentences with the imperfect form of **avoir** + past participle are in the pluperfect tense.

(d) Mes parents sont gentils. Comment sont les vôtres?

    ....

(e) Ma sœur a de bonnes notes, elles sont meilleures que les miennes.

    ....

> **Meilleur** is the comparative of **bon**.

Aiming higher ⬆

Using possessive pronouns is a feature of top grade answers.

⑩ Using stressed and possessive pronouns   Grades 4–9 ✒

2. Translate the following sentences **into French**.

(a) He is less patient than me.

    ....

(b) They are richer than us.

    ....

(c) My keys are here but theirs are over there.

    ....

(d) My room was quite small, but hers was big.

    ....

(e) My brother had his ticket, but I had left mine at home.

    ....

✓ Made a start   ✓ Feeling confident   ✓ Exam ready

Relative and demonstrative pronouns

5 Quick quiz

Complete the following sentences using the correct word for *the one* or *the ones* from the box below.

ceux	celle	celles-ci	celui

These are demonstrative pronouns. Make sure the pronoun agrees with the noun to which it refers.

1. Tu vas acheter un pull? – Oui, je prendrai .... en coton.

2. Il y a un grand choix de légumes au marché. J'achèterai .... qui sont les plus frais.

3. La voiture de mon père est très petite, mais .... de ma mère est grande.

4. Je veux acheter des chaussures. .... sont plus chères que celles-là.

10 Relative pronouns   Grades 4–9

1. Underline the relative pronoun in the following sentences and translate the sentences **into English**.

(a) Voici l'église <u>où</u> mes parents se sont mariés.

Here is the church ....

(b) Où est la fille <u>qui</u> a gagné?

Where is ....

(c) C'est le magasin qu'on peut voir à côté de la poste.

....

(d) Le cadeau que j'ai acheté n'était pas trop cher.

....

*Relative pronouns are words like who, that, which, where and whose. They are used to link two parts of a sentence. Use **dont** when linking phrases containing verbs followed by **de**, such as **parler de** and **avoir besoin de**.*

(e) Je suis allé voir le film dont il a parlé.

....

(f) L'homme dont la femme travaille dans mon collège est malade.

....

(g) Je ne trouve pas les documents dont j'ai besoin.

....

10 Using relative pronouns   Grades 4–9

2. Translate the following sentences **into French**.

(a) It's the man I saw at the station. ....

(b) The book I need is not in the library. ....

(c) That's the woman who helped me. ....

(d) The hotel where we stayed was small. ....

Pronouns *y* and *en*

⑤ Quick quiz

Read the French sentence pairs. What does **en** refer to in the second sentence of each pair? Choose the correct meaning from the box.

any	it	of it	of them	some

1. As-tu de l'argent? – Oui, j'en ai. ....

2. Est-ce qu'elle a peur des serpents? – Non, elle n'en a pas peur. ....

3. Tu as des biscuits? – Non, je n'en ai pas. ....

4. Est-ce qu'il peut travailler en équipe? – Oui, il en est capable. ....

5. Tu te souviens de l'anniversaire de ta grand-mère? – Oui, je m'en souviens. ....

⑩ Using *y* and *en* in a sentence

1. Rewrite these sentences, replacing the underlined words with **y** or **en**.

(a) Je vais <u>en ville</u> en bus. ..J'y vais................................

(b) Je me souviens <u>du concert</u>. ....

(c) Je vais acheter <u>des pommes</u>. ....
....

(d) Nous passons une semaine <u>au bord de la mer</u>. ....
....

(e) Il a participé <u>au concours</u>. ....
....

(f) Je n'ai pas pensé <u>à visiter Lyon</u>. ....
....

> If you are replacing an expression that uses **de**, use **en**. If it uses **à**, use **y**. Remember that the pronoun goes in front of the verb. When there are two verbs in the sentence, the pronoun must go in front of the infinitive verb.

> In the perfect tense, the pronoun goes immediately in front of the auxiliary verb.

⑩ Using *y* and *en* · Grades 4–9

2. Translate the following sentences **into French**.

(a) Here's the cheese. Would you like some more?

....

(b) Have you been to France? – Yes, I went there last week.

....

(c) Does he participate in extra-curricular activities? – Yes, he participates in them on Mondays.

....

(d) Did she reply to his email? – Yes, she replied to it yesterday.

....

(e) Would you like some milk with your tea? – Yes, I would like a lot.

....

✓ Made a start	✓ Feeling confident	✓ Exam ready

Conjunctions and connectives

BBC

⑤ Quick quiz

Draw lines to match up the pairs.

(a)

ensuite	or
et	if
ou	when
si	then
lorsque	and

(b)

à cause de	otherwise
afin de	in order to
pourtant	including
sinon	however
y compris	because of

⑩ Choosing conjunctions and connectives — Grades 4–9

1. Circle the conjunction or connective that best completes each sentence. Translate the sentences **into English**.

(a) Veux-tu aller au cinéma ce soir **mais / ou / si** rester à la maison?

🚩 Do you want ....

> If you are not sure which to use, try substituting each of the options and see which one makes the most sense when you translate it.

(b) J'ai écouté de la musique **sinon / pourtant / pendant que** je faisais mes devoirs.

....

> When there is a verb in the imperfect tense after one in the perfect tense, it indicates that the two actions were happening at the same time.

(c) J'étais malade **donc / parce que / comme** je ne suis pas allé à l'école.

....

(d) Nous voulions faire une randonnée **par conséquent / mais / car** il pleuvait.

....

(e) Je veux absolument aller à ce spectacle **même si / alors / ainsi** c'est très cher.

....

⑩ Using conjunctions and connectives — Grades 4–9

2. Translate the following sentences **into French**.

(a) I always do my homework before watching television.

....

(b) When we went to France we visited a lot of museums.

....

(c) Since I woke up late, I didn't get to school on time.

....

(d) In my opinion, reality TV shows are fun. However, my parents don't agree.

....

(e) I think the most serious problem is global warming, whereas my friend thinks it is deforestation.

....
....

The present tense

5 Quick quiz

Read the following sentences. Circle the correct option so each sentence is correct.

1. Vous **visiter / visitez / visitons** un musée?
2. Nous **mange / mangent / mangeons** bientôt.
3. Il **envoyent / envoie / envoies** des lettres.
4. Les garçons **jetons / jettent / jettes** les déchets.
5. On **achète / achetez / achètent** du pain.
6. Nous **commence / commençons / commencent** le film.
7. La fille **lève / levons / levez** la main.
8. Tu **employons / emploie / emploies** quelqu'un?

10 Regular and irregular verbs

1. Fill in the gaps with the correct form of the verb in brackets. Then translate the sentences **into English**.

(a) Ils (réagir) *réagissent* très vite.

They react very quickly.

(b) On (vendre) .... des magazines au kiosque.

....

(c) Le train (ralentir) ....

....

(d) Nous (choisir) .... des cadeaux.

....

(e) Je ne (dormir) .... pas bien.

....

(f) Mon frère (écrire) .... tous les jours à sa copine.

....

(g) Ils (lire) .... le journal.

....

(h) Normalement je (prendre) .... un café.

....

> The present tense can be translated by both the simple and continuous form of the present tense in English, for example **il boit** could mean *he drinks* or *he is drinking*.

> **On** uses the same ending as **il** or **elle**.

> **Ralentir** and **choisir** are regular **–ir** verbs.

> **Dormir**, **écrire**, **lire** and **prendre** don't follow the pattern of regular **–ir** or **–re** verbs.

10 Translating short sentences using the present tense — Grades 1–5

2. Translate the following sentences **into French**.

(a) I send text messages to my friends every day. ....

(b) Normally, we go for a walk in the morning. ....

(c) I don't know him very well. ....

(d) What are you (pl) drinking? ....

(e) I have been learning French for five years. ....

(f) We are going to the cinema today. ....

Made a start | Feeling confident | Exam ready

Key verbs

5 Quick quiz

Translate the following **avoir** and **être** phrases **into English**.

1. avoir peur ....

2. avoir raison ....

3. avoir besoin de ....

4. avoir envie de ....

5. avoir soif ....

6. avoir faim ....

7. être d'accord ....

8. être en train de ....

10 *Devoir, pouvoir* and *vouloir*

1. In each of the following sentences, circle the modal verb and underline the infinitive. Then, translate the sentences **into English**.

(a) Cet été, nous (voulons) aller en Espagne. We want to go to Spain in the summer.

(b) Je pourrais améliorer mon français. ....

(c) On doit respecter le règlement scolaire. ....

> Use *you* or *we* to translate **on**.

(d) Nous devons partir quand il fait jour. ....

> **Devons** and **dois** are forms of the verb **devoir**. Translate them as *must* or *have to.*

(e) Ils veulent faire grève la semaine prochaine. ....

> **Il fait jour** means *when it is light* and **faire grève** means *to go on strike*.

(f) Je ne dois pas faire de bêtises. ....

(g) Ils peuvent venir avec nous. ....

10 Preparing for the speaking exam   Grades 1–9

2. You want to say the following sentences in your speaking exam. Translate them **into French**.

(a) He wants to have a party at the weekend.

(b) I can't come tomorrow.

(c) He doesn't agree with me.

(d) You can see a lot of sights in Paris.

(e) Can you help me?

(f) Yesterday evening, I had to pack my bags.

(g) My parents want to go to Italy.

(h) I wanted to stay at home.

Made a start   Feeling confident   Exam ready   87

The perfect tense

5 Quick quiz

Fill in the gaps with the correct part of the verb **avoir** or **être**.

1. il .... bu
2. nous .... visité
3. vous .... partis
4. je / j'............................... pris

5. tu................................. reçu
6. ils .... allés
7. on .... rentrés
8. elle .... tombée

9. elle .... lu
10. nous............................ arrivés
11. elles .... dit
12. je / j'............................. voulu

10 *Avoir* and *être* verbs

1. Fill in the gaps with the perfect tense of the verb in brackets.

   (a) Nous (manger) avons mangé une pizza.

   (b) Je / J' (choisir) .... le poulet.

   (c) Nous (faire) .... du shopping.

   (d) Je / J' (mettre) .... un pull.

   (e) On (boire) .... du café.

   (f) Elle (écrire) .... un article.

   (g) Mes parents (aller) .... en vacances.

   (h) Je / J' (venir) .... en bus.

   (i) Ma famille et moi (arriver) .... à l'heure.

   (j) Tu (lire) .... la lettre?

   (k) Tu (perdre) .... ton passeport?

   (l) Mes frères (voir) .... le film.

   (m) Ma tante (tomber) .... malade.

> Check whether the verb takes **avoir** or **être** in the perfect tense.

> **Choisir** is a regular **–ir** verb. Take off the **r** to form the past participle.

> **Aller** takes **être**, so the past participle should agree.

> **Perdre** is a regular **–re** verb. The past participle ends in **–u**.

> **Tomber** takes **être**, so the past participle should agree.

10 Describing recent events — Grades 4–9

2. You are preparing a response to the following bullet points in a speaking task.

   - Activités récentes
   - Incident avec des amis

   Translate this passage **into French**.

> Yesterday, I did a lot of things. In the morning, I went into town and bought some magazines. I ate lunch in a little café with my friends, and after that we played football. One of my friends fell and we had to call an ambulance. They took him to hospital and he spent the night there.

....
....
....
....
....
....
....

| ✓ | Made a start | ✓ | Feeling confident | ✓ | Exam ready |

The imperfect tense

5 Quick quiz

Circle the verbs in the imperfect tense in the following sentences.

1. Il a fini ses devoirs pendant que sa mère préparait le dîner.

2. Je vais être ingénieur mais quand j'étais petit, je voulais être pilote.

3. Nous attendions le bus quand l'incident s'est passé.

4. Pendant nos vacances, il y avait du soleil et il faisait chaud.

10 Forming the imperfect tense

1. Complete the following phrases with the correct form of the imperfect tense. Then, translate the sentences **into English**.

(a) J'(habiter) ...habitais... dans une petite maison.

I used to live in a small house.

....

(b) Elle ne (manger) .... pas de poisson.

....

(c) Les cours (finir) .... tôt.

....

(d) Nous (apprendre) .... le français depuis quatre ans.

....

(e) Il (venir) .... d'arriver.

....

> Use the **nous** form of the present tense to form the imperfect tense. Remember to keep the **e** in **nous mangeons** in the imperfect tense. **Finir** in the present **nous** form is **nous finissons**.

> Sentences with an imperfect verb + **depuis** are translated by *had been (doing something)*.

> The imperfect of **venir** followed by **de** + infinitive is used to say that someone *had just (done something)*.

10 Using the imperfect tense   Grades 4–9

2. Translate the following sentences **into French**.

(a) My sister didn't use to like bananas.

....

(b) I had just finished my homework when the phone rang.

....

(c) We were going for a walk in the park when it started to snow.

....

(d) They were preparing dinner while I was laying the table.

....

(e) He had been working at the bank for two years.

....

(f) The weather was fine when we were on holiday.

....

✓ Made a start   ✓ Feeling confident   ✓ Exam ready   **89**

The pluperfect tense

BBC

5 Quick quiz

Write the following verbs in the pluperfect form.

1. penser – j' ....

2. aller – elle ....

3. voir – ils ....

4. dire – nous ....

5. manger – vous ....

6. partir – ils ....

10 Noticing and understanding the pluperfect — Grades 4–9

1. Underline the verbs in the pluperfect tense. Then, translate the passage **into English**.

> Un jour, mon frère est arrivé à l'école en retard parce qu'il ne s'était pas réveillé à l'heure. Puis il avait raté le bus et il avait dû aller au collège à pied. Le directeur s'était fâché et l'avait puni. Mon frère ne pouvait pas sortir à la récré et il était resté dans la salle de classe. Avant ce jour-là, il n'avait jamais eu de problèmes à l'école.

> One day, my brother arrived late at school because ....
>
> ....
>
> ....
>
> ....
>
> ....

> You can recognise the pluperfect tense by looking for verbs made up of the imperfect of **avoir** or **être** + past participle.

10 Saying what you had done — Grades 4–9

2. Translate the following sentences **into French**.

(a) Before visiting Paris, I had never been to France.

....

(b) We couldn't have a cup of tea because my mother had forgotten to buy some milk.

....

(c) She couldn't walk very well because she had broken her leg.

....

(d) I wanted to go shopping but I had lost my wallet.

....

(e) He told me he hadn't read the text I had sent.

....

Made a start | Feeling confident | Exam ready

The immediate future tense

⑤ Quick quiz

Translate the following future time phrases **into French**.

1. tomorrow evening

....

2. this afternoon

....

3. next Tuesday

....

4. in ten days

....

⑩ Saying what is going to happen   Grades 1–5

1. Rewrite the following sentences in the immediate future tense, and then translate them **into English**.

(a) Je vois mes cousins. *Je vais voir mes cousins. – I am going to see my cousins.*

(b) Il pleut. ....

(c) Il fait chaud. ....

(d) Nous nous réveillons tôt. ....

....

(e) Ils choisissent le menu pour la fête. ....

....

(f) Est-ce que tu achètes des souvenirs? ....

....

> Use **aller** + infinitive to make the immediate future tense.

> The reflexive pronoun should come before the infinitive.

⑩ Saying what you are going to do   Grades 1–5

2. You want to say the following sentences in your speaking exam. Translate them **into French**.

(a) What are you (informal sing.) going to do next week?

....

(b) I think it is going to be cold at the weekend.

....

(c) Where are you (pl.) going to spend your holidays this year?

....

(d) They are going to enjoy themselves at the beach.

....

(e) My sister is going to leave early tomorrow morning.

....

(f) We are going to watch a film on Friday.

....

The future tense

⏱ ⑤ Quick quiz

Write the infinitive of the verb for each of the following future tense verbs. The verb stem is bold.

1. j'**aur**ai ....

2. tu **ser**as ....

3. je **recevr**ai ....

4. nous **fer**ons ....

5. il **enverr**a ....

6. vous **pourr**ez ....

7. ils **deviendr**ont ....

8. elle **ir**a ....

9. nous **verr**ons ....

10. elles **saur**ont ....

⏱ ⑩ Saying what will happen

1. Fill in the gaps with the correct future tense form of the verbs in brackets.

(a) Vous *ferez* .... (faire)

(b) Elle .... (avoir)

(c) Tu .... (prendre)

(d) Nous .... (choisir)

(e) Vous .... (aller)

(f) Mes amis .... (être)

(g) Mathieu .... (acheter)

(h) Je .... (jeter)

(i) Ils .... (revenir)

(j) Je .... (employer)

> **Faire**, **avoir**, **aller** and **être** all have an irregular future tense stem.

> Some **-er** verbs make slight changes to the stem in the future tense. **Acheter** has a grave accent, **jeter** has a double **t** and **employer** changes the **y** to an **i**.

⏱ ⑩ Saying what will or won't happen   Grades 4–9

2. Translate the following sentences **into French**.

(a) Will you (informal sing.) see him tomorrow?

....

(b) If I'm lucky, I will win the lottery.

....

(c) He won't buy anything.

....

(d) We will have to take the bus.

....

(e) They will be going to the theatre tonight.

....

(f) Will you (pl.) go cycling at the weekend?

....

(g) If it's fine tomorrow, we'll have a picnic.

....

☑ **Made a start**   ☑ **Feeling confident**   ☑ **Exam ready**

The conditional

5 Quick quiz

Circle the verb in the conditional in each sentence.

1. Si j'avais beaucoup d'argent, je ferais un don à une association caritative.

2. Si je prenais une année sabbatique en France, je pourrais perfectionner mon français.

3. S'il était de meilleure humeur, il aurait plus d'amis.

4. Si nous vivions en France, nous parlerions bien français.

10 Using the conditional

1. Fill in the gaps using the conditional of the verbs in brackets. Then, write the sentences **in English**.

(a) Je ..voudrais.. visiter le musée (vouloir) . I would like to visit the museum.

(b) Est-ce que vous .... m'aider? (pouvoir) ....

(c) On .... se coucher tôt. (devoir) ....

(d) Nous .... en Italie. (aller) ....

(e) J'............................... des souvenirs. (acheter) ....

(f) Ils .... contents. (être) ....

(g) Qu'est-ce que tu .... faire? (vouloir) ....

(h) Je vous .... de téléphoner. (conseiller) ....

(i) Je .... qu'il a tort. (dire) ....

(j) On n' .... pas le temps. (avoir) ....

The following verbs have an irregular conditional stem: **pouvoir** (**pourr–**), **devoir** (**devr–**), **aller** (**ir–**), **être** (**ser–**), **vouloir** (**voudr–**) and **avoir** (**aur–**). **Acheter** has a grave accent in the conditional stem.

10 Describing your ideal home   Grades 4–9

2. Translate the following passage **into French**.

If I had lots of money, I would like to live in a big house. There would be ten bedrooms and a huge swimming pool. My friends would come and visit me and we would relax in the garden or we would go horse-riding. If the weather was fine, we could go for walks.

....

....

....

....

....

Negative forms

5 Quick quiz

What do the following French negative forms mean in English?

1. ne … jamais ....
2. ne … plus ....
3. ne … ni … ni ....
4. ne … personne ....
5. ne … que ....
6. ne … guère ....

10 Using *ne … pas*   Grades 1–5

1. Rewrite the following sentences, using **ne … pas**.

(a) Le chinois est difficile. *Le chinois n'est pas difficile.* ....

(b) Il parle clairement. ....

(c) Nous le comprenons très bien. ....

(d) J'achète des provisions. ....

(e) Nous avons mangé de bonne heure. ....

(f) On va faire des courses demain. ....

> **Ne** must go in front of a direct or indirect object pronoun in a sentence.

> In a negative sentence, **des** changes to **de**.

> **Ne** and **pas** go either side of the auxiliary verb when using the perfect tense.

> If there are two verbs in a sentence **ne** and **pas** go around the first verb, not the infinitive.

10 Using negatives   Grades 4–9

2. Translate the following sentences **into French**.

(a) I haven't got any milk left.

....
....

(b) I only have one bottle of water.

....
....

(c) We are not doing anything this evening.

....
....

(d) They have never won the lottery.

....
....

(e) No one came to the party.

....
....

(f) I don't like either apples or pears.

....
....

(g) My father no longer works.

....
....

(h) We didn't go to the museum.

....
....

(i) He didn't stay there.

....
....

(j) I don't want to go out this evening.

....
....

> **Ne … ni … ni** is used to connect two negative things and translates both *neither … nor…* and *not either … or.*

Reflexive verbs

⏱ 5 Quick quiz

Write the following verbs in the present tense.

1. je .... (se lever)

2. ils .... (se disputer)

3. nous .... (se reposer)

4. tu .... (s'ennuyer)

5. vous .... (s'inquiéter)

6. mes amies .... (s'entendre)

⏱ 10 Perfect tense of reflexive verbs

Grades 1–5

1. Rewrite the following sentences in the perfect tense.

🚩 **(a)** Je m'excuse pour le retard. *Je me suis excusé(e) pour le retard.* ....

> The past participle must agree with the subject of the verb.

(b) Ma sœur s'assied près de la fenêtre. ....

(c) Ils s'entendent bien avec leurs amis. ....

(d) Nous nous disputons de temps en temps avec nos parents. ....

(e) Mes copines se fâchent avec lui. ....

(f) Luc et David ne s'amusent pas au parc d'attractions. ....
....

> No agreement is needed when a reflexive verb is used with parts of the body.

(g) Elle se brosse les dents. ....

⏱ 10 Describing a photo

Grades 4–9

2. Translate this passage **into French**.

> The weather is very nice and it is very hot, and the sea is blue! There are a lot of people on the beach, and they have multi-coloured beach towels and parasols. Most people are sunbathing and relaxing on the beach but a few are swimming and having fun in the water.
>
> Normally, we go to the south of France. Last year, I bathed in the sea, but this year, I would like to go sailing with my parents. We never argue when we are on holiday.

Vocabulary A–Z
Se baigner means *to bathe*.

....
....
....
....
....
....

The imperative

⑤ Quick quiz

Fill in the gaps with the correct form of the imperative for the verbs in brackets.

1. .... tes devoirs. (faire)
2. .... en silence. (travailler – tu)
3. .... en ville (aller – tu)
4. .... à la cantine. (manger – nous)
5. .... gentils. (être – vous)
6. .... maintenant! (se réveiller – vous)

⑩ Using the imperative   Grades 4–9

1. Translate the following sentences **into French**.

(a) Go out of the station and turn left. (tu) *Sors de la gare et tourne à gauche.*
....

> The **tu** form of an **-er** verb loses the **s** in the imperative.

(b) Let's go to the theatre. ....
....

(c) Don't wait for me. (vous) ....
....

> Use the **nous** form of the imperative to say *let's*. Remember that the **nous** form of **manger** has an **e** in it.

(d) Get up early tomorrow. (sing) ....
....

> With reflexive verbs, the reflexive pronoun goes after the verb.

(e) Let's eat now. ....
....

(f) Don't be late. (vous) ....
....

> The imperative form of the verb *to be* is irregular.

(g) Choose a main course and a dessert. (vous) ....
....

⑩ Protecting the environment   Grades 4–5

2. While on holiday, you are given a leaflet. Translate this passage **into English**.

> Pour protéger l'environnement, achetez des produits sans emballage. Triez les ordures et recyclez-les autant que possible. Éteignez la lumière quand vous quittez une pièce et si personne n'est à la maison, baissez le chauffage central. Déplacez-vous à pied ou à vélo pour les petits trajets. N'oubliez pas d'encourager les autres à prendre les mêmes mesures.

....
....
....
....
....
....
....

☐ **Made a start**   ☐ **Feeling confident**   ☐ **Exam ready**

Impersonal verbs

⑤ Quick quiz

Translate the following impersonal verbs **into French**.

1. il gèle ....
2. il fait froid ....
3. il y aura ....
4. il suffit de ....
5. il s'agit de ....
6. il semble ....

⑩ Using impersonal verbs — Grades 4–9

1. Underline the impersonal verb in the following sentences. Then, translate the sentences **into English.**

(a) Je pense qu' il fera beau demain. *I think it will be fine tomorrow.* .... [Fera is the future tense of faire.]

(b) Il n'est pas facile d'apprendre cette langue. ....

(c) À mon avis, il faut trouver des solutions à ce problème. ....

(d) On peut y aller en bus mais il vaut mieux prendre le train. ....

(e) Il s'agit de la Première Guerre mondiale. ....

(f) Il suffit de suivre la recette. ....

⑩ Translating short sentences using impersonal verbs — Grades 4–5

2. Translate the following sentences **into French**.

(a) It snowed during the holidays.

....

(b) There was no milk left.

....

(c) We must leave early.

....

(d) It was about his childhood spent in Spain.

....

(e) There were about a hundred participants.

....

(f) It is important to do exercise regularly.

....

The infinitive

⑤ Quick quiz

Are these verbs followed by **de** or **à** when followed by an infinitive? Write **de** or **à** after each one.

1. décider ....
2. aider ....
3. oublier ....
4. se mettre ....

5. continuer ....
6. s'arrêter ....
7. hésiter ....
8. essayer ....

9. inviter ....
10. s'amuser ....
11. s'intéresser ....
12. refuser ....

⑩ Translating infinitives in sentences | Grades 4–9

1. Underline the infinitive in the following sentences, then translate them **into English**.

(a) Il commence à <u>pleuvoir</u>. *It's beginning to rain.* ....

> **Venir** + **de** + infinitive means *to have just done something.*

(b) Je viens d'apprendre de nouveaux mots. ....

(c) Nous irons au musée pour voir la nouvelle exposition. ....

(d) J'ai essayé d'acheter des souvenirs pour ma famille. ....

(e) Après avoir joué au tennis, ils étaient très fatigués. ....

(f) Après être arrivés au collège, nous sommes entrés dans notre salle de classe. ....

⑩ Using infinitives in context | Grades 4–9

2. Translate the following sentences **into French**.

(a) My brother usually does his homework before watching TV.

....
....

(b) He decided to play tennis instead of going swimming.

....
....

(c) I am going to Spain to improve my Spanish.

....
....

(d) We would prefer to spend our holidays by the sea.

....
....

(e) Having gone out late, the girls missed the bus.

....
....

(f) After having finished eating, he left the room without saying goodbye.

....
....

(g) I used to like playing football.

....
....

(h) My little brother loves reading.

....
....

(i) He forgot to send a birthday card to his grandmother.

....
....

☑ **Made a start** ☑ **Feeling confident** ☑ **Exam ready**

The present participle

⑤ Quick quiz

Write the present participle for the following verbs.

1. finir ....
4. écrire ....
7. dire ....

2. travailler ....
5. boire ....
8. faire ....

3. être ....
6. avoir ....
9. savoir ....

⑩ By / While / On doing something — Grades 4–9

1. Translate the following sentences **into French.**

(a) By searching in his room, he found his keys.

🚩 *En cherchant dans sa chambre, il a trouvé ses clés.*
....

(b) He did his homework while eating a sandwich.

....
....

> There is an **e** in the present participle of **manger**.

(c) On seeing the accident, we stopped immediately.

....
....

> **Vocabulary** A–Z
> Use the verb **s'arrêter** for *stopped*.

(d) She broke her leg by falling on the pavement.

....
....

> **Vocabulary** A–Z
> **Trottoir (m)** means *pavement*.

> **Se casser la jambe** means *to break one's leg*. The past participle does not agree with the subject when it is used with parts of the body.

(e) Not having much money, I didn't go into town with my friends.

🚩 N'
....
....

> **Ne** and **pas** go around the present participle when translating *not having*.

⑩ A healthy lifestyle — Grades 4–9

2. Translate this passage **into English**.

> Mon copain a retrouvé la forme en mangeant moins de féculents et de matières grasses, en buvant huit verres d'eau par jour et en faisant beaucoup d'exercice. Par contre, je l'ai fait en faisant du jogging chaque matin, en prenant des portions plus petites au dîner et en évitant le chocolat.

....
....
....
....
....
....
....

☐ **Made a start**   ☐ **Feeling confident**   ☐ **Exam ready**

The passive voice

⑤ Quick quiz

Which of the following sentences use the passive **in English**? Tick the correct answers.

1. The houses were destroyed in the earthquake.

2. I saw an accident on my way to school.

3. The church was built in the tenth century.

4. The film has been promoted.

5. I will spend my gap year in France.

⑩ Using the passive voice   Grades 4–9

1. Underline the verbs in the passive form in the following sentences. Then, translate the passive sentences **into English**. Watch out: not all of the sentences use the passive.

(a) L'hôtel Grand Palais <u>a été construit</u> en 1900.

The Grand Palais hotel was constructed in 1900.

> In French, the passive form of the verb is made up of **être** in a tense appropriate for the context and a past participle.

(b) Il a été détruit par un incendie en 2012.

....

(c) On a reconstruit le bâtiment deux ans plus tard.

....

> You can avoid the passive by using **on**.

(d) Dans le nouvel hôtel, le petit déjeuner est servi à partir de sept heures.

....

(e) Les chambres doivent être libérées avant midi.

....

(f) Les chambres seront nettoyées par le personnel pendant la journée.

....

(g) On a déjà accueilli des milliers de clients.

....

> **Exam focus**
> You will need to be able to recognise the passive voice in both Foundation and Higher tier.

⑩ Martinique   Grades 4–9

2. Translate this passage **into English**.

> La Martinique a été découverte par Christophe Colomb en 1502. En 1635, l'île a été occupée par des Français et une colonie a été établie. Maintenant, elle est administrée comme département d'outre-mer et elle est peuplée par presque quatre-cent-mille habitants. L'ancienne capitale Saint-Pierre a été détruite par une éruption volcanique en 1902, et la capitale a été déplacée à Fort-de-France.

....

....

....

....

☑ **Made a start**   ☑ **Feeling confident**   ☑ **Exam ready**

The subjunctive mood

5 Quick quiz

Draw lines to match up the pairs. In French, they are all followed by the subjunctive.

il faut que	until
afin que	although
bien que	it is necessary that
jusqu'à ce que	in order that

10 Recognising the subjunctive — Grades 7–9

1. Read the extracts from *Le Grand Meaulnes* by Alain-Fournier. Underline all of the subjunctive verbs. Then, translate these subjunctive phrases **into English**.

Je continue à dire « chez nous », bien que la maison ne nous appartienne plus. Nous avons quitté le pays depuis bientôt quinze ans et nous n'y reviendrons certainement jamais. Nous habitions les bâtiments du Cours de Sainte-Agathe.

Augustin, si calme en général, était maintenant dans un état de nervosité et d'impatience extraordinaires: «Ah! Mais oui, sans doute, je puis le sauver. Mais il faut que ce soit tout de suite. Il faut que je le voie, que je lui parle, qu'il me pardonne et que je répare tout... Autrement, je ne peux plus me présenter là-bas...»

> Look for the phrases that introduce the subjunctive. Sometimes one conjunction can introduce more than one verb.

> The subjunctive form of **-er** verbs is often identical to the indicative present tense.

> **Il faut** can be translated as *must* or *have to*.

Exam focus
You only need to be able to recognise the subjunctive at Higher tier. If you feel confident, you could use it in your writing and speaking exams.

... although the house doesn't belong to us any more.

....

....

....

....

10 Understanding the subjunctive — Grades 7–9

2. Translate the following sentences **into English.**

(a) Je veux que tu viennes me voir demain.

....

....

(b) Il faut que je lui écrive et que je fasse ça tout de suite.

....

....

(c) J'attendrai jusqu'à ce que vous soyez prêts.

....

....

(d) Bien qu'il ait le vertige, il montera en haut de la tour.

....

....

....

(e) Il semble qu'il sache la vérité.

....

....

Practice paper: Listening (Foundation)

This listening paper is shorter than the real exam. Allow yourself 18 minutes to answer all of the questions. You will hear the extract twice. You may write at any time during the tests. There will be a pause between each question.

Section A   Questions and Answers **in English**

Job priorities

1. Your exchange partner and her friends are talking about job priorities. What do they say? Listen to the recording and put a cross ☒ next to each one of the **three** correct statements.

		Safia	Guy	Djamila
Example	interesting work	☒	☐	☐
A	good salary	☐	☐	☐
B	flexible working hours	☐	☐	☐
C	close to home	☐	☐	☐
D	pleasant colleagues	☐	☐	☐
E	opportunity to travel	☐	☐	☐
F	opportunity to use languages	☐	☐	☐
G	fixed working hours	☐	☐	☐

[Total for Question 1 = 3 marks]

Museum announcements

2. You are visiting a museum in France. What information are you given? Listen to the recording and complete these statements by putting a cross ☒ in the correct box for each question.

Example: The exhibition of paintings is…

☐	**A** on the first floor
☐	**B** in a separate building
☒	**C** in the basement
☐	**D** on the ground floor

(ii) The guided tour of the museum…

☐	**A** covers all floors of the museum
☐	**B** lasts an hour
☐	**C** is at four o'clock
☐	**D** doesn't cost anything

(i) You have to pick up your things from the cloakroom by…

☐	**A** six o'clock
☐	**B** a quarter to six
☐	**C** a quarter past six
☐	**D** half past six

(iii) While visiting the museum, you…

☐	**A** are not allowed to take photos
☐	**B** cannot take photos with a flash
☐	**C** cannot use a selfie stick
☐	**D** can take photos using a flash

[Total for Question 2 = 3 marks]

News reports

3. You hear the following reports on the radio. What is mentioned? Listen to the recording and put a cross ☒ in each one of the **three** correct boxes.

Example	a lottery win	☒
A	a cyber attack	☐
B	a demonstration	☐
C	a murder	☐
D	a storm	☐
E	a terrorist attack	☐
F	a bank robbery	☐
G	a train accident	☐

[Total for Question 3 = 3 marks]

Online shopping

4. You hear a radio phone-in programme where people are discussing internet shopping.

Listen to the recording and answer the following questions **in English**.

(a) What does Natalie particularly like about online shopping? [1 mark]

(b) What does she say is a disadvantage? [1 mark]

(c) What kind of people find online shopping particularly convenient according to Pascal? [1 mark]

(d) What happened to Pascal recently? [1 mark]

[Total for Question 4 = 4 marks]

Les Misérables

5. Having seen the film, you have decided to listen to an audio book recording of *Les Misérables* by Victor Hugo.

Listen to the recording and put a cross ☒ in each one of the **three** correct boxes.

Example	This story takes place at the start of a month.	☒
A	The stranger arrived in Digne before sunset in summer.	☐
B	He had travelled by public transport.	☐
C	His appearance was uninviting.	☐
D	The people of Digne were pleased to see him.	☐
E	He looked as if he had spent a lot of time out of doors.	☐
F	He had walked to Digne.	☐
G	He was smartly dressed.	☐

[Total for Question 5 = 3 marks]

Section B   Questions and Answers **in French**

Jeune paralympienne

6. Une jeune paralympienne parle de ses expériences.

Complète les phrases en choisissant un mot dans la case. Il y a des mots que tu n'utiliseras pas.

ambitieuse	~~Belgique~~	déprimée	deuxième	devenue	
en	vélo	née	premier	danser	ski	souffrir	Suisse

Exemple: Léna Leclerc vient de la ...Belgique...

(a) La course en fauteuil roulant est son .... choix de sport. [1 mark]

(b) Elle est .... handicapée. [1 mark]

(c) À cause de son état physique, elle ne peut plus faire de .... [1 mark]

(d) Elle est très .... [1 mark]

(e) Elle passe la majeure partie de sa vie à .... [1 mark]

[Total for Question 6 = 5 marks]

Practice paper: Speaking (Foundation)

This speaking paper follows the structure of the real exam. In total, you will be expected to speak to the teacher for 7–9 minutes. You will have 12 minutes to prepare.

Role play

Listen to the teacher's part on the recording. This will be followed by a model answer, so pause the recording first so you can respond.

Topic: Travel and tourist transactions

Instructions to candidates:

You are making a reservation in a hotel in France. The teacher will play the role of the receptionist and will speak first.

You must address the receptionist as *vous*.

You will talk to the teacher using the five prompts.

- where you see – **?** – you must ask a question
- where you see – **!** – you must respond to something you have not prepared.

Task

> *Vous êtes dans un hôtel. Vous parlez avec le / la réceptionniste.*
>
> 1. Chambre – nombre de personnes
> 2. Genre de chambre
> 3. **!**
> 4. Activité préférée en ville + raison
> 5. **?** Restaurant – heures d'ouverture

Picture-based task

Topic: Daily life

Instructions to candidates:

- Study the photo carefully during the preparation time.
- You may make notes on a separate sheet of paper.
- Listen to the teacher's part on the recording. You will hear questions and model answers about the photo and about topics related to **the use of technology in everyday life**. Before each model answer, pause the recording so you can give your own response.

Regarde la photo et prépare des réponses sur les points suivants:

- la description de la photo
- ton opinion des médias sociaux
- l'utilisation récente de ton portable
- comment tu vas utiliser Internet ce soir
- ton site internet préféré

Conversation

The conversation follows on from the picture-based task and will cover two themes not covered by the picture-based task. It will last between three and five minutes.

The first theme of the conversation task is chosen by you. You must ask a question at some point during the course of the conversation.

Listen to the teacher's part on the recording. You will hear questions and model answers about the topics. Before each model answer, pause the recording so you can give your own response.

Conversation themes:

- Future aspirations, study and work
- Local area, holiday and travel

END OF QUESTIONS

Practice paper: Reading (Foundation)

> This reading paper is shorter than the real exam. Allow yourself 26 minutes to answer all of the questions.

Vegetarianism

1. Read the comments about vegetarianism on a website.

> **Fabrice:** À mon avis, quand on mange au restaurant, le choix de plats est trop limité. À la maison il faut être créatif quand on fait la cuisine.
>
> **Sandrine:** Je sais que c'est bon pour la planète et pour la santé, mais j'adore la viande, alors je ne suivrai pas ce régime alimentaire.
>
> **Jérôme:** Être végétarien m'a permis de faire des économies.

What do they say about vegetarianism? Enter either **Fabrice**, **Sandrine** or **Jérôme**.

You can use each person more than once.

Example: Sandrine .... likes meat.

(a) .... complains of a lack of choice when eating out.   **[1 mark]**

(b) .... says that it is cheaper to be a vegetarian.   **[1 mark]**

(c) .... knows about the benefits of vegetarianism but ignores them.   **[1 mark]**

(d) .... says that vegetarians prepare food more imaginatively.   **[1 mark]**

[Total for Question 1 = 4 marks]

Shopping habits

2. Read the results of an online survey published on a French website.

> La fête de Pâques est une des plus importantes occasions d'acheter du chocolat en France. 80% des gens récemment sondés ont dit qu'ils ont l'intention d'offrir du chocolat à Pâques.
>
> Voici les autres résultats du sondage:
>
> - La plupart des gens (77%) vont au supermarché ou à l'hypermarché pour acheter du chocolat. 38% achètent du chocolat dans une boutique spécialisée et 28% dans une boulangerie ou une pâtisserie. Seulement 6% font leurs achats en ligne.
> - Les œufs en chocolat sont les achats les plus populaires (47%), suivis par les lapins (31%), les poules (20%), autre chocolat (15%) et autres animaux (10%).
> - 19% des gens sondés n'ont aucune intention d'acheter du chocolat.

Complete the gap in each sentence using a word or words from the box below. There are more words than gaps.

at the baker's	~~chocolate~~	Christmas	Easter	flowers	hen
online	supermarket	specialist shop	rabbit	10%	19%

Example: The report is about buying chocolate ....

(a) The report is about people's shopping habits at ....   **[1 mark]**

(b) Most people make their purchases in a ....   **[1 mark]**

(c) A very small number of people buy chocolate ....   **[1 mark]**

(d) The second most popular form of chocolate to buy is a ....   **[1 mark]**

(e) .... of people surveyed don't plan to buy any chocolate.   **[1 mark]**

[Total for Question 2 = 5 marks]

Television

3. Read these online comments about television.

> Tout le monde parle de la nouvelle émission de télé-réalité mais je ne comprends pas pourquoi. Ils disent que c'est très divertissant mais pour moi, c'est une perte de temps ! En fait, de telles émissions ne m'intéressent pas du tout. Puisque je n'ai jamais le temps de regarder les émissions au moment où elles sont diffusées, je ne regarde que les trucs qui valent la peine sur ma tablette. **Céline**

Answer the following questions **in English**. You do not need to write in full sentences.

(a) What does Céline think about reality TV? [1 mark]

(b) What does she say about her television-viewing habits? Give **two** details. [2 marks]

[**Total for Question 3 = 3 marks**]

A journey

4. Read this extract from *Le Tour du monde en quatre-vingts jours* by Jules Verne.

Passepartout, a manservant, is talking to a detective, Fix, about his master Phileas Fogg's plans.

Quelques instants après, Fix lui disait :

« Vous avez donc quitté Londres précipitamment ?

— Je le crois bien ! Mercredi dernier, à huit heures du soir, contre toutes ses habitudes, Mr. Fogg est revenu de son cercle, et trois quarts d'heure après nous étions partis.

— Mais où va-t-il donc, votre maître ?

— Toujours devant lui ! Il fait le tour du monde !

— Le tour du monde ? a crié Fix.

— Oui, en quatre-vingts jours ! Un pari*, dit-il, mais, entre nous, je n'en crois rien. Cela n'aurait pas le sens commun. Il y a autre chose.

— Ah ! c'est un original, ce Mr. Fogg ?

— Je le crois. (…)

— Et vous le connaissez depuis longtemps, votre maître ?

— Moi ! répondit Passepartout, je suis entré à son service le jour même de notre départ. »

*un pari = a bet

Answer the following questions **in English**. You do not need to write in full sentences.

(a) On what day and at what time did Passepartout and Phileas Fogg set off? [2 marks]

(b) Where does Phileas Fogg plan to travel? [1 mark]

(c) How long does Phileas Fogg plan to be away? [1 mark]

(d) What is perhaps unusual about the fact that Passepartout is accompanying Phileas Fogg on his journey? Give **two** details. [2 marks]

[**Total for Question 4 = 6 marks**]

Un mail

5. Lis ce blog de Fabrice au sujet d'une initiative à laquelle il a participé.

> Salut!
>
> La semaine dernière, c'était la semaine européenne de la réduction des déchets. J'ai participé à cette initiative internationale avec d'autres personnes car le problème le plus grave dans ma commune est celui des ordures laissées sur la plage par les gens qui sont en vacances. Nous avons passé notre samedi matin avec des sacs-poubelle à ramasser toutes sortes de déchets pour nettoyer la plage.
>
> Cette petite action est notre contribution à cette initiative. Dans l'avenir, nous devons bien sûr encourager les supermarchés à vendre des produits sans emballage et encourager les producteurs à utiliser des matériaux compostables. De cette façon, on pourrait réduire les déchets qui défigurent nos villes et nos villages. Cependant, avant tout, il faut s'occuper du problème des plastiques dans les océans; ils menacent les animaux qui y vivent.

Mets une croix ☒ dans la case correcte.

Exemple: Fabrice a participé à cette initiative…

☐	**A** pendant une semaine
☐	**B** pendant un week-end
☒	**C** samedi dernier
☐	**D** le matin en semaine

(i) Fabrice décrit…

☐	**A** une initiative uniquement locale
☐	**B** une initiative pour aider les autres
☐	**C** une initiative environnementale
☐	**D** une initiative organisée par les supermarchés

(ii) Selon Fabrice la cause du problème local est…

☐	**A** les visiteurs
☐	**B** la commune
☐	**C** les producteurs
☐	**D** les supermarchés

(iii) Selon Fabrice les pires conséquences des déchets plastiques sont qu'ils…

☐	**A** durent trop longtemps
☐	**B** tuent la vie marine
☐	**C** abîment l'environnement
☐	**D** sont difficiles à recycler

[Total for Question 5 = 3 marks]

Section C   Translation **into English**

6. Translate this passage **into English**.

> Dans mon collège, il y a une grande piscine. J'aime faire de la natation après les cours. Samedi dernier, j'ai participé à un concours. C'était passionnant. Pendant les vacances, je vais réviser pour mes examens.

[Total for Question 6 = 7 marks]

Practice paper: Writing (Foundation)

> This writing paper follows the structure of the real exam. Allow yourself 1 hour and 10 minutes to answer questions 1, 2, either 3(a) or 3(b) and 4. Write your answers on a separate sheet of paper.

Une fête

1. Tu es à une fête avec ta famille. Tu postes cette photo sur des médias sociaux pour tes amis.

   Écris une description de la photo **et** exprime ton opinion sur les fêtes en famille.

   Écris 20–30 mots environ **en français.**   **[Total for Question 1 = 12 marks]**

Travail en France

2. Vous allez faire un stage en entreprise en France.

   Écrivez un mail à votre employeur avec les informations suivantes:

   - les détails de votre arrivée
   - la durée de votre séjour
   - vos activités pendant votre temps libre
   - pourquoi vous voulez travailler en France.

   Écrivez 40–50 mots environ **en français.**   **[Total for Question 2 = 16 marks]**

Choose either Question 3(a) or Question 3(b)

Les vacances

3. (a) Tu écris un article sur les vacances pour ton blog.

   Tu **dois** faire référence aux points suivants:

   - tes vacances préférées
   - ton logement habituel en vacances
   - une expérience récente en vacances
   - tes prochaines vacances.

   Écris 80–90 mots environ **en français.**   **[Total for Question 3(a) = 20 marks]**

Les activités extrascolaires

3. (b) Tu écris un article pour le magazine de ton école partenaire sur les activités extrascolaires et bénévoles de ton collège.

   Tu **dois** faire référence aux points suivants:

   - les activités extrascolaires qu'on peut faire
   - l'importance de ces activités
   - une action récente au collège pour collecter des fonds pour une association caritative
   - tes projets pour une activité extrascolaire dans l'avenir.

   Écris 80–90 mots environ **en français.**   **[Total for Question 3(b) = 20 marks]**

Chez moi

4. Traduis les phrases suivantes **en français.**

   (a) My mother is small.   **[2 marks]**

   (b) I like to do some cooking.   **[2 marks]**

   (c) In the summer I work in the garden.   **[2 marks]**

   (d) There are a lot of trees in the park near my house.   **[3 marks]**

   (e) Yesterday evening I went for a walk in the countryside.   **[3 marks]**

   [Total for Question 4 = 12 marks]

Practice paper: Listening (Higher)

This listening paper is shorter than the real exam. Allow yourself 29 minutes to answer all of the questions. You will hear the extract twice. You may write at any time during the tests. There will be a pause between each question.

À l'office de tourisme

1. Une employée de l'office de tourisme parle des hôtels dans sa ville. Comment sont les hôtels? Choisis entre: **grand**, **démodé**, **bruyant** et **cher**. Chacun des mots peut être utilisé plusieurs fois.

    Exemple: L'Hôtel Voltaire est ...grand...........

    (a) L'Hôtel Centre est .... **[1 mark]**

    (b) L'Hôtel Bellevue n'est pas .... **[1 mark]**

    (c) L'Hôtel Opéra est .... **[1 mark]**

    (d) L'Hôtel Royal est .... **[1 mark]**

    (e) L'Hôtel de la Cour n'est pas .... **[1 mark]**

    [Total for Question 1 = 5 marks]

Musical genres

2. You hear this podcast of Yannick talking about zouglou. Put a cross ☒ in each one of the **two** correct boxes for each question.

(i) What does Yannick say about zouglou music in general?

Example	It was created by students.	☒
A	It's a form of popular protest music.	☐
B	It's a form of music sung at sporting events in the Ivory Coast.	☐
C	The songs are about dancing.	☐
D	The songs are about unsatisfactory living and working conditions.	☐
E	It's a recent development.	☐

[2 marks]

(ii) What does Yannick say about zouglou songs?

A	They never have a political message.	☐
B	The words of the songs are often amusing.	☐
C	They are preoccupied with the history of the language.	☐
D	They are made up of a mix of languages.	☐
E	They are not difficult to understand.	☐

[2 marks]

(iii) What does he say about zouglou music today?

A	Zouglou singers in France risk losing their African identities.	☐
B	Zouglou singers in France risk being separated from their families.	☐
C	It has spread to other countries in West Africa.	☐
D	It's very well-known in France.	☐
E	Zouglou singers in France live apart from their families.	☐

[2 marks]

[Total for Question 2 = 6 marks]

Mobile phones

3. You hear this discussion about mobile phone use on the radio.

    Listen to the recording and answer the following questions **in English**.

    (a) Why won't Mélanie find it difficult to take part in 'no phone use' day? **[1 mark]**

    (b) What is her attitude to this day? **[1 mark]**

    (c) What does Gérard think about this initiative? Give **two** details. **[2 marks]**

    [Total for Question 3 = 4 marks]

Role models

4. You hear your French friend and his classmates talking about role models. Which type of people do they admire? Listen to the recording and put a cross ☒ in each one of the **three** correct boxes.

		Hassan	Alésia	Jérôme	Charlotte
Example	people who raise a lot of money for charity	☒	☐	☐	☐
A	people who are always honest	☐	☐	☐	☐
B	women with careers in the sciences	☐	☐	☐	☐
C	people who campaign regardless of personal safety	☐	☐	☐	☐
D	people with a lot of musical talent	☐	☐	☐	☐
E	athletes who train long and hard	☐	☐	☐	☐
F	people who have a lot of artistic talent	☐	☐	☐	☐

[Total for Question 4 = 3 marks]

Volunteering

5. You hear this radio report in which Simone talks about an initiative by volunteers in Calais. Listen to the report and answer the following questions **in English**.

   (a) What specific problems does Simone say that the homeless have in Calais? Give **two** details. [2 marks]

   (b) In what way do the volunteers use social media? Give **two** details. [2 marks]

   (c) What does Simone say is the motivation for some volunteers? [1 mark]

   (d) What reason does Simone give for personally taking part in this action? [1 mark]

[Total for Question 5 = 6 marks]

Urban transport

6. You hear this advert on the radio. Listen to the recording and put a cross ☒ in the correct box for each question.

Example: This advert is about…

☒	**A** travel
☐	**B** accommodation
☐	**C** sightseeing
☐	**D** eating out

(i) This advert is mainly aimed at people who…

☐	**A** want to keep fit
☐	**B** normally make short journeys by car
☐	**C** don't like walking
☐	**D** want to save money

(ii) When you cycle in towns, you….

☐	**A** sometimes get caught in traffic jams
☐	**B** get to your destination more easily than by other means
☐	**C** should only use the cycle paths
☐	**D** are not allowed to cycle on the pavement

[Total for Question 6 = 2 marks]

Paris Olympics

7. You hear some people speaking on the radio about the Paris Olympics.

   Listen to the recording and answer the following questions **in English**.

   (a) What impact will the Olympics have on tourism according to Monsieur Parmentier? Give **two** examples. [2 marks]

   (b) Who will benefit and in what way according to him? Give **two** examples. [2 marks]

   (c) What does Mme Lefèvre think that the impact of the Olympics will be after the games? [1 mark]

   (d) What does she say about how things will be before the games? Give **one** example. [1 mark]

[Total for Question 7 = 6 marks]

END OF QUESTIONS

Practice paper: Speaking (Higher)

> This speaking paper follows the structure of the real exam. In total, you will be expected to speak to the teacher for 10–12 minutes. You will have 12 minutes to prepare.

Listen to the teacher's part on the recording. A model answer will follow, so pause the recording first so you can respond.

Topic: Daily life

Instructions to candidates:

You are talking about shopping with a French friend. The teacher will play the role of the French friend and will speak first.

You must address your French friend as *tu*.

You will talk to the teacher using the five prompts below.

- where you see – **?** – you must ask a question
- where you see – **!** – you must respond to something you have not prepared.

Task

> ***Tu parles du shopping avec ton ami(e) français(e).***
> 1. Achats – où et quand
> 2. Achats en ligne – opinion
> 3. **!**
> 4. **?** Acheter – quoi
> 5. **?** Magasin préféré

Picture-based task

Topic: What school is like

Instructions to candidates:

- Study the photo carefully during the preparation time.
- You may make notes on a separate sheet of paper.
- Listen to the teacher's part on the recording. You will hear questions and model answers about the photo and about topics related to **what school is like**. Before each model answer, pause the recording so you can give your own response.

> Regarde la photo et prépare des réponses sur les points suivants:
> - la description de la photo
> - ton opinion du règlement scolaire
> - tes activités extrascolaires récentes
> - une activité que tu feras à l'école l'année prochaine
> - **!** (*Qu'est-ce que tu changerais dans ton collège si tu étais directeur / directrice?*)

Conversation

The conversation follows on from the picture-based task and will cover two themes not covered by the picture-based task. It will last between five and six minutes.

The first theme of the conversation task is chosen by you. You must ask a question at some point during the course of the conversation.

Listen to the teacher's part on the recording. You will hear questions and model answers about the topics. Before each model answer, pause the recording so you can give your own response.

Conversation themes:

- Identity and culture
- Local area, holiday and travel

Practice paper: Reading (Higher)

> This reading paper is shorter than the real exam. Allow yourself 45 minutes to answer all of the questions.

Mobile phone use

1. Read these comments from an online forum about mobile phone use.

> **Ria:** J'ai un smartphone que j'utilise tout le temps, même en cours où j'arrive à envoyer des SMS sans que le prof le voie.
>
> **Malik:** Je suis tout à fait accro à mon portable. Je l'utilise dès le matin pour me réveiller jusqu'au soir, sauf quand je suis en cours. Pendant le trajet pour aller au collège je joue à des jeux vidéo sur mon portable, mais c'est quelque chose que je trouvais bête il y a quelques années.
>
> **Solange:** Mes copains aiment beaucoup les applis où on peut partager des photos pour une période limitée. Je préfère celles qui permettent de regarder des vidéos car celles-ci m'aident à me détendre.
>
> **André:** J'adore prendre et partager des photos avec mon portable, alors les applis qui facilitent ce genre de choses sont les plus utiles. Les meilleures sont celles où les photos disparaissent au bout de 24 heures.

Who says what about mobile phone use? Enter either **Ria**, **Malik**, **Solange** or **André**.

You can use each person more than once.

> **Example:** Ria .... has a smartphone.

(a) .... doesn't use photo sharing apps.   **[1 mark]**

(b) .... has changed their mind about video games.   **[1 mark]**

(c) .... uses their phone during lessons.   **[1 mark]**

(d) .... uses apps where you can only share photos for a limited period.   **[1 mark]**

Answer the following questions **in English**.

(e) Which practical use of mobile phones to help organise daily life is mentioned on the forum?   **[1 mark]**

(f) What does André consider to be important in his choice of apps?   **[1 mark]**

[Total for Question 1 = 6 marks]

School life in Senegal

2. Read Mariama's blog post about her school life in Senegal.

> Ma journée scolaire commence tôt, vers six heures, parce que je dois préparer le petit déjeuner pour mes frères avant de me laver et de prendre le chemin de l'école. Les cours commencent à huit heures mais quelques filles arrivent en retard parce qu'elles doivent aller chercher de l'eau pour leur famille. Les cours durent jusqu'à midi et reprennent l'après-midi vers trois heures. Pendant cette pause, la partie la plus chaude de la journée, on peut manger et se reposer. Normalement, je rentre chez moi et j'aide ma mère dans la cuisine.
>
> On est cinquante élèves dans ma classe; il n'y a pas assez de tables donc on est assis très serrés sur des bancs. En plus, il nous manque du matériel scolaire comme des livres. Cependant, je pense qu'il est très important d'aller à l'école pour avoir de meilleures chances dans la vie. Je connais des filles qui ont arrêté l'école parce qu'elles ont dû se marier ou travailler dans les champs.

Answer the following questions **in English**. You do not need to write in full sentences.

(a) Why does Mariama have to get up early?   **[1 mark]**

(b) What does Mariama do in the break in the middle of the school day? Give **one** detail.   **[1 mark]**

(c) What does she say about facilities at her school? Give **two** details.   **[2 marks]**

(d) What is Mariama's attitude to education?   **[1 mark]**

(e) What reason does she give for this?   **[1 mark]**

(f) Why do some girls not continue with their education according to Mariama? Give **one** detail.   **[1 mark]**

[Total for Question 2 = 7 marks]

Social issues

3. Read this article about a social problem in France.

> Je m'appelle Dominique et je suis lycéenne. Ce que la plupart des gens au lycée ne savent pas, c'est que je suis aussi sans-abri. Peut-être que quelques profs le soupçonnent car il m'arrive de m'endormir en classe. Je ne sais pas comment je vais pouvoir préparer mon bac parce que je suis tellement fatiguée tout le temps. La nuit, il m'est impossible de fermer l'œil quand je suis dans la rue parce que j'ai peur de me faire agresser. Les nuits sont toujours longues et froides, même en été. Mes problèmes ont commencé quand ma mère a perdu son emploi et que nous habitions dans un logement de fonction fourni par son travail. Ensuite, nous étions logés chez un oncle mais après quelques mois, il nous a dit de partir. Nous avons essayé sans succès d'obtenir un logement dans un centre d'hébergement d'urgence. Pourtant le pire, c'est l'hostilité et l'indifférence des passants.

Answer the following questions **in English**. You do not need to write in full sentences.

(a) What is the main problem that affects Dominique's life at the moment? **[1 mark]**

(b) What does she say about her teachers and her situation? **[1 mark]**

(c) How does her situation affect her at school? **[1 mark]**

(d) What event was the start of all her problems? **[1 mark]**

(e) What is the worst aspect of her situation? **[1 mark]**

[Total for Question 3 = 5 marks]

Gap year

4. Read Philippe's blog post below.

> Je viens de prendre une année sabbatique et je dirais que cela a été une expérience qui m'a aidé à prendre des décisions sur mes priorités dans la vie. Je sais que ce n'est pas pour tout le monde, et si l'on a l'intention de suivre une carrière qui demande une longue formation, il vaudrait mieux commencer cette formation tout de suite. Pourtant, j'étais sûr que je ne voulais pas ce genre de carrière et en plus, je voulais faire une pause après avoir étudié très dur pour le bac pendant plusieurs années. Au début, mes parents ont hésité à m'encourager parce qu'ils pensaient que je devais commencer mes études tout de suite. Quelques-uns de mes copains ont passé leur année sabbatique à voyager, mais cela n'était pas possible pour moi car je devais gagner de l'argent. Alors, j'ai travaillé en France pendant six mois et l'autre partie de l'année, j'ai travaillé comme bénévole dans une école à l'étranger. **Philippe**

What does he tell us? Put a cross ☒ next to each one of the **three** correct statements.

☒	**Example:** Philippe has just had a gap year.
☐	**A** Philippe thinks that everyone should have a gap year to sort out their priorities.
☐	**B** Philippe's gap year was a positive experience.
☐	**C** Philippe had a gap year because he wanted a break from studying.
☐	**D** Philippe spent his gap year travelling.
☐	**E** Philippe's parents were totally supportive of his plans from the outset.
☐	**F** Philippe spent his entire gap year earning money.
☐	**G** Philippe spent part of his gap year helping others.

[Total for Question 4 = 3 marks]

L'Assommoir **d'Émile Zola**

5. Lis cet extrait. Mets une croix ☒ dans la case correcte.

> Gervaise avait attendu Lantier jusqu'à deux heures du matin. Puis, toute froide elle s'était jetée sur le lit les joues pleines de larmes. Depuis huit jours, au sortir du *Veau à deux têtes*, où ils mangeaient, il l'envoyait se coucher avec les enfants et ne reparaissait que tard dans la nuit, en racontant qu'il cherchait du travail. Ce soir-là, pendant qu'elle attendait son retour, elle croyait l'avoir vu entrer au bal du Grand-Balcon, et, derrière lui, elle avait aperçu la petite Adèle, une brunette qui dînait à leur restaurant, marchant à cinq ou six pas, les mains ballantes, comme si elle venait de lui quitter le bras pour ne pas passer ensemble sous la clarté crue des globes de la porte.

Exemple: Il semble que Gervaise et Lantier mangent…

☐	**A**	tous les huit jours au restaurant
☒	**B**	régulièrement au restaurant
☐	**C**	rarement au restaurant
☐	**D**	le matin au restaurant

(i) Gervaise attend Lantier…

☐	**A**	au bal du Grand-Balcon
☐	**B**	au restaurant
☐	**C**	dans sa chambre
☐	**D**	toute seule dans sa maison

(ii) Il paraît que Lantier…

☐	**A**	est allé au *Veau à deux têtes*
☐	**B**	cherche du travail
☐	**C**	passe la nuit seul
☐	**D**	n'est pas fidèle

(iii) Gervaise se sent...

☐	**A**	malheureuse
☐	**B**	contente
☐	**C**	inquiète
☐	**D**	calme

[Total for Question 5 = 3 marks]

Identité

6. Lis cet article de Josette sur l'identité.

> Je n'aurais pas pu continuer dans mon ancien collège car depuis un an, j'étais presque tous les jours victime de harcèlement. Les autres filles me lançaient des insultes à cause de la couleur de ma peau puisque mon père est français alors que ma mère vient du Mali.
>
> En fait je suis très fière de mon double héritage car c'est une expérience vraiment enrichissante de faire partie de deux cultures. Au moins une fois par an je rends visite à mes grands-parents maliens et j'apprends quelque chose de la vie dans leur village. À la maison on fête Noël et Pâques ainsi que les fêtes musulmanes à la fin de ramadan et Tabaski (la fête du mouton). Surtout je pense que mon double héritage m'a appris à traiter chaque être de manière égale et sans préjugé.

Réponds aux questions **en français**. Il n'est pas nécessaire d'écrire des phrases complètes.

(a) Comment est-ce que Josette s'est probablement sentie avant de changer d'école?   **[1 mark]**

(b) De quel genre d'insultes a-t-elle souffert avant de changer d'école?   **[1 mark]**

(c) Pourquoi Josette dit-elle que son double héritage est une expérience positive? Mentionne **un détail**.   **[1 mark]**

(d) Comment est-ce que Josette décrirait son attitude envers les autres?   **[1 mark]**

[Total for Question 6 = 4 marks]

7. Translate this passage **into English**.

> J'attends avec impatience ta visite chez nous dans une quinzaine de jours. Mes parents et moi avons pensé aux activités qu'on pourrait faire pendant la semaine de ton séjour. S'il fait beau le dimanche, ce serait génial d'aller au parc d'attractions près d'ici. Sinon, il vaudrait mieux faire du patin à roulettes. Avant ton arrivée, je dois finir un projet pour l'école.

[Total for Question 7 = 7 marks]

Practice paper: Writing (Higher)

This writing paper follows the structure of the real exam. Allow yourself 1 hour and 20 minutes to answer the questions as instructed.

Choose either Question 1(a) or Question 1(b).

Les loisirs

1. **(a)** Ton ami(e) français(e) t'a posé des questions au sujet de tes loisirs.

   Écris une réponse à ton ami(e). Tu **dois** faire référence aux points suivants:

   - ta musique préférée
   - tes activités en famille le week-end
   - une sortie récente au cinéma
   - tes projets pour les vacances scolaires.

   Écris 80–90 mots environ **en français**.   **[Total for Question 1(a) = 20 marks]**

En vacances

1. **(b)** Tu es en vacances et tu écris un mail à ton ami(e) français(e).

   Tu **dois** faire référence aux points suivants:

   - ton logement et les environs
   - tes activités récentes pendant les vacances
   - tes projets pour les vacances l'année prochaine
   - le genre de vacances que tu préfères – pourquoi?

   Écris 80–90 mots environ **en français**.   **[Total for Question 1(b) = 20 marks]**

Choose either Question 2(a) or Question 2(b).

Les fêtes

2. **(a)** Vous écrivez un article pour le magazine de votre école partenaire au sujet des fêtes.

   Écrivez un article pour intéresser les lecteurs.

   Vous **devez** faire référence aux points suivants:

   - les différentes fêtes dans votre pays
   - votre expérience d'une fête récente
   - l'importance des fêtes – votre opinion
   - une future fête.

   Justifiez vos idées et vos opinions.

   Écrivez 130–150 mots environ **en français**.   **[Total for Question 2(a) = 28 marks]**

Les initiatives caritatives

2. **(b)** Vous écrivez un article pour le magazine de votre école partenaire au sujet des actions caritatives au collège.

   Écrivez un article pour intéresser les lecteurs.

   Vous **devez** faire référence aux points suivants:

   - une initiative caritative récente au collège
   - une autre initiative dans l'avenir
   - l'importance des actions caritatives
   - les actions différentes qu'on peut faire.

   Justifiez vos idées et vos opinions.

   Écrivez 130–150 mots environ **en français**.   **[Total for Question 2(b) = 28 marks]**

3. Traduis le passage suivant **en français**.

   > A lot of people like living in my town because you can go for long walks in the big park. I used to live in the town centre but last year we moved to the suburbs. Next month my uncle is going to visit us and we will go to the theatre. I would prefer to see a comedy.

        [Total for Question 3 = 12 marks]

Transcripts

Page 1 Numbers

2. En 2016, près de 83 millions d'étrangers ont visité la France. Par contre, le chiffre pour 2015 était 85 millions. Cette chute est due aux attentats terroristes, surtout à Paris.

Ce sont les touristes d'Extrême-Orient qui ont le plus peur, car le nombre de touristes chinois à Paris a baissé de 22% et celui des touristes japonais de 42%.

On estime que les visiteurs chinois dépensent 1400 euros en moyenne dans les grands magasins.

Page 2 The French alphabet

1. – *Quel est votre nom?*

– Charpentier

– *Comment ça s'écrit?*

– C – H – A – R – P – E – N – T – I – E – R

– *Et votre prénom?*

– Béatrice

– *Comment est-ce que vous épelez ça?*

– B – E (accent aigu) – A – T – R – I – C – E

– *Et votre adresse courriel?*

– B (tiret bas) C – H – A – R – P (arrobase) F – R (point) N – E – T

2. Bonjour, je voudrais faire une réservation pour deux personnes au nom de Leclerc.

Ça s'écrit L – E – C – L – E – R – C, prénoms Gérard G – É – R – A – R – D et Julie, J – U – L – I – E.

C'est pour la nuit du 28 au 29 juillet. Pourriez-vous confirmer ma réservation par e-mail, s'il vous plaît? Mon adresse courriel est maisonleclerc@free.fr, ça s'écrit M – A – I – S – O – N – L – E – C – L – E – R – C (arrobase) F – R – E – E (point) F – R.

Page 3 Dates

2. En 1969, le président Georges Pompidou a décidé que le plateau Beaubourg deviendrait le site d'un centre culturel entièrement nouveau. En 1971, on annonce qu'une équipe internationale d'architectes serait responsable de la conception du bâtiment.

Les travaux de construction ont commencé en mai 1972 et ont duré cinq ans, jusqu'à l'ouverture du centre au public le 2 février 1977.

Dès le début, le centre a rencontré un grand succès avec plus de 150 millions de visiteurs, de sorte qu'il a fallu entreprendre un programme de rénovation entre octobre 1997 et décembre 1999.

Chaque année, le Centre Pompidou organise de grandes expositions. Le record du nombre de visiteurs a été enregistré pour l'exposition consacrée à Dali en 2013. L'exposition la plus populaire sur le thème de l'architecture a été celle sur Le Corbusier en 2015.

Page 4 Telling the time

1. Demain, on va faire une excursion à Dinan. Alors, il faut être au collège à sept heures et quart. Le car va partir à sept heures et demie précises. Ne soyez pas en retard!

Le trajet va durer deux heures et demie mais on va faire un arrêt vers neuf heures. Vous aurez vingt-cinq minutes pour vous rafraîchir.

Notre visite guidée de la ville est prévue pour onze heures et dure une heure et demie. À midi et demi, vous aurez du temps libre pour le déjeuner. Il y a beaucoup de petits restaurants où vous pourrez acheter des crêpes.

L'après-midi, on va visiter le château et on y sera vers deux heures moins le quart. Vous aurez quatre-vingt-dix minutes pour la visite et il faudra être devant le château à trois heures et demie pour notre retour au collège.

Page 5 Greetings

2. • Bonne chance! N'oubliez pas tout ce que vous avez appris, et surveillez l'heure. Vous n'avez que quarante-cinq minutes!

• Félicitations, Laurent. Tu es le premier de mes petits-enfants à réussir ton permis de conduire.

• Alors, va dire bonjour à Mamie. Elle regarde un film à la télé dans le salon. Ton grand-père se repose en ce moment parce qu'il était fatigué après le voyage.

• Bonsoir, messieurs-dames. Alors, vos places sont à gauche au deuxième rang. Le programme va commencer dans cinq minutes. Bon film!

Page 8 Describing people

1. Salut. Je m'appelle Félix. J'ai quinze ans et je cherche un correspondant anglophone qui a le même âge que moi.

J'aime bien rencontrer de nouvelles personnes et je n'hésite jamais à engager la conversation.

Par contre, je ne suis pas tellement enthousiaste quand ma mère prépare des plats que je connais pas et je les évite autant que possible.

Page 9 Family

2. – *Fabien, parlez-moi de votre famille.*

– On est six dans ma famille et je trouve ça génial car on a toujours quelqu'un à qui parler et je m'entends bien avec tout le monde. Cependant, ma sœur aînée se dispute souvent avec mon frère cadet. C'est dommage parce que moi, je le trouve mignon comme tout!

– *Laure, parlez-moi de votre famille.*

– J'aime bien être membre d'une famille nombreuse, surtout quand on est tous réunis pour manger. Il y a des inconvénients quand même, par exemple quand on veut être seul car nous n'avons pas notre propre chambre.

Page 11 When I was younger

1. Je suis né en Côte d'Ivoire à Abidjan, la capitale, où mon père travaillait au port. Quand j'étais jeune j'aimais jouer avec mes copains devant ma maison car il n'y avait ni terrain de foot à l'école ni club pour les jeunes. En plus, je jouais souvent pied nus puisque mes parents n'avaient pas assez d'argent pour l'équipement.

Cependant, ils se sont rendus compte que j'avais du talent et ils m'ont envoyé en France à l'âge de sept ans pour vivre chez mon oncle. Lui, il était footballeur professionnel dans un club en Bretagne. Trois ans plus tard j'ai joué dans l'équipe des jeunes de ce club pour la première fois.

Page 12 Food

1. Les Français aiment beaucoup manger de la viande, mais leurs préférences changent quand même. Selon un sondage réalisé pendant la Semaine du Goût, le bœuf bourguignon n'est plus le plat le plus populaire. À sa place, on trouve le magret de canard, un plat du sud-ouest de la France, suivi par la côte de bœuf et la raclette.

Les préférences suivent souvent les goûts régionaux: par exemple, la choucroute est très populaire dans l'est et les crêpes dans l'ouest.

Quant aux fruits et légumes, seulement 12% des Français consomment les cinq portions par jour conseillées. Parmi les légumes les plus populaires, on trouve les oignons, les carottes et les endives.

Page 15 Social media

2. – *Chloé, vous utilisez souvent les réseaux sociaux?*

– Tout le temps, surtout pour partager des images avec mes copains, c'est très pratique. Pourtant, je sais qu'il faut être prudent car notre identité peut être volée et nos profils piratés.

– *Et vous, Léo?*

– À mon avis, c'est chouette pour les entreprises car elles peuvent communiquer directement avec leurs clients et partager leurs informations. Cependant, on voit trop de choses méchantes ou blessantes en ligne, alors je les évite.

Page 16 Mobile technology

1. – *Nous parlons aujourd'hui avec un enseignant, Philippe Leroy, qui permet à ses élèves d'utiliser leurs portables en cours de langues. Philippe Leroy, ça pose des problèmes, non?*

– Pas forcément. On a discuté des avantages et des inconvénients et on a établi des règles très strictes pour l'utilisation des portables. Par exemple, il est interdit d'accéder aux réseaux sociaux ou d'utiliser les sites de traduction en ligne.

– *Et s'ils ne respectent pas les règles?*

– Dans ce cas-là, ils savent que je leur enlèverai leur portable et que j'appellerai leurs parents, alors ça arrive rarement.

– *Alors, vos élèves, comment est-ce qu'ils utilisent leurs portables?*

– Ils lisent des textes authentiques et trouvent les expressions intéressantes. Ils peuvent aussi utiliser des applis pour apprendre du vocabulaire et vérifier l'orthographe d'un mot.

– *Qu'est-ce que vos collègues pensent de l'utilisation des portables?*

– En fait, plusieurs de mes collègues permettent à leurs élèves d'écouter de la musique avec leur portable pendant qu'ils travaillent parce que ça les aide à se concentrer.

Page 17 French customs

2. En France, la fête des Morts n'a pas lieu le deux novembre comme au Mexique, mais le premier novembre, le jour de la Toussaint, un des jours fériés les plus importants pour les familles françaises. Ce jour-là, il est de tradition d'aller sur les tombes familiales. Traditionnellement, on plaçait une bougie allumée sur la tombe mais depuis la fin de la Première Guerre mondiale, on ne le fait plus. Maintenant, on met des chrysanthèmes sur les tombes. Ces fleurs résistent au froid et symbolisent l'immortalité au Japon, leur pays d'origine.

Page 18 French festivals

2. La Chandeleur est une fête chrétienne d'origine romaine qu'on fête en France quarante jours après Noël, c'est-à-dire le deux février. Traditionnellement, on ne range pas la crèche de Noël avant cette date.

C'est aussi le jour où on allume des bougies et on mange des crêpes le soir à la maison. On dit que la forme et la couleur des crêpes ressemblent au soleil et évoquent la fin de l'hiver et le retour du printemps.

Page 20 Music

2. J'attendais avec impatience le nouvel album de Stromae, car j'adore ceux qu'il a déjà sortis, mais je dois dire que je suis déçue. Les paroles sont trop simples, je dirais même banales, et la musique n'est pas du tout accrocheuse, de sorte qu'on l'oublie presque tout de suite. Il n'y a qu'une chanson sur l'album qui vaut la peine.

Page 21 Sport

1. – *Noah, quand vous étiez jeune, le foot était votre passion, non?*

– Oui, quand j'étais jeune, je jouais au foot régulièrement, mais quand il a fallu que je m'entraîne pour les compétitions de natation cinq fois par semaine, j'ai quitté l'équipe de foot. Cependant, j'aime toujours ce sport et je vais voir un match deux fois par an.

– *Alors, vous préférez les sports individuels?*

– Oui, je dirais que je préfère les sports où l'on est le seul responsable des résultats, par exemple si on gagne ou on perd. Pourtant, les sports d'équipe vous aident à développer des compétences qui vous serviront dans chaque sphère de votre vie plus tard. Par exemple, en jouant dans une équipe, on apprend à coopérer et communiquer avec les autres.

– *Je suppose que vous pouvez identifier d'autres avantages du sport?*

– Bien sûr, ça contribue à la réduction des cas d'obésité et de diabète, mais avant tout, il est important d'être actif et le sport, ça vous aide à bouger.

– *Et comment voyez-vous le rôle des entraîneurs, surtout avec les jeunes?*

– Il y en a qui se concentrent sur la compétition et la performance, mais il faut éviter ça. Les meilleurs entraîneurs encouragent la participation et l'effort.

Page 24 Holiday plans and preferences

2. • Normalement, je passe mes vacances au bord de la mer mais cette année, j'ai l'intention de faire un stage à la campagne. On fera de l'escalade et des randonnées à pied et à cheval.

• L'année dernière, j'ai passé de belles vacances dans un gîte en Italie. Cela m'a tellement plu que j'ai décidé d'y retourner cet été.

• Si on avait beaucoup d'argent, on passerait des vacances à l'étranger. Cependant, ce n'est pas le cas, alors nous prendrons notre tente et nous ferons un tour dans le nord du pays.

- La chance de visiter plusieurs endroits différents et de passer la nuit à bord d'un bateau m'attire beaucoup. Je partirai en vacances en juin et j'espère que je n'aurai pas le mal de mer!

Page 26 Travel and transport

2. (a) Le train en provenance de Strasbourg, arrivée prévue pour quatorze heures trente, arrivera à quatorze heures quarante-cinq.

(b) Attention aux passagers sur le quai numéro 3. Le prochain train qui arrivera dans cinq minutes s'arrêtera ici, à son terminus. Ne franchissez pas la ligne jaune.

Page 27 Accommodation

1. Bonjour, je m'appelle Monsieur Grandet, ça s'écrit G – R – A – N – D – E – T. Je voudrais réserver une chambre pour deux nuits, du 8 au 10 mars. Nous sommes deux adultes, et si possible, nous voudrions une chambre au premier étage avec vue sur le lac. Je voudrais aussi savoir si vous avez un parking.

Page 28 Dealing with problems

2. – *Hervé, l'échange s'est bien passé?*

– Oui et non. J'ai passé de bons moments chez mon correspondant, mais on a eu plusieurs problèmes. Une fois, je n'ai pas pu trouver de distributeur d'argent et j'ai dû emprunter de l'argent à un copain. Mais Béatrice, la pauvre! Nous sommes arrivés à notre destination et elle ne trouvait pas son passeport! Après avoir cherché pendant une demi-heure, elle l'a trouvé dans sa valise. Ensuite, comme les conducteurs de train avaient interrompu leur travail, on a dû voyager en bus de l'aéroport à notre école partenaire! En train le trajet aurait été plus rapide!

Page 30 Eating out

2. (a) – *Excusez-moi, monsieur. Notre table est à côté de la porte et il fait froid. Est-ce qu'il y a une autre table où on peut se mettre?*

– Certainement, la table dans le coin est libre. Voulez-vous vous asseoir là-bas?

(b) – *Messieurs-dames, je suis désolé mais il n'y a plus de poisson. Vous voulez choisir autre chose?*

– Qu'est-ce que vous recommandez, le steak ou le poulet?

– *Ils sont tous les deux très bons.*

– Bon, on prendra un steak chacun.

Page 32 Where I live

2. Aujourd'hui, il existe environ 4,8 millions de logements à loyer modéré, c'est-à-dire des logements HLM, dans lesquels dix millions de personnes sont logées. Financées par l'État, ces habitations sont destinées aux individus et aux familles dont les ressources financières sont limitées.

38% des logements sont occupés par une seule personne, 17% par une famille monoparentale avec un ou deux enfants et 13% par un couple sans enfants.

Page 33 The neighbourhood

2. – *Gérard, vous aimez habiter ici?*

– On dit qu'il y a beaucoup d'activités pour les jeunes, et c'est vrai si on aime le sport. Pour moi, ça ne compte pas car je ne suis pas du tout sportif. Mes intérêts sont plutôt culturels et il n'y a ni musée ni théâtre. Cependant, on n'est pas loin de Paris, alors on peut y aller quand on veut.

– *Et vous Safia?*

– Avant, j'habitais à Paris où il y avait toujours des embouteillages, surtout aux heures de pointe. Heureusement, ça n'existe pas ici. Cependant, j'aimerais bien qu'il y ait des pistes cyclables le long des rues, car en ce moment, il est trop dangereux de se déplacer à vélo.

Page 35 Francophone countries

2. (a) À partir de 2018, on ne verra plus les fameux «cars rapides» dans les rues de Dakar, la capitale du Sénégal. Depuis plus de quarante ans, ces minibus jaunes et bleus décorés d'inscriptions islamiques, d'images d'animaux et d'yeux, ont transporté les Dakarois à travers leur capitale.

(b) Ils seront remplacés par des bus blancs moins polluants et moins dangereux qui ont été fabriqués en Inde ou en Chine. Ceux qui utilisent les cars rapides ne sont pas contents parce qu'ils devront payer un tarif plus élevé.

Page 36 Seasons and weather

1. Voici la météo pour demain. Après des brumes matinales, l'ouest de la France deviendra ensoleillé, avec des températures plus basses qu'hier mais toujours agréables pour cette période de l'année.

Le nord du pays restera couvert toute la journée avec risque d'orage vers la fin de l'après-midi. Le soir, des averses seront fort probables.

Dans l'est, vous avez eu du beau temps aujourd'hui mais demain, le temps sera pluvieux pendant toute la journée avec un vent froid assez fort. N'oubliez pas votre parapluie!

Dans le sud de la France, le ciel sera couvert le matin avec risque d'averses. Vers la fin de la matinée, le ciel s'éclaircira et l'après-midi, il fera très beau.

Page 38 Your school

1. – *Julien, que pensez-vous du règlement intérieur?*

– On a le droit d'avoir un portable sur soi, et je trouve ça juste car on en a parfois besoin à la sortie des cours, mais je ne serais pas du tout content si mes cours étaient interrompus par la sonnerie d'un portable.

– *Et vous, Amélie?*

– On ne porte pas d'uniforme, alors je ne comprends pas pourquoi le maquillage est interdit. Une de mes copines a reçu une retenue récemment à cause de ça. Heureusement, le prof n'a pas remarqué que je m'étais aussi maquillée en cours. Autrement, je respecte toutes les règles.

– *Et finalement, Baptiste?*

– Quelques-unes des règles sont acceptables, comme l'interdiction des portables en cours, par exemple. Mais celles qui prennent pour cible des aspects de votre identité, comme le maquillage et le tatouage, sont bêtes. Je me demande pourquoi ils sont interdits. Le pire, c'est qu'on n'a pas le droit de se couvrir la tête!

Page 39 School trips, events and exchanges

1. Cette année j'ai participé à l'échange avec notre collège partenaire en France. L'échange a eu lieu juste avant les grandes vacances et il a duré une quinzaine de jours. J'ai eu de la chance car ma famille d'accueil était vraiment sympa et les parents ont fait des efforts pour parler clairement et pas trop vite avec moi. Pendant l'échange on a fait des visites aux musées et nous avons aussi donné un concert. Pour moi c'était une expérience tout à fait géniale.

Page 41 Ambitions

1. – *Bienvenue à notre programme. Aujourd'hui, nous discutons de comment les jeunes voient leur avenir. Alors, Lucy?*

– Quand j'étais jeune, je rêvais d'être actrice. Cependant, c'est un métier instable où on n'est jamais certain d'être employé. Je voudrais me marier et fonder une famille dans quelques années, donc je chercherai un emploi qui m'offre un bon salaire.

– *Et vous, Alice?*

– J'avais décidé que travailler à la maison serait mieux que travailler dans un bureau, mais je viens de faire mon stage professionnel dans une petite entreprise et je me demande maintenant si je veux poursuivre cette route.

– *Et finalement, Guy?*

– Après avoir obtenu mon diplôme à l'université, j'ai l'intention de prendre une année sabbatique, car je n'ai pas besoin de travailler immédiatement. J'ai envie de faire du bénévolat avec des gens dans le besoin. Si je faisais ça en Amérique du Sud, je pourrais également perfectionner mon espagnol. Je crois que ça m'aidera dans ma future carrière.

Page 42 Education post-16

2. – *Adam, qu'est-ce que tu vas faire l'année prochaine?*

– À la rentrée prochaine, je ne serai plus à l'école parce que je commencerai un apprentissage. Cela me permettra de développer de nouvelles compétences pratiques et en même temps je gagnerai de l'argent. Et toi, Lola?

– *Bon ben, puisque je ne suis pas forte en maths, j'ai choisi le bac L car on n'est plus obligés d'en faire. J'étudierai donc les matières dont j'aurai besoin dans ma future carrière d'interprète.*

Page 43 Charity and voluntary work

1. – *Écoutons d'abord Maurice.*

– Moi, je fais du bénévolat depuis six mois pour une association caritative qui soigne les chats abandonnés. Je fais ça pour enrichir mes compétences.

– *Et vous Angélique?*

– Je collecte des fonds pour une association caritative qui aide les enfants qui n'ont rien à manger en Afrique. À mon avis, il faut penser aux autres.

– *Et pour terminer, Paul?*

– Je fais du bénévolat pour un groupe environnemental dans mon quartier. Cela me permet de participer à la vie de la société.

Page 45 International events

2. On ne peut pas prendre ce concours au sérieux mais je l'adore quand même. Chaque année je passe cette soirée avec mes copains devant la télé et on fait la critique de chaque artiste, soit pour la musique, les paroles, le costume ou la mise en scène. Je trouve les remarques des commentateurs très amusantes et je partage mes pensées sur des réseaux sociaux. La seule partie de la soirée que je trouve ennuyeuse, c'est l'annonce des résultats des votes. Ça dure trop longtemps et on sait à l'avance que beaucoup de pays donnent toujours leurs douze points à leurs voisins!

Page 46 Campaigns and good causes

1. Mon père écrit des lettres à des prisonniers, à l'étranger. Il dit que c'est un petit geste que tout le monde peut faire et qui est énormément apprécié, surtout par ceux qui n'ont aucune chance de sortir de prison. Ma mère, par contre, pense qu'il est plus important de soutenir les enfants en difficulté. Chaque mois elle donne des vêtements que nous ne portons plus à une boutique solidaire. De temps en temps, elle donne aussi de l'argent à une association française qui soutient des projets sanitaires en Afrique pour améliorer les conditions de vie des filles démunies.

Page 47 Global issues

1. – *Laurent, qu'est-ce que vous pensez des problèmes dans le monde?*

– Ça m'énerve quand des gens disent que le réchauffement de la Terre n'existe pas. Est-ce qu'ils refusent d'accepter toutes les preuves mises à leur disposition?

– *Et vous Amina?*

– Laurent a raison. Cette année, on a vu des inondations catastrophiques en Asie, surtout en Inde où plus d'un millier de gens sont morts, ainsi que les ouragans qui ont déplacé des milliers de gens dans les Caraïbes.

Page 48 The environment

2. Chaque seconde, 175 bouteilles d'eau sont vendues en France. Cette consommation d'eau en bouteille pose des problèmes énormes pour l'environnement car moins de 20% des bouteilles sont recyclées et il faut attendre au moins 450 ans pour que les bouteilles se décomposent.

La solution? C'est de boire de l'eau du robinet plutôt qu'en bouteille. Après dix ans de campagne pour encourager les Français à changer leurs habitudes, ceux qui le font sont maintenant la majorité.

Page 49 Pronunciation strategies

Quick quiz:

1 Est-ce qu'ils ont une table pour six personnes?
2 Est-ce que vous avez voyagé en avion?
3 Ces assiettes sont assez sales.
4 Ils adorent les oignons.
5 À la fin, on était fatigués mais très heureux.
6 Mes amis n'aiment pas cet acteur.

1. (a) Il fait assez froid dans le nord et un peu plus chaud dans le sud du pays en hiver.

(b) Samedi, j'ai été très surpris parce qu'un flashmob a eu lieu devant l'arrêt d'autobus!

(c) Ma sœur vient d'acheter un anorak vert pour son petit ami.

(d) Le chef a préparé le bœuf et les choux de Bruxelles avec des noix d'une façon tout à fait délicieuse.

(e) Après le repas, il avait mal à l'estomac parce qu'il avait trop mangé.

(f) De nos jours, il est impossible de vivre sans portable.

2. Sur cette photo, on voit beaucoup d'enfants africains qui sont dans leur salle de classe. Ils portent un uniforme bleu. Il n'y a pas assez de place pour tous les élèves et ils doivent partager un banc. Certains n'ont ni cahier ni crayon. Je pense qu'ils sont assez pauvres.

À mon avis, l'éducation est très importante. Alors, il faut absolument continuer à l'école jusqu'à l'âge de dix-huit ans pour développer ses compétences et avoir de meilleures chances dans la vie.

Page 51 Asking for clarification strategies

2. ● Si j'ai bien compris votre question, vous m'avez demandé quels métiers seront les plus importants dans l'avenir.

● Facteur? Je suis désolé, je ne comprends pas le mot «facteur». Vous pouvez me l'expliquer, s'il vous plaît?

● Pardon, je n'ai pas bien entendu la question, pouvez-vous la répéter, s'il vous plaît?

● Je suis désolé, qu'est-ce que vous voulez dire? Vous pouvez me l'expliquer, s'il vous plaît?

Page 56 Listening strategies

1. ● Le Leu Tempo festival, qui a lieu pendant quatre jours au mois de mai, est le plus ancien et le plus important des festivals de La Réunion. Plus de 30 000 spectateurs assistent à des spectacles variés de théâtre et de cirque ainsi qu'à des concerts.

● Safiko, festival de musique rock et reggae qui se déroule pendant trois jours en juin, accueille des artistes locaux et internationaux. Pendant ce festival, on conseille aux touristes de réserver leur hôtel à l'avance.

● Le Grand Raid attire environ 2500 participants chaque mois d'octobre. Avec un parcours de 162 kilomètres et des ascensions cumulatives de plus de 9000 mètres, c'est une des courses à pied les plus difficiles du monde, mais elle permet aux concurrents de découvrir la beauté naturelle de l'île.

2. – *Autrefois, la pension était considérée comme une punition. Mais c'est comment la vie en internat, aujourd'hui? Nous allons parler avec des pensionnaires. D'abord, à toi, Éloïse.*

– La journée est bien organisée avec l'étude obligatoire après les cours. Je trouve ça bien car on peut travailler sans distractions. Par contre, on mange trop tôt le soir et j'ai encore faim avant de me coucher.

– *Et toi, Daniel?*

– On nous offre un choix énorme d'activités périscolaires, tout sur place. Ce qui m'embête, c'est qu'on doit éteindre les lumières à vingt-deux heures trente!

Page 57 Listening 1

2. – *Une enquête récente a révélé que notre jeunesse souffre. Aujourd'hui, les jeunes nous parlent de leurs problèmes. D'abord, Ariane.*

– Avant, j'avais des problèmes scolaires car j'avais toujours de mauvaises notes et mes parents se fâchaient. J'ai dû redoubler, ce qui m'a énormément aidée. Cependant, j'ai remarqué récemment que mes anciennes copines ne me parlent plus et je me sens de plus en plus isolée et déprimée.

– *Et vous Raoul?*

– Depuis l'âge de treize ans, je fume et j'ai toujours peur que mes parents découvrent mes cigarettes. Je sais que c'est mauvais pour la santé mais jusqu'ici, je n'ai pas réussi à abandonner le tabac. Ça sent mauvais, alors j'applique toujours beaucoup de déodorant après avoir fumé. Mes copains expérimentent avec des drogues maintenant, mais je ne veux pas y participer.

– *Et finalement, Fatima.*

– Tous les jours, je dois aider ma mère qui souffre d'un cancer et qui passe toute la journée au lit. En plus, je dois préparer tous les repas, faire des courses et emmener ma petite sœur à l'école. Mes parents se sont séparés parce que mon père dépensait tout son argent dans l'alcool et qu'il n'en restait plus assez pour la famille.

3. Nous voici dans le vieux quartier. Ici il y a beaucoup à voir. À droite vous voyez le musée. Vous y trouverez plein de choses intéressantes. L'entrée ne coûte qu'un euro. Juste à côté il y a l'hôtel de ville mais les touristes ne peuvent pas y entrer. Si vous avez du temps, visitez le château situé au bout de cette rue. Vous ne vous ennuierez pas! Tout près, il y a aussi un parc où vous pouvez vous promener. Il est ouvert toute la journée. Finalement, vous pouvez marcher jusqu'au fleuve pour voir le pont, après notre visite guidée. Il date du seizième siècle.

Page 58 Listening 2

2. – *Bienvenue à notre forum sur les métiers. Écoutons d'abord Riley.*

– Si vous vous intéressez aux langues, pensez à une carrière de traducteur. Certains de mes collègues travaillent pour des organisations internationales, mais moi, je préfère le travail indépendant parce que je peux choisir mes horaires et les projets qui m'intéressent. La plupart du temps, c'est un travail intéressant mais parfois, il y a des mois où je n'ai pas beaucoup de travail et où je dois faire attention à ce que je dépense.

– *Merci, Riley. Et maintenant, Céline.*

– Je voudrais vous encourager tous à considérer une carrière dans les sciences. Vous participerez souvent à des projets variés et intéressants qui valent vraiment la peine, comme trouver un remède contre le cancer ou une solution aux problèmes environnementaux. De temps en temps, il faut travailler de très longues heures, ce qui peut avoir des conséquences sur votre vie sociale.

3. Normalement, je vais au collège à pied, parce que c'est bon pour la santé et je pense qu'il faut contribuer à la protection de l'environnement. Cependant, c'est un trajet d'une bonne demi-heure et ce matin, je me suis réveillé en retard. J'ai demandé à mon père de m'emmener au collège en voiture. Malheureusement, la batterie de la voiture était à plat, alors j'ai dû prendre le bus.

Page 102 Practice paper: Listening (Foundation)

1. Example: – (00:05) Safia, comment vois-tu ton avenir?

　　　　　– Je voudrais du travail intéressant bien sûr.

– (00:35) J'aime bien parler anglais et espagnol. Je voudrais utiliser ces langues au travail. Et toi Guy?

– Je voudrais un emploi qui me permette de visiter d'autres pays. Et toi Djamila?

– Pour moi, avoir des collègues aimables est plus important qu'un bon salaire.

2. Example: (01:32) L'exposition des peintures du dix-neuvième siècle se trouve au sous-sol.

(01:57) Si vous avez déposé vos affaires au vestiaire, veuillez les récupérer avant six heures moins le quart.

La visite guidée gratuite commencera à quatorze heures dans la galerie située au rez-de-chaussée et passera ensuite au premier étage, mais la salle des collections au deuxième étage est fermée aujourd'hui.

Vous pouvez prendre des photos pendant votre visite, mais l'utilisation du flash est interdite.

3. **Example:** (03:15) Un Français a gagné quatre-vingts-millions d'euros lors du tirage de l'Euro Millions vendredi soir. Le gagnant n'a pas encore décidé de ce qu'il va faire avec cet argent.

(03:56) Environ 25 000 grévistes ont participé à la manifestation qui a eu lieu hier à la place de la République. Ils se sont rassemblés parce qu'ils veulent des salaires plus élevés.

À la suite du déraillement d'un TGV hier, le gouvernement a lancé une enquête sur la sécurité des chemins de fer. Dix personnes ont été gravement blessées.

On estime que des pirates informatiques ont volé les informations personnelles de milliers de gens lors de l'attaque informatique récente. De nombreuses entreprises ont également été touchées.

4. – (05:36) *Bienvenue à notre discussion sur le shopping en ligne. D'abord, Natalie. Qu'en pensez-vous?*
   – C'est le choix énorme de produits que j'aime le plus, mais souvent, on a besoin de beaucoup de temps pour trouver les meilleurs prix.
   – *Merci Natalie. Maintenant, Pascal.*
   – À mon avis, le shopping en ligne est très pratique pour les gens qui habitent dans des régions rurales loin des grands magasins. Cependant, j'ai récemment acheté un jean que j'ai dû renvoyer parce qu'il était trop petit; c'était embêtant.

5. (07:14) Dans les premiers jours du mois d'octobre, une heure environ avant le coucher du soleil, un homme qui voyageait à pied entrait dans la petite ville de Digne. Les habitants qui se trouvaient en ce moment à leurs fenêtres regardaient ce voyageur avec une sorte d'inquiétude. Il était difficile de rencontrer un passant d'un aspect plus misérable. C'était un homme de moyenne taille. Il pouvait avoir quarante-six ou quarante-huit ans. Une casquette cachait en partie son visage brûlé par le soleil.

6. (08:41) Léna Leclerc, la championne belge de course en fauteuil roulant, avait toujours rêvé de représenter son pays aux Jeux olympiques en cyclisme, un sport qu'elle a dû abandonner à cause d'un accident de la route dont elle a été victime à l'âge de onze ans. Elle a dû se faire amputer d'une jambe, mais déterminée à poursuivre son ambition sportive et malgré une douleur presque constante, elle a commencé son entraînement en fauteuil roulant aussitôt que possible.

Page 104 Practice paper: Speaking (Foundation)
Role play 00:05 (Model answer)

– *Vous parlez avec le / la réceptionniste dans un hôtel en France. Je suis le / la réceptionniste.*

   Bonjour. Je peux vous aider?
– Je voudrais une chambre pour deux personnes.
– *Très bien, et vous voulez quelle sorte de chambre?*
– Je voudrais une chambre avec balcon et vue sur le parc.

– *D'accord. Vous voulez rester pour combien de temps?*
– Je voudrais rester pour deux nuits.
– *Pas de problème. Qu'est-ce que vous aimez faire en ville?*
– J'aime visiter les musées parce que c'est intéressant.
– *Il y a beaucoup de musées dans notre ville.*
– À quelle heure est-ce que le restaurant est ouvert le soir?
– *De sept heures à dix heures et demie.*

Picture-based task 01:04 (Model answer)

– *Décris-moi la photo.*
– Sur la photo il y a des ados qui regardent leurs portables. Je pense qu'ils envoient des textos ou surfent sur Internet. Je pense qu'il fait beau temps parce qu'ils portent tous un jean et un tee-shirt ou une chemise.
– *Que penses-tu des réseaux sociaux?*
– À mon avis les réseaux sociaux sont super parce qu'on peut rester en contact avec ses amis. Mon réseau social préféré est Instagram parce que j'aime prendre et partager des photos.
– *Comment est-ce que tu as utilisé ton portable hier?*
– Hier j'ai utilisé mon portable pour envoyer des textos à mes copains et pour écouter de la musique.
– *Que fais-tu d'habitude sur Internet?*
– Normalement j'utilise Internet pour faire mes devoirs car je dois quelquefois faire des recherches. J'aime aussi télécharger des films et de la musique.
– *Quel est ton site internet préféré? Pourquoi?*
– Je n'ai pas de site préféré mais en général j'aime tous les réseaux sociaux parce que j'adore tchatter avec mes amis. Je pense que Wikipédia est très utile pour les devoirs mais mes profs n'aiment pas ça!

Conversation (Possible questions and answers)

Theme: Future aspirations, study and work; **Topic:** School (02:38)

– *Quelle est ta matière préférée?*
– J'adore la chimie parce que je la trouve facile et intéressante. En fait j'aime toutes les sciences parce que les profs sont vraiment géniaux.
– *Et la matière que tu détestes le plus?*
– Je déteste l'histoire parce que le prof est nul et je pense que c'est une matière ennuyeuse.
– *Qu'est-ce que tu as fait au collège hier?*
– Hier j'ai eu cours en maths, anglais et sciences le matin. Pendant la récré, j'ai bavardé avec mes copains et on a mangé à la cantine.
– *Qu'est-ce que tu vas étudier l'an prochain?*
– L'an prochain je vais étudier les sciences parce que je veux être médecin. On doit étudier ces matières pour avoir une place à l'université.
– *Que penses-tu des langues?*
– Je pense que les langues comme le français, l'espagnol et l'allemand sont importantes, mais je suis faible en langues alors je ne les aime pas tellement. Et vous? Est-ce que les langues sont importantes à votre avis?
– *Oui, je pense qu'elles sont très importantes.*

Theme: Local area, holiday and travel; **Topic:** Town, region and country (04:11)

– *Parle-moi de ta maison et ton quartier.*
– J'habite une assez grande maison dans un quartier très tranquille. J'aime bien y habiter parce qu'il y a beaucoup d'arbres et d'espaces vertes.

- *Comment es-tu venu(e) au collège aujourd'hui?*
- Aujourd'hui, je suis venu en voiture avec mon père parce qu'on était en retard, mais normalement je viens à pied.
- *Qu'est-ce qu'il y a pour les jeunes dans ta ville?*
- Il y a un centre sportif et un cinéma dans ma ville mais les magasins ne sont pas tellement bons.
- *Qu'est-ce que tu feras dans ta région le week-end prochain?*
- Le week-end prochain je ferai une sortie avec ma famille à la campagne. Elle est très pittoresque et on va faire une promenade.
- *Que penses-tu des transports dans ta ville?*
- À mon avis, les transports en commun sont assez bons car il y a des bus et des trains fréquents. Mais les billets sont chers!

Page 109 Practice paper: Listening (Higher)

1. **Example:** (00:05) Vous trouverez toujours une chambre à l'Hôtel Voltaire, il y a plus de cent-cinquante chambres.

   (00:32) Les chambres dans l'Hôtel Centre sont très modernes, mais il est situé à côté de la gare alors vous entendrez les trains tout le temps.

   Si vous avez des moyens limités un séjour dans L'Hôtel Bellevue est à recommander, mais il est situé loin du centre-ville.

   L'Hôtel Opéra, dans le vieux quartier, a des chambres tranquilles mais elles ne sont pas très modernes.

   Dans le vieux quartier il y a aussi l'Hôtel Royal avec ses grandes chambres de luxe. Un séjour dans cet hôtel ne sera pas bon marché!

   Pour un hôtel plus intime l'Hôtel de la Cour, avec seulement douze chambres, sera peut-être pour vous.

2. - (02:25) *Dans nos séries de podcasts sur les genres musicaux, Yannick Sako va nous expliquer le zouglou. C'est quoi, exactement?*
   - Le zouglou est un genre de musique populaire créé par des étudiants de Côte d'Ivoire il y a trente ans, dans les années quatre-vingt. La musique a ses origines dans la danse et dans les chants qui encouragent des équipes pendant les compétitions sportives. Dans les chansons, les étudiants ont protesté contre leurs conditions de vie et de travail.
   - *Les chansons, de quoi parlent-elles maintenant?*
   - Les paroles reflètent toujours les préoccupations et l'histoire de la jeunesse ivoirienne. Parfois, elles portent un message politique et elles sont très humoristiques. Cependant, les chansons ne sont pas toujours faciles à comprendre parce qu'on utilise des expressions argotiques et populaires en français ainsi que dans la langue régionale.
   - *On rencontre le zouglou uniquement en Côte d'Ivoire?*
   - Ben, maintenant, on trouve des artistes de zouglou toujours en Côte d'Ivoire et aussi dans d'autres pays d'Afrique de l'Ouest comme le Cameroun, le Burkina Faso et le Gabon. Depuis quelques années, des chanteurs de zouglou se sont installés en France, mais le zouglou y est moins connu que d'autres genres de musiques africaines. À mon avis, ces artistes de zouglou risquent de se séparer de leurs origines africaines.
3. - (05:49) *Le six février est la journée mondiale sans portable. Nous demandons aux jeunes s'ils vont y participer. Mélanie, vous y participez?*
   - En fait, je n'ai pas le choix, car mes parents me supprimeront le portable. Alors, je ne serai pas tentée

d'y jeter un coup d'œil. Cependant, je suis contente, c'est une seule journée!
   - *Et vous, Gérard?*
   - Je pense que c'est une bonne initiative car on est obligé d'avoir de vraies conversations avec ses amis! En plus, c'est bien de passer un repas en famille sans être distrait par son portable!

4. **Example:** - (07:35) *Hassan, qui représente un modèle pour toi?*
   - Les gens qui collectent des fonds énormes pour les associations caritatives sont mes modèles car ils pensent toujours aux autres.
   - *Et toi, Alésia?*
   - Je trouve les personnes qui sont prêtes à confronter les injustices de notre société, même si elles se mettent en danger, très inspirantes.
   - *Jérôme, qu'est-ce que tu en penses?*
   - Puisque je veux participer aux Jeux olympiques dans huit ans, les sportifs qui s'entraînent dur et qui réussissent grâce à leurs propres efforts m'inspirent toujours beaucoup.
   - *Et finalement, Charlotte?*
   - Alors, on dit qu'en général les filles ne poursuivent pas de carrières scientifiques. Donc, pour moi, les femmes comme ma mère, qui est professeur de médecine à l'université, sont des modèles importants.

5. (10:00) Dans notre ville, nous manquons de centres d'hébergement d'urgence. L'hiver approche et la vie est très dure pour ceux qui sont obligés de dormir dans les rues.

   Les bénévoles se rassemblent à un rendez-vous annoncé sur Facebook avant de circuler parmi les sans-abri. On peut aussi indiquer à l'avance ce qu'on va apporter, par exemple des vêtements chauds qu'on a collectés ou un repas chaud qu'on a préparé.

   Certains bénévoles sont motivés par des sentiments religieux mais à mon avis, il faut tout simplement penser aux personnes qui n'ont pas les mêmes chances que vous dans la vie.

6. (11:35) Saviez-vous qu'un quart des déplacements urbains se font pour des trajets de moins d'un kilomètre? Réfléchissez avant de sauter dans votre voiture, il y a de meilleurs moyens pour vous déplacer! Pour les trajets inférieurs à trois kilomètres, le vélo est le moyen de transport le plus efficace, parce que c'est rapide et vous pouvez éviter les embouteillages. En plus, il y a beaucoup de pistes cyclables maintenant. Pour les déplacements de moins d'un kilomètre, il vaut mieux marcher. Un grand avantage: ça ne coûte rien et vous pouvez rester en forme!

7. - (13:26) *Alors c'est décidé, Paris sera la ville hôte des Jeux olympiques en 2024! Mais comment réagissent les Parisiens à cette nouvelle, Monsieur Parmentier?*
   - On dit que c'est bon pour le tourisme, mais je pense que les touristes hésiteront à venir pendant les Jeux olympiques parce que les hôtels seront trop chers. Cependant, pour les Parisiens qui cherchent du travail, il y aura beaucoup d'opportunités, soit dans le secteur de la construction, soit dans celui de l'hôtellerie.
   - *Et vous, Madame Lefèvre, qu'en pensez-vous?*
   - À mon avis, le pays qui organise les Jeux olympiques remporte normalement beaucoup de médailles, ce qui encourage la participation sportive dans les mois qui

suivent. Cependant, les Parisiens doivent vivre avec la perturbation et le bruit provoqués par les travaux pendant la période de construction.

Page 111 Practice paper: Speaking (Higher)

Role play 00:04 (Model answer)

– *Salut, tu fais souvent du shopping?*

– Je fais des achats le week-end en ville.

– *Moi aussi. Que penses-tu des achats en ligne?*

– J'aime bien faire des achats en ligne parce que c'est très pratique.

– *Qu'est-ce que tu as acheté récemment?*

– Récemment j'ai acheté un pull bleu en laine.

– *C'est chouette ça.*

– Qu'est-ce que tu aimes acheter?

– *Des vêtements et des magazines.*

– Quel est ton magasin préféré?

– *J'aime bien les grands magasins.*

Picture-based task 00:47 (Model answer)

– *Décris-moi la photo.*

– Sur la photo il y a cinq filles qui sont au collège. Elles portent leur uniforme scolaire, une jupe à carreaux bleus et noirs, une veste bleu foncé et une chemise bleu clair. Je pense qu'elles sont en train d'aller à un cours, car elles portent leurs sacs et dossiers. Elles bavardent et elles ont l'air heureuses.

– *Que penses-tu du règlement scolaire?*

– À mon avis le règlement scolaire est important pour maintenir l'ordre et la discipline. Nous ne devons pas courir dans les couloirs par exemple; ça c'est une règle tout à fait raisonnable car il pourrait être dangereux si tout le monde courait d'un endroit à un autre. Cependant, je ne comprends pas pourquoi la couleur de nos gants en hiver est importante, c'est bête!

– *Qu'est-ce que tu as fait comme activités extrascolaires récemment?*

– Je n'ai pas le temps de participer à beaucoup d'activités extrascolaires parce je suis très occupé(e) par les préparations pour mes examens. Cependant, je suis membre de la chorale et hier nous avons eu une répétition pour un concert la semaine prochaine.

– *Qu'est-ce que tu feras au collège l'année prochaine?*

– L'année prochaine je participerai à la chorale parce que j'aime bien chanter. Je ferai aussi des visites scolaires au théâtre et aux musées.

– *Qu'est-ce que tu changerais dans ton collège si tu étais directeur / directrice?*

– Si j'étais directeur / directrice je changerais l'uniforme parce que je déteste la couleur de notre uniforme actuel. En plus, je permettrais aux filles de se maquiller et de porter des boucles d'oreilles.

Conversation (Possible questions and answers)

Theme: Identity and culture; **Topic:** Cultural life (03:04)

– *Comment est-ce que tu aimes passer ton temps libre?*

– Pendant mon temps libre j'aime me détendre en écoutant de la musique sur mon portable. J'aime toutes sortes de musique, mais celle que je préfère est le pop parce que je trouve les rythmes très accrocheurs. Parfois j'utilise des services de streaming, mais je télécharge aussi des chansons de mes groupes et chanteurs préférés.

– *Quel genre de film est-ce que tu aimes regarder?*

– J'adore les comédies romantiques parce que je les trouve divertissantes. Cependant, j'aime aussi les adaptations cinématographiques des livres car elles m'encouragent à lire le livre. D'autre part je déteste les films d'horreur parce qu'ils me font peur.

– *Parle-moi d'un livre que tu as lu récemment.*

– Récemment j'ai lu un roman historique que j'ai trouvé très captivant. L'action a eu lieu en France pendant la Première Guerre mondiale et il s'agissait d'un soldat blessé sur le champ de bataille qui est tombé amoureux de la femme qui le soignait. C'est un livre que je recommanderais.

– *Qu'est-ce que tu feras ce week-end?*

– Ce week-end j'irai en ville pour voir la nouvelle exposition sur l'histoire de notre ville au musée. Je pense que ce sera très intéressant. L'après-midi je retrouverai mes amis au café et ensuite nous irons au parc parce qu'il y aura un feu d'artifice le soir. J'adore les feux d'artifice parce qu'ils sont pleins de couleurs.

Theme: Local area, holiday and travel; **Topic:** Town, region and country (05:07)

– *Décris la ville / le village où tu habites.*

– J'habite dans une ville de cent-mille habitants non loin de Londres. Dans ma ville, il y a beaucoup de choses à faire et à voir comme le musée, les ruines de la ville ancienne et la cathédrale. Si on veut sortir le soir, il y a un cinéma et un théâtre ainsi que beaucoup de restaurants où on peut déguster la cuisine de toutes les régions du monde.

– *Que penses-tu des transports dans ta région?*

– À mon avis, les transports en commun sont excellents dans ma ville parce qu'on peut facilement aller à Londres en train, un trajet d'une vingtaine de minutes. En plus, on n'est pas loin des autoroutes et des aéroports.

– *Quels sont les avantages de la vie en ville?*

– Je pense que c'est bien de vivre en ville parce que c'est plus facile de faire des achats et il y a toujours beaucoup de choses à faire. Mais la ville peut être plus bruyante et polluée que la campagne où la vie est plus calme et lente. Où est-ce que vous voudriez vivre?

– *Moi, je voudrais vivre à la campagne parce que c'est plus tranquille. Qu'est-ce que tu as fait dans ta ville / ton village le week-end dernier?*

– Le week-end dernier, j'ai retrouvé mes copains / copines en ville. Après avoir bu un café, nous sommes allé(e)s voir une nouvelle exposition au musée. Ensuite, nous sommes allé(e)s au cinéma voir un film qui était vraiment amusant. On a beaucoup ri!

– *Qu'est-ce tu voudrais changer dans ta ville / ton village? Et pourquoi?*

– Ce que je voudrais faire pour changer ma ville, c'est créer un skate-park pour les jeunes parce qu'en ce moment, il n'y a rien pour ceux qui aiment faire du skate. Ça serait génial d'avoir aussi un meilleur marché de Noël en décembre. Celui qui a lieu chaque année est trop petit. Je pense que l'année prochaine, il faudra plus de chalets avec une plus grande variété de marchandises.

Answers

Page 1 Numbers
Quick quiz:
une trentaine – about thirty; le douzième – the twelfth; vingt pour cent – 20%; deux-cent-cinquante – 250; soixante-quinze – 75

Questions:
1. (a) Il y a trois-cent-trente-deux chambres dans l'hôtel.

(b) Le restaurant est au vingtième étage.

(c) Une chambre (simple / individuelle) coûte entre soixante-seize et quatre-vingt-huit euros la nuit.

(d) Deux-mille-cinq-cents personnes travaillent dans des hôtels dans cette ville.

2. (a) 85 million

(b) terrorist attacks

(c) 42% fewer tourists

(d) 1400 euros

Page 2 The French alphabet
Quick quiz:
C – say; E – euh; G – jhay; I – ee; J – jhee; K – kah; Q – kuh; Y – ee-grek

Questions:
1. Compare your pronunciation with the audio recording.

2. (a) C   **(b)** B   **(c)** D

Page 3 Dates
Quick quiz:
1. en février

2. le jeudi soir

3. mercredi prochain

4. août dernier

Questions:
1. (a) 5th November

(b) 13th June

(c) 21st May

2. (a) A team of international architects would design the building.

(b) 2nd February 1977

(c) renovations

(d) 2013

Page 4 Telling the time
Quick quiz:
1. 1 pm / 13.00; **2.** 12.30 pm; **3.** 7.45; **4.** 11.55; **5.** 7.15; **6.** 2.40

Questions:
1. (a) 25 minutes

(b) 12.30

(c) in front of the castle (1) in order to return home (1)

2. (a) At 6.30 pm

(b) He has rugby training until 7.15.

(c) 7.45 pm

(d) It will be too late to go to the cinema – she wanted to see the film.

(e) To go to the cinema, meeting at 8.15 pm.

Page 5 Greetings
Quick quiz:
1. vous   **2.** vous   **3.** tu
4. vous   **5.** tu

Questions:
1. Chère Christine,

Joyeux anniversaire! J'espère que tu passes une bonne journée. Quels cadeaux as-tu reçu? Je suis désolée, je ne peux pas venir dîner chez toi avec ta famille ce soir mais je vais te voir le week-end prochain et nous allons fêter ton anniversaire à ce moment-là.

À samedi.

À bientôt, Annette

2. B; D; A

Page 6 Opinions
Quick quiz:
1. on the other hand

2. however

3. in my opinion

4. that gets on my nerves

5. I like that

Questions:
1. (a) J'adore le football parce que c'est un jeu passionnant et j'aime bien aller regarder des matchs le week-end. La semaine dernière mon équipe a gagné. / Je n'aime pas du tout le football parce que je trouve ça très ennuyeux et les matchs sont trop longs. Je préfère les sports rapides, par exemple l'athlétisme.

(b) À mon avis, la musique classique est plus agréable que les autres genres de musique comme le jazz car elle m'aide à me détendre. Je vais souvent à des concerts et je joue aussi du violon dans un orchestre.

(c) À mon avis, Internet est très pratique pour obtenir des informations et pour communiquer avec les autres. Il y a bien sûr des inconvénients et on peut perdre pas mal de temps en ligne. Il faut être prudent.

2. B; D; G

Page 7 Asking questions
Quick quiz:
Est-ce qu'il y a un supermarché près d'ici? – Oui, en face du parking.

Quand est-ce que le film commence? – À dix-neuf heures trente.

Avec qui vas-tu en France? – Avec ma famille.

Pourquoi as-tu choisi ce livre? – Parce qu'il est intéressant.

Quelle saison est-ce que tu préfères? – Le printemps.

Où est-ce que tu as mis le livre? – Sur la table.

Questions:
1. (a) Comment est-ce que vous trouvez la cuisine française? Comment trouvez-vous la cuisine française?

(b) Qu'est-ce que tu veux faire ce soir? Que veux-tu faire ce soir?

(c) Avez-vous de l'eau? Est-ce que vous avez de l'eau?

(d) Quel genre (Quelle sorte) de musique est-ce que tu aimes?
Quel genre (Quelle sorte) de musique aimes-tu?

(e) Est-ce qu'il y a des toilettes près d'ici?

(f) Où est-ce qu'on peut acheter un sandwich? Où peut-on acheter un sandwich?

2. (a) Que nous conseillez-vous de faire?

(b) Est-ce que tu fais souvent de l'exercice?

(c) Quand est-ce que le musée est ouvert? / Quels sont les horaires d'ouverture du musée?

(d) Où est-ce qu'on peut bien manger? Est-ce que tu connais (vous connaissez) un bon restaurant?

(e) Qu'est-ce que tu fais (vous faites) pour protéger l'environnement?

(f) Qu'est-ce que tu as pensé du concert? Comment as-tu trouvé le concert?

Page 8 Describing people
Quick quiz:
1. J'ai seize ans.

2. Je suis né(e) en 2002.

3. Je suis mince et de taille moyenne.

4. Je porte des lunettes.

Questions:
1. (a) B   **(b)** C

2. (a) C   **(b)** B   **(c)** D

Page 9 Family
Quick quiz:
1. My elder brother is single.

2. I have a younger sister.

3. My stepfather's children are twins.

4. My half-brother is younger than me.

Questions:
1. Je suis fille unique. Nous sommes quatre à la maison parce que ma grand-mère habite (vit) chez (avec) nous. Je trouve ça génial parce qu'elle est gentille et nous aimons regarder la télé ensemble. Le week-end, nous faisons toujours une promenade. Hier, nous sommes allés au restaurant pour fêter l'anniversaire de mon beau-père.

2. (a) It is a positive experience / He likes having someone to talk to.

(b) His elder sister and younger brother don't get on. (1)

He gets on well with his younger brother. (1)

(c) At meal times / When they eat together.

(d) She and her siblings don't have their own bedrooms.

Page 10 Friends and relationships
Quick quiz:
1. N   **2.** P/N   **3.** P   **4.** N   **5.** P

Questions:
1. (a) (Model answer) Normalement, on ne se dispute pas mais parfois, on n'est pas d'accord au sujet d'un film qu'on va voir.

(b) (Model answer) Je m'entends bien avec la plupart des élèves de ma classe, surtout avec ceux qui ont les mêmes centres d'intérêt que moi, mais je trouve les élèves bruyants très agaçants.

(c) (Model answer) Quand je me dispute avec mes parents, c'est normalement au sujet de l'argent de poche, des heures de sorties ou de l'heure à laquelle je me couche. La semaine dernière, j'ai voulu sortir avec mes copains (copines) et mes parents ont dit 'non'. Ce n'est pas juste!

2. Chez moi, en général, on s'entend bien parce que nous avons tous les mêmes centres d'intérêt et les disputes sont heureusement rares. Je n'aime pas quand tout le monde s'énerve parce que l'atmosphère à la maison devient désagréable et ça me rend triste. Cependant, je me dispute parfois avec mes parents au sujet des devoirs et de la télévision. La semaine dernière, ma sœur et moi voulions regarder des émissions différentes et mes parents ont dit que celle qui aurait fini ses devoirs la première pourrait choisir!

Mon copain (ma copine) idéal(e) serait quelqu'un avec qui je pourrais facilement parler et avec qui je m'amuserais bien.

Page 11 When I was younger
Quick quiz:
1. je jouais

2. je n'aimais pas

3. j'étais assez timide

4. je voulais être

5. Il n'avait pas beaucoup d'ami(e)s.

Questions:
1. (a) C   **(b)** B   **(c)** D

(d) A   **(e)** B

2. Quand j'étais plus jeune, mes parents avaient une ferme et je les aidais avec les animaux le week-end. Le matin je devais me lever tôt pour arriver au collège (à l'école) à l'heure. Je ne pouvais pas passer du temps avec mes copains (copines / amis / amies) après les cours (le collège / l'école) parce que je devais prendre le bus pour rentrer chez moi.

Page 12 Food
Quick quiz:
1. sucre   **2.** fraise

3. beurre   **4.** œufs

Questions:
1. (a) C   **(b)** A

2. (a) Henri   **(b)** Céline

(c) Céline   **(d)** Henri

Page 13 Meals
Quick quiz:
1. Je prends le petit déjeuner à sept heures et demie.

2. J'ai mangé de la soupe au déjeuner.

3. Je bois du thé au goûter.

4. On mange du poisson au dîner.

Questions:
1. A; C; G

2. (a) À mon avis, il est important de manger en famille au moins plusieurs fois par semaine, par exemple le soir ou pour le déjeuner le dimanche, parce que c'est bien d'être ensemble et de discuter de ce qui s'est passé pendant la journée. Cependant, ce n'est pas toujours pratique. Mon père, par exemple, part tôt le matin et rentre parfois tard le soir.

(b) On mange toujours un repas spécial pour les fêtes comme les anniversaires et Noël. Sinon, c'est quand on a des invités à la maison, comme le week-end dernier. Mes grands-parents sont venus nous voir.

(c) J'aime les plats salés et savoureux, mais je n'aime pas tellement les plats épicés. Cependant, mon frère, qui est allé en Inde, les adore.

Page 14 Shopping
Quick quiz:
Je veux me faire rembourser. – I want a refund.

Je voudrais échanger ce pull. – I would like to exchange this jumper.

Je n'ai plus mon ticket de caisse. – I haven't got my receipt any more.

Je voudrais essayer ce pull. – I would like to try on this jumper.

Je ne veux pas dépenser trop d'argent. – I don't want to spend too much money.

Questions:
1. (Model answer)

1. *Je peux vous aider?*

Je cherche un tee-shirt bleu.

Les tee-shirts sont là-bas.

2. *Pourquoi est-ce que vous avez choisi notre magasin?*

Les vêtements ne sont pas chers.

3. *Qu'est-ce que vous avez déjà acheté en France?*

J'ai acheté une casquette pour mon frère.

Bon… Vous aimez ce tee-shirt?

4. C'est combien?

Douze euros.

5. Est-ce que vous avez un tee-shirt à ma taille / de taille moyenne?

Bien sûr – voilà.

2. (a) You can waste a lot of time.

(b) Clothes are often cheap in the sales. / You can see what you are getting. / You can make sure the size and colour are right. (any 2)

Page 15 Social media
Quick quiz:
1. réseaux sociaux   **2.** contact

3. amis   **4.** partager

5. en ligne   **6.** tchatté

7. demi-heure   **8.** réfléchir

9. poster

Questions:
1. J'adore les réseaux sociaux et je passe plusieurs heures par jour à tchatter avec mes amis et à mettre des photos en ligne. Mes parents diraient probablement que j'y suis accro, mais je ne suis pas d'accord avec eux. Je ne suis jamais distrait(e) en classe et je fais toujours mes devoirs. Hier, j'ai organisé une soirée avec mes ami(e)s (copains / copines) en utilisant un réseau social.

2. (a) to share photos

(b) identity theft / hacking

(c) businesses can communicate directly with customers

(d) hurtful comments / online bullying

Page 16 Mobile technology
Quick quiz:
1. télécharger de la musique

2. appeler mes amis

3. obtenir des renseignements

4. envoyer des SMS / textos

Questions:
1. (a) Students are not allowed to use social media. (1)

They are not allowed to use online translation websites. (1)

(b) They know their mobile phone will be taken away. (1)

Their parents will be called. (1)

(c) Reading authentic texts (1) and using apps to learn and check the spelling of words. (1)

(d) Pupils listen to music. (1)

It helps them to concentrate. (1)

2. (a) Christelle   **(b)** Didier

(c) Didier   **(d)** Laurent

(e) Maya

Page 17 French customs
Quick quiz:
la messe – Mass; la fête – party; le cadeau – gift; le réveillon – Christmas Eve / New Year's Eve dinner / party; l'église – church

Questions:

1. (a) plus   **(b)** un arbre

     (c) 29%   **(d)** Peu

2. B; E

Page 18 French festivals
Quick quiz:
1. parade / procession

2. firework display

3. Easter

4. a public (bank) holiday

Questions:
1. (Model answer)

- Sur la photo, on voit beaucoup de gens dans la rue qui sont en costumes multicolores. Ils se sont maquillés et certains portent un parapluie. Ils s'amusent bien et je pense qu'ils fêtent le carnaval.

- À mon avis, les fêtes sont importantes parce que c'est l'occasion de se retrouver et de s'amuser. On peut aussi célébrer les moments importants dans la vie d'une nation.

- Non, je ne suis jamais allé(e) à une fête traditionnelle en France, mais je voudrais bien aller à Paris pour la fête nationale du quatorze juillet parce que j'ai vu des photos des défilés militaires sur les Champs-Élysées, et je pense que c'est un spectacle formidable.

- Je fêterai Noël en famille. Nous décorerons la maison et nous aurons un beau sapin de Noël. Le jour de Noël, nous mangerons un grand repas après être allés à l'église. Ensuite, j'offrirai des cadeaux à ma famille et j'ouvrirai ceux qu'on me donnera. À Pâques, mes parents me donneront un œuf en chocolat et nous irons à l'église. Après ça, nous rendrons visite à mes grands-parents pour le déjeuner.

- Dans ma région, on célèbre les fêtes avec une fête foraine qu'on installe sur la place du marché. On joue aussi de la musique en plein air et on peut acheter quelque chose à manger aux marchands ambulants. Ils vendent souvent des plats et produits régionaux.

2. (a) chrétiens   **(b)** garder

     (c) illuminées   **(d)** saison

Page 19 Reading
Quick quiz:
1. Normalement je lis le soir.

2. J'aime télécharger des romans sentimentaux.

Questions:
1. (a) Félix   **(b)** Hugo

     (c) his parents

     (d) to keep up to date / abreast of the news

     (e) write a novel

2. (Model answer)

(a) J'aime lire toutes sortes de livres, mais surtout des romans. La lecture m'aide à me détendre et les romans stimulent mon imagination. Récemment j'ai lu un roman de JK Rowling. Je pense qu'elle écrit bien et je trouve que ses personnages sont réalistes.

(b) À mon avis les livres électroniques sont très pratiques quand on est en vacances car on peut emporter beaucoup de livres. Cependant, je préfère tourner les pages d'un vrai livre imprimé. De cette façon on peut voir très facilement combien de pages on a lues.

(c) Quand j'étais jeune je lisais beaucoup, surtout des romans pour les jeunes. Maintenant je n'ai pas assez de temps et je lis très peu. Cependant j'espère que j'aurai plus de temps pour lire dans l'avenir.

(d) Récemment j'ai lu un roman historique. Il s'agissait d'un roi d'Angleterre et de ses reines et c'était une histoire à la fois intéressante et passionnante. L'écrivain a donné une impression très vivante de la vie à cette époque-là.

Page 20 Music
Quick quiz:
1. Je joue du piano depuis deux ans.

2. Je jouais de la guitare.

3. Quand j'étais plus jeune, j'aimais la musique classique.

4. Mon genre de musique préféré est le rock. / Mon genre musical préféré est le rock.

Questions:
1. When I was young, I didn't understand why my grandmother loved classical music. However, I have been playing the violin in an orchestra for three years and I have learned to appreciate this kind of music. At the moment, we have rehearsals for a concert that will take place at the end of the month.

2. (a) B   **(b)** C

Page 21 Sport
Quick quiz:
1. le surf   **2.** le volleyball

3. l'équitation   **4.** l'escalade

Questions:
1. (a) B   **(b)** A   **(c)** C

2. (Model answer) À l'école, on doit faire du sport régulièrement, au moins trois fois par semaine. Je fais partie d'une équipe de hockey et on joue des matchs tous les samedis. La semaine dernière, nous avons dû jouer contre une équipe très forte et nous avons perdu le match. Nous étions tous très fatigués et très déçus. Cependant, je trouve que faire du sport aide à rester en forme et à se détendre. Le mois prochain, nous allons participer à un tournoi qui aura lieu à Londres. Nous nous entraînerons plusieurs fois dans la semaine car nous voudrions bien être champions!

Page 22 Cinema
Quick quiz:
1. a screen   **2.** scary

3. to take place   **4.** the film star

Questions:
1. (a) (Model answer) Je préfère regarder un film au cinéma parce que l'écran est plus grand et c'est mieux pour apprécier les effets spéciaux, mais j'aime aussi regarder des films chez moi. C'est génial de s'installer confortablement sur le canapé avec des amis.

(b) (Model answer) Je n'aime pas les films d'horreur parce que je les trouve effrayants et qu'ils me font peur. Je n'aime pas tellement les films de science-fiction car ils ne sont pas du tout réalistes et je préfère les histoires qui pourraient être vraies.

(c) (Model answer) La semaine dernière je suis allé(e) voir une comédie romantique avec mes copines. Les acteurs étaient bons et on a beaucoup ri. Cependant, je pense que l'histoire était un peu bête.

2. (a) Albert

     (b) les effets spéciaux

     (c) le drame des deux personnages

Page 23 Television
Quick quiz:
un feuilleton – Une série dramatique qu'on peut regarder plusieurs fois dans la semaine.

un dessin animé – Une émission pour les enfants.

les actualités – Une émission pour savoir ce qui se passe dans le monde.

la météo – Une émission qu'on regarde pour savoir le temps qu'il va faire.

Questions:
1. (Model answer) J'adore les émissions, comme les jeux télévisés, parce qu'elles sont divertissantes. Normalement je regarde la télé dans le salon avec mes parents. En semaine je regarde seulement une heure de télé le soir, mais le week-end dernier je suis allé(é) chez un(e) copain / copine pour regarder une série policière. Ça a duré six heures!

Je pense que j'utiliserai plus les services de rattrapage dans l'avenir parce que je dois souvent faire autre chose quand mes émissions préférées sont diffusées. Je déteste les publicités parce qu'elles sont bêtes.

2. (a) (Model answer) Ça dépend de l'émission. J'adore les émissions où on doit faire des gâteaux ou préparer un repas, mais celles où il y a des concurrents sur une île déserte ou enfermés dans une maison, je les trouve bêtes et je ne les regarde jamais.

(b) (Model answer) Je regarde la télé de rattrapage quand je ne peux pas regarder une émission à une heure précise. J'utilise souvent ma tablette pour regarder ces émissions.

Page 24 Holiday plans and preferences
Quick quiz:
1. plage

2. visiter un musée

3. faire du ski

4. faire ses bagages

Questions:
1. (Model answer)

- Sur la photo on voit des gens qui font du camping en été. Je pense que c'est un groupe d'amis. Il y a six filles et deux garçons. Je pense qu'il fait chaud parce qu'ils portent des tee-shirts. Ils sont assis et ils préparent le repas du soir. Je pense qu'ils sont heureux parce qu'ils sont en vacances.

- À mon avis les vacances dans un camping peuvent être super si le camping est bien aménagé, par exemple avec piscine, terrain de jeux, restaurant et magasin. C'est moins cher que rester dans un hôtel, mais s'il fait mauvais temps c'est moins agréable.

- Récemment j'ai passé des vacances au Costa Rica. J'ai fait des randonnées dans les forêts tropicales et j'ai vu des animaux exotiques, tels que des toucans et des singes. Pour me rafraîchir, j'ai nagé dans la mer et j'ai fait de la plongée avec masque et tuba.

- L'année prochaine, je partirai en vacances avec mes amis. On logera dans une auberge de jeunesse parce que c'est moins cher qu'un hôtel mais plus confortable que le camping! Cependant je n'aime pas tellement les lits superposés!

- Je crois que les vacances sont essentielles pour se détendre. De nos jours, tout le monde est très occupé avec le travail, la famille et même les réseaux sociaux. C'est vraiment trop facile d'être stressé.

2. E; B; F

Page 25 Holiday experiences
Quick quiz:
1. il y a un an

2. juillet dernier

3. pendant mon séjour

4. quand il pleuvait

Questions:
1. (a) Il est arrivé trop tard pour le repas du soir / dîner.

(b) la variété des activités à sa disposition

(c) parce qu'il pleuvait / il faisait mauvais temps

2. (Possible answer) Tout le monde a besoin de vacances pour s'amuser, se détendre et pour récupérer.

En août, j'ai passé mes vacances dans le sud de la France avec mes parents. Nous avons loué un gîte près de la côte, donc nous sommes très souvent allés à la plage. Mes parents aiment bien se bronzer mais je préfère nager dans la mer ou jouer au volleyball sur la plage. C'est au cours d'une partie de volleyball que j'ai rencontré quelques jeunes Français avec qui j'ai souvent parlé. C'était super pour améliorer mes compétences linguistiques.

À mon avis, les vacances à l'étranger sont une chance exceptionnelle de découvrir une nouvelle culture et une nouvelle cuisine. On peut également voir des choses qu'on ne peut pas voir chez soi comme les pyramides en Égypte et les temples de la Grèce antique. D'autre part, on peut avoir des problèmes si on ne parle pas la langue du pays.

L'année prochaine j'irai en Espagne parce que je veux avoir la chance d'améliorer mon espagnol.

Page 26 Travel and transport
Quick quiz:
1. waiting room

2. ticket office

3. toll on the motorway

4. fasten your seatbelt

Questions:
1. (Model answer)

1. *Bonjour, je peux vous aider?*

   Je voudrais deux allers simples pour Marseille, s'il vous plaît.

2. *Bon. Pourquoi voulez-vous voyager en train?*

   Parce que c'est rapide et confortable. *Vous avez raison.*

3. *Qu'est-ce que vous avez déjà fait en France?*

   Je suis allé à Paris et j'ai visité des musées.

   Bon. Voici vos billets. Ça fait quatre-vingt-dix euros.

4. Est-ce que je peux payer avec ma carte bancaire?

   Bien sûr.

5. Combien de temps dure le voyage?

   Trois heures.

2. (a) B   **(b)** C

Page 27 Accommodation
Quick quiz:
1. an air-conditioned room

2. with a sea view

3. with a safe

4. a family room

Questions:
1. (a) A room for 2 adults on the 1st floor (1) with a view of the lake (1).

(b) Dates of stay are 8th–10th March.

(c) Does the hotel have a car park?

2. (Model answer) Voici ma chambre dans mon hôtel. Il y a un balcon avec vue sur la mer et les montagnes. J'aime l'hôtel parce qu'il est très moderne et confortable.

Page 28 Dealing with problems
Quick quiz:
1. achat

2. gîte

3. formulaire

4. choix

Questions:
1. (Model answer)

1. *Bonjour, je peux vous aider?*

   Mon vélo a un pneu crevé / Les freins de mon vélo ne fonctionnent pas.

   Je suis désolé. On va le(s) réparer.

2. *Où est-ce que vous logez dans notre ville?*

   Je loge à l'auberge de jeunesse.

3. *Où êtes-vous déjà allé(e) pendant votre séjour en France?*

   Je suis déjà allé(e) en Normandie.

   Ça, c'est chouette.

4. Combien de temps est-ce que ça va prendre la réparation?

   Une journée.

5. Ça coûte combien?

   Trente euros.

2. (a) financier

(b) pièce d'identité

(c) une grève

(d) plus

Page 29 Directions
Quick quiz:
Traversez la place. – Cross the square.

Allez jusqu'au rond-point. – Go as far as the roundabout.

Suivez le panneau. – Follow the sign.

De l'autre côté du pont. – On the other side of the bridge.

Au carrefour va tout droit. – Go straight ahead at the crossroads.

Questions:
1. (Model answer)

1. *Bonjour, je cherche la poste. Où est-elle?*

   Elle est entre la pharmacie et le supermarché.

2. *Qu'est-ce qu'il y a à voir dans cette ville?*

   Il y a un musée. Il est très intéressant.

3. *Quand est-ce qu'il est ouvert?*

   Il est ouvert de dix heures à dix-sept heures.

4. *Et comment est-ce qu'on peut y aller?*

   Allez tout droit et puis prenez la première rue à gauche.

   Bon, merci.

5. Combien de temps est-ce que vous passez en Grande-Bretagne?

   Une semaine seulement.

2. (a) D   **(b)** C

Page 30 Eating out
Quick quiz:
1. l'addition   **2.** un verre

3. une assiette   **4.** content

Questions:

1. (Model answer)

- Sur la photo, il y a cinq personnes, deux hommes et trois femmes. Ils sont jeunes et je pense qu'ils sont amis. Ils sont au restaurant et ils prennent le petit déjeuner. Je pense qu'ils mangent des croissants et des fruits. Ils boivent du café et du jus d'orange. Ils ont l'air heureux car ils rigolent ensemble.

- J'adore la cuisine française parce qu'il y a des plats tout à fait délicieux. Si j'avais le choix, je mangerais dans un restaurant parisien à côté de la tour Eiffel. J'aimerais beaucoup essayer les escargots et les cuisses de grenouille parce qu'on m'a dit qu'ils sont délicieux.

- La dernière fois que je suis allé(e) au restaurant c'était pour l'anniversaire de ma mère. Nous sommes allés dans un restaurant italien et j'ai mangé une soupe aux légumes comme entrée, une pizza aux fruits de mer comme plat principal et une glace au chocolat comme dessert. C'était un repas très appétissant.

- Le week-end prochain nous irons au restaurant parce mon frère vient de recevoir son diplôme universitaire. Nous irons manger dans un restaurant chinois parce que c'est sa cuisine préférée. J'aime bien le canard préparé à la mode chinoise.

- J'aime bien la cuisine indienne parce que j'adore les plats épicés. Par contre, mes parents la détestent et n'en mangent jamais.

2. (a) (i) it's near the door (1) and it's too cold (1)

    (ii) a table in the corner

(b) (i) fish   **(ii)** steak

Page 31 Shopping on holiday
Quick quiz:

1. Est-ce qu'il y a un distributeur d'argent près d'ici?

2. J'ai besoin de timbres.

3. Avez-vous des cartes postales?

Questions:

1. (Model answer)

- Sur la photo on voit des touristes qui sont en train d'acheter des souvenirs. Je pense qu'ils regardent des peintures en plein air et choisissent peut-être des cadeaux pour leur famille. Il fait beau temps et ils portent des vêtements décontractés.

- À mon avis les souvenirs sont importants parce qu'ils nous aident à nous souvenir de nos vacances. On peut acheter des objets décoratifs ou quelque chose de typique du pays qu'on a visité.

- Quand j'ai visité Paris j'ai acheté un porte-clés de la tour Eiffel et un aimant de la cathédrale Notre-Dame que j'ai donné à mes parents. J'aurais aimé acheter un tee-shirt mais je n'avais pas assez d'argent!

- Je ne sais pas où je vais aller mais j'achèterai peut-être une casquette et un petit objet.

- Je prends toujours beaucoup de photos, y compris des selfies devant les monuments importants. Je partage ces photos avec mes amis sur les réseaux sociaux. Cependant, j'aime aussi acheter un petit objet comme souvenir.

2. It's normal to bring back holiday souvenirs but be careful if you want to avoid expensive mistakes. Check that your purchases fit into your luggage and that they are not too heavy, otherwise you will have to pay additional charges if you are travelling by air. So it's best to choose small objects such as jewellery, key rings or light items of clothing.

Page 32 Where I live
Quick quiz:

1. on the ground floor

2. a terraced house

3. the basement

4. the hall

5. a room

6. the attic

7. low-cost home

8. a wardrobe

Questions:

1. Il y a un mois, nous avons déménagé dans un appartement tout neuf situé dans un immeuble au centre-ville. Notre ancienne maison était plus grande mais elle était aussi très démodée. Nous sommes au cinquième étage et j'ai ma propre chambre à côté de celle de mes parents. Nous avons un balcon, mais je préférerais avoir un jardin.

2. (a) low-cost housing

(b) There are more than 10 million of them (1); they have limited financial means / they don't have much money (1).

(c) They are single people / they live on their own.

(d) They are couples without any children.

Page 33 The neighbourhood
Quick quiz:

1. rush hour

2. public transport

3. zoo

4. shopping centre

5. lively

6. neighbourhood / area / quarter

Questions:

1. (Possible answers)

- Sur la photo, on voit trois amis, un homme et deux femmes, qui sont assis par terre dans un parc. Ils ont l'air cool! Ils regardent quelque chose

d'amusant sur une tablette, ils rient beaucoup! Il fait beau et je pense que c'est le printemps parce que les arbres sont verts.

- Je trouve que les environs de mon quartier sont très agréables parce qu'il y a beaucoup d'espaces verts. Si on veut être actif il y a de bonnes installations parce qu'il y a un centre sportif et une belle piscine. D'autre part il y a seulement quelques petits magasins et pas de supermarché. Alors, il faut prendre le bus et aller en ville si on veut trouver des magasins plus grands.

- Le week-end dernier j'ai fait une promenade avec mes copains et nous avons acheté des glaces au café qui se trouve dans le parc. Nous avons aussi joué au tennis au centre sportif.

- Dans un mois il y aura un festival de musique dans le parc près de chez moi. Il durera deux jours et beaucoup de gens y assisteront. Un de mes chanteurs préférés sera là!

- Si j'avais le choix, je réduirais la limitation de vitesse dans les rues près de chez moi parce que les rues deviennent trop dangereuses pour les piétons. À mon avis les gens roulent trop vite et récemment il y a eu un accident.

2. (a) There are no theatres or museums.

(b) He lives not too far from Paris (1); he can go there whenever he wants (1).

(c) There are no traffic jams in the rush hour.

(d) They could do with some cycle paths next to the roads.

Page 34 Town and region
Quick quiz:

1. le champ   **2.** la colline

3. se déplacer   **4.** à la montagne

5. l'usine (f)   **6.** la ferme

Questions:

1. I've just come back from Provence. If you don't know this region, it's worth the effort to make a visit / it's worth visiting for its picturesque villages perched among the mountains, as well as for the vineyards that stretch as far as the big rivers. I really liked it, despite the aches I've suffered after touring around the region by bike.

2. (Model answer) J'habite dans le sud de l'Angleterre dans une région rurale. J'aime bien habiter ici parce que le paysage est très pittoresque avec de jolis villages situés parmi les collines ou au bord d'une rivière. Aussi, il fait beau en été, mais en hiver il pleut quelquefois et il fait assez froid. Si on a une voiture on peut se déplacer très facilement dans ma région, mais sinon les transports en commun ne sont pas tellement fréquents. La semaine dernière j'ai visité un château qui date du douzième siècle. Pendant les vacances j'irai à Londres car j'ai envie de visiter des musées et des monuments. Je pense que ce sera génial.

Page 35 Francophone countries
Quick quiz:
1. Ivory Coast   **2.** Morocco
3. French-speaking   **4.** West Africa
5. overseas   **6.** an island

Questions:
1. (a) 8 French-speaking countries (1) in sub-Saharan Africa (1).

  (b) Lessons were taught in French. (1); French was not their first language / French was a second language for them. (1); They mainly spoke an African (national) language. (1) (any 2)

  (c) They will receive a bilingual education / they will be taught in their native language and French.

2. (a) A; D   **(b)** C; E

Page 36 Seasons and weather
Quick quiz:
1. brouillard   **2.** orageux
3. soleil   **4.** météo

Questions:
1. (a) C   **(b)** D   **(c)** B

2. (a) Je préfère l'automne parce que j'aime bien les couleurs des arbres pendant cette saison, les feuilles deviennent rouges, jaunes et orange.

  (b) L'été prochain, je voudrais visiter l'Italie parce qu'il fait toujours très chaud et qu'il y a beaucoup de soleil là-bas.

  (c) En général, je n'aime pas l'hiver parce qu'il fait trop froid. Mais l'an dernier, il a neigé et j'ai trouvé ça très joli. J'espère qu'il va neiger cette année.

Page 37 My studies
Quick quiz:
1. Ma matière préférée est l'histoire parce que c'est fascinant.

2. Je trouve les maths difficiles, mais c'est une matière obligatoire.

Questions:
1. (a) (Model answer) À mon avis, les langues et les maths sont les matières les plus importantes parce qu'elles aident à trouver un emploi. Par contre, si j'avais le choix, je n'aurais pas de cours d'éducation religieuse car c'est une matière qui n'est pas tellement utile.

  (b) (Model answer) Cette année, j'ai trouvé l'espagnol très facile parce que j'ai fait une visite scolaire en Espagne il y a six mois. Cela m'a permis de développer mes compétences linguistiques.

  (c) (Model answer) En général, je m'entends bien avec tous mes profs sauf le prof de dessin qui est toujours de mauvaise humeur. Je trouve la prof de maths vraiment sympa car elle nous comprend quand nous avons des difficultés dans cette matière.

2. A, D

Page 38 Your school
Quick quiz:
1. school rules   **2.** school facilities
3. badly equipped   **4.** extra-curricular activities

Questions:
1. (a) B

  (b) C

2. (a) Mon collège est très grand.

  (b) Je pense que la journée scolaire est trop longue.

  (c) Je n'aime pas les règles scolaires.

  (d) Je porte un uniforme tous les jours, mais les Français ne portent pas d'uniforme.

  (e) Hier je suis allé(e) au club de dessin après le collège.

Page 39 School trips, events and exchanges
Quick quiz:
1. to take part in a show
2. prize-giving ceremony
3. an orchestra rehearsal
4. to be homesick
5. to act in a play
6. to sing in a choir

Questions:
1. (a) deux semaines

  (b) bien

  (c) facile

  (d) culturelles

  (e) positive

2. (Model answer) Le succès scolaire n'est pas la seule chose importante à l'école! Il faut aussi participer aux événements culturels et sportifs parce que c'est la chance d'être membre d'une équipe, de faire la connaissance des autres et de développer de nouvelles compétences. Il faut rappeler aux jeunes que ces compétences peuvent les aider à trouver un emploi dans l'avenir.

À la fin du dernier trimestre, après avoir répété pendant plusieurs semaines, on a donné un concert pour célébrer les différentes cultures représentées dans mon collège. On a joué de la musique africaine et asiatique ainsi que des morceaux de musique classique européenne. Plusieurs élèves ont porté le costume de leur pays d'origine et à la fin de la soirée on a bien applaudi.

L'année prochaine, en septembre, on va fêter la journée européenne des langues. Je participerai à un concours de chant qui aura lieu ce jour-là. On fera aussi des présentations en plusieurs langues pendant l'assemblée de l'école. Cela aidera les élèves à apprécier la diversité culturelle.

Page 40 Using languages
Quick quiz:
1. Belgique
2. couramment
3. me débrouille
4. prononciation
5. comprendre

Questions:
1. (Model answer)
Monsieur / Madame,

En juillet prochain, je voudrais faire un stage dans votre école de langues. J'apprends le français depuis quatre ans, mais je trouve difficile de parler et de comprendre les gens car ils parlent trop vite. Je voudrais améliorer mes compétences parce que plus tard j'aimerais travailler en France. Pendant mon séjour, je voudrais aussi faire des activités sportives.

Cordialement,

2. (Possible answers)

  (a) Je parle couramment l'arabe puisque ma mère est tunisienne et qu'on l'utilise à la maison. Depuis cinq ans, j'apprends également le français au collège. À l'avenir je voudrais aussi apprendre l'espagnol et le chinois. Je pense que ces langues sont très utiles parce que beaucoup de gens les parlent.

  (b) Je trouve assez facile d'apprendre des langues, mais parfois il est difficile de comprendre les personnes qui parlent trop vite. L'autre chose que je trouve difficile, c'est de mémoriser le vocabulaire surtout si un nom est masculin ou féminin.

  (c) À mon avis il est très important de parler une autre langue parce qu'on a plus de choix quand on cherche un emploi et quelquefois on est mieux payé. Je pense aussi que c'est important car cela nous aide à faire la connaissance de personnes d'une autre culture. Je trouve que les gens apprécient beaucoup quand on fait l'effort de parler leur langue.

  (d) Oui, je voudrais devenir ingénieur et je voudrais travailler sur des projets à l'étranger, alors mes compétences linguistiques seront indispensables.

Page 41 Ambitions
Quick quiz:
1. J'ai l'intention d'aller à l'université.
2. Je veux fonder une famille.
3. Mon rêve est d'acheter une voiture.
4. J'espère devenir coiffeur / coiffeuse.

Questions:
1. (a) A   **(b)** C

2. (Model answer) Je dirais que je suis bien organisé(e), travailleur (travailleuse) et plein(e) d'ambition car je voudrais avoir ma propre entreprise dans dix ans. Je rêve aussi d'être marié(e) et d'avoir des enfants. Cependant, j'ai l'intention de continuer mes études à l'université pour obtenir des qualifications. Récemment, j'ai fait mon stage à l'office de tourisme de ma ville. J'ai dû parler aux gens qui sont venus demander des renseignements sur la ville. À mon avis, une carrière est importante parce que cela nous offre la chance de gagner plus d'argent et d'obtenir de l'avancement.

Page 42 Education post-16
Quick quiz:
1. Next year, we will be able to drop several subjects.
2. I want to become an apprentice because I would like to do something practical.

Questions:
1. J'ai décidé d'entrer en première en septembre pour étudier pour mon bac. J'ai l'intention de laisser tomber les sciences mais je continuerai les maths et les langues parce que je veux une carrière dans le commerce. Certains de mes amis prendront une année sabbatique après avoir passé leur bac, mais je voudrais aller à l'université aussitôt après.
2. **(a)** He will acquire some practical skills. (1); He will earn some money. (1)
   (b) She won't have to do maths any more. (1); She will be doing subjects useful for her future career (as an interpreter). (1)

Page 43 Charity and voluntary work
Quick quiz:
1. to fundraise
2. to support someone
3. to be supportive
4. to gain confidence in oneself

Questions:
1. Maurice - D; Angélique - A; Paul - E
2. (Model answer) Chaque semaine, je vais faire du bénévolat dans un centre pour les personnes âgées. La dernière fois que j'y suis allé(e), je leur ai préparé du thé et j'ai bavardé avec une vieille dame qui n'a jamais de visiteurs. Je trouve ça triste quand personne ne leur rend visite. Elle m'a parlé de son enfance et de la vie d'autrefois. Je pense que le bénévolat est très important parce que ça nous donne une chance d'aider les autres, de participer à la société et d'acquérir de nouvelles compétences. Le mois prochain, je participerai à une course de dix kilomètres pour collecter des fonds. Ça va être dur!

Page 44 Jobs and careers
Quick quiz:
1. Je voudrais être médecin.
2. Mon père est ingénieur.
3. J'ai eu un entretien hier.

Questions:
1. (Model answer)
   - Sur la photo on voit dix personnes assises autour d'une table dans un bureau. Elles sont jeunes et je pense qu'elles sont en train de discuter d'un projet. La femme aux cheveux longs paraît très animée.

- À mon avis le salaire est important, mais je voudrais aussi des collègues agréables et faire du travail varié et satisfaisant.
- Pendant l'été, j'ai fait un stage dans une agence de voyages. J'ai dû répondre au téléphone, trier les courriels et comparer les prix des vols et des hôtels. Parler avec les clients de leurs vacances m'amusait beaucoup.
- J'adore les animaux, alors je voudrais être vétérinaire dans l'avenir. Je suis très fort(e) en sciences et j'aime beaucoup aider les autres. Il est vrai que ce métier peut être assez triste, mais je crois que j'ai la bonne personnalité pour devenir un(e) excellent(e) vétérinaire.
- Je ne voudrais pas travailler à l'extérieur parce qu'on pourrait avoir trop froid ou trop chaud. Travailler sous la pluie ne me dirait pas grand-chose non plus.
2. I've just got a casual job in a restaurant. It's not well paid but I like it because I am part of a team and it will enable me to develop new skills. You have to communicate well with the customers and be very attentive. Yesterday, I got 80 euros in tips!

Page 45 International events
Quick quiz:
1. to bring people together
2. to bring in money
3. the crowd
4. to attract visitors
5. increased prices
6. improved infrastructure

Questions:
1. (Model answer)
   - Sur la photo on voit des jeunes qui sont à un festival de musique en plein air. Ils sont assis sur l'herbe et écoutent la musique. À droite de l'image on voit la scène où les musiciens chantent et jouent. Il fait beau et je pense aussi qu'il fait chaud parce que les gens portent un tee-shirt. Certains portent aussi un chapeau.
   - À mon avis, je pense qu'on devrait laisser les jeunes aller à des festivals de musique. Cependant, ils doivent être prudents. Pour les concerts en plein air il faut se protéger contre le soleil en mettant de la crème solaire et en portant un chapeau et des lunettes de soleil. On doit également boire beaucoup d'eau et éviter de prendre de la drogue.
   - Je ne suis jamais allé(e) à un festival de musique, mais pendant l'échange scolaire je suis allé(e) avec mon partenaire voir le championnat de tennis à Paris. Il y avait des gens de pays différents, mais avant tout de nombreux Espagnols et Autrichiens car les joueurs qui s'affrontaient en finale étaient de ces nationalités. L'ambiance était tout à fait géniale et le match passionnant.
   - L'année prochaine j'espère aller voir un match de rugby international. J'irai voir

le match entre la France et l'Angleterre. J'espère que l'Angleterre va gagner!
   - Bien sûr, ce n'est pas tout à fait la même chose quand on regarde un tel événement à la télé car on n'est pas entouré par une grande foule, mais souvent on n'a pas le choix. Beaucoup d'événements ont lieu à l'étranger et ça coûte cher d'y aller. En plus, on doit aussi obtenir des billets, ce qui n'est pas toujours facile.
2. **(a)** It's fun / you can't take it seriously.
   (b) the music / words / artists' costumes / performance (any 2)
   (c) the commentator's remarks
   (d) It takes too long. (1) Many countries always vote for their neighbours. (1)

Page 46 Campaigns and good causes
Quick quiz:
1. commerce équitable
2. pauvres
3. prix
4. l'argent
5. améliorer
6. vie

Questions:
1. B; C
2. **(a)** On leur donne un repas / des aliments.
   (b) Il y avait trop de gaspillage alimentaire / on détruisait les surplus agricoles.
   (c) On aide les gens par d'autres moyens, par exemple en les aidant à trouver un logement.

Page 47 Global issues
Quick quiz:
1. séisme
2. guerre
3. déboisement
4. incendie

Questions:
1. **(a)** people who say that climate change does not exist / climate change deniers
   (b) frustration / anger / annoyance
   (c) There have been floods in Asia, particularly India (1) and hurricanes in the Caribbean (1).
2. (Model answer)
   (a) On devrait faire des efforts pour arrêter le déboisement des forêts tropicales parce que beaucoup d'espèces d'animaux et de plantes vivent dans ces forêts. Si on achète des produits en bois, on devrait vérifier l'origine du bois.
   (b) Quand il y a des catastrophes naturelles, on peut aider les victimes en faisant un don ou en collectant des fonds. On pourrait faire des gâteaux et les vendre au collège,

ou on pourrait participer à une course sponsorisée, par exemple.

(c) On contribue au réchauffement de la Terre en brûlant trop de combustibles fossiles et en nous déplaçant tout le temps en voiture. Nous devrions utiliser le soleil et le vent pour produire de l'électricité, et nous devrions faire les petits trajets à pied, à vélo ou en utilisant les transports en commun.

Page 48 The environment
Quick quiz:
Triez les ordures pour faciliter le recyclage.

Fermez le robinet en vous brossant les dents pour ne pas gaspiller d'eau.

Éteignez les appareils électriques pour économiser de l'énergie.

Ne faites pas de petits trajets en voiture pour réduire la pollution de l'atmosphère.

Questions:
1. Chaque semaine, on jette (nous jetons) trop de choses à la poubelle. Depuis l'année dernière, ma famille refuse d'acheter des fruits et des légumes emballés dans du plastique, et hier, j'ai réutilisé un sac en plastique quand j'ai fait des courses. On a (Nous avons) réduit notre consommation d'énergie en baissant le chauffage central. L'année prochaine, on espère (nous espérons) protéger l'environnement en installant des panneaux solaires sur le toit.

2. (a) the sale of water in plastic bottles

    (b) Only 20% of bottles are recycled. / The plastic takes 450 years to decompose.

    (c) to drink tap water

    (d) advertising campaigns over 10 years

Page 49 Pronunciation strategies
Quick quiz:
1. Est-ce qu'ils ont une table pour six personnes?

2. Est-ce que vous avez voyagé en avion?

3. Ces assiettes sont assez sales.

4. Ils adorent les oignons.

5. À la fin, on était fatigués mais très heureux.

6. Mes amis n'aiment pas cet acteur.

Questions:
1. (a) Il fait assez froid dans le nord et un peu chaud dans le sud du pays en hiver.

    (b) Samedi, j'ai été très surpris parce qu'un flashmob a eu lieu devant l'arrêt d'autobus!

    (c) Ma sœur vient d'acheter un anorak vert pour son petit ami.

    (d) Le chef a préparé le bœuf et les choux de Bruxelles avec des noix d'une façon tout à fait délicieuse.

    (e) Après le repas, il avait mal à l'estomac parce qu'il avait trop mangé.

    (f) De nos jours, il est impossible de vivre sans portable!

2. Listen to the audio recording to check your pronunciation.

Page 50 Speaking strategies
Quick quiz:
If you don't know the French word for something, you could paraphrase or describe the item.

When answering a question, you could repeat words and phrases from the question to give yourself time to think.

If you need time to think, you could use a filler phrase such as **eh bien**.

Questions:
1. (a) (Model answer) Je n'aime pas l'automne parce qu'il y a du vent et qu'il pleut souvent. Par contre, ma saison préférée est l'été, parce que normalement, il fait beau temps et je peux faire des activités en plein air comme des randonnées et du cyclisme.

    (b) (Model answer) Les SDF n'ont pas beaucoup d'argent alors ils doivent dormir dans la rue même s'il fait mauvais temps. En plus, ils ne mangent pas bien et ils tombent souvent malades.

2. (a) (Model answer) Pour moi, la date la plus importante de l'année, c'est Noël parce que toute la famille est ensemble et tout le monde est heureux. J'adore décorer le sapin de Noël et offrir des cadeaux. L'année dernière, mes grands-parents étaient chez nous et après le repas, on a joué à des jeux.

    (b) (Model answer) Mon copain / ma copine idéal(e) serait quelqu'un qui me comprend et qui m'écoute quand j'ai des problèmes. Il / Elle doit aussi être quelqu'un avec un bon sens de l'humour et avec qui on peut bien s'amuser.

    (c) (Model answer) Le week-end dernier, le matin, nous sommes allés en ville pour faire des courses. L'après-midi, on a fait une randonnée à vélo pendant une heure avant de faire un barbecue dans le jardin. Ma mère avait préparé de la viande et des légumes à griller, c'était délicieux!

Page 51 Asking for clarification strategies
Quick quiz:
1. Could you repeat the question, please?

2. How do you say 'playground' in French?

3. What does that mean?

Questions:
1. (a) Pouvez-vous / Peux-tu expliquer le mot 'peluche'?

    (b) Je ne sais pas comment dire 'to squabble' en français.

    (c) Je ne comprends pas le mot 'facteur'.

    (d) Comment ça s'écrit?

    (e) Qu'est-ce que vous voulez dire quand vous dites / tu dis...?

2. A; B; D

Page 52 General conversation
Questions:
1. Answers will vary. You may want to note down some topic vocabulary, appropriate verbs in a range of tenses and question structures.

2. (Model answer)

    (a) À mon avis les fêtes sont très importantes pour réunir ma famille. Récemment je suis allé(e) au mariage de ma cousine dans une petite église à la campagne. C'était un très beau mariage et ma cousine portait une belle robe blanche. Après la cérémonie nous sommes allés dans un hôtel où on a mangé un repas délicieux. Malheureusement il faisait mauvais temps et nous ne pouvions pas sortir dans le jardin, mais nous avons pu danser dans une grande salle jusqu'à minuit.

    (b) De nos jours il y a beaucoup de problèmes environnementaux tels que la pollution de l'air par les véhicules et le réchauffement de la planète, mais à mon avis un des problèmes les plus graves c'est notre utilisation du plastique. Il y a partout trop de déchets en plastique qui détruisent notre environnement. Nous devrions être plus responsables, par exemple on ne devrait pas utiliser de sacs en plastique quand on fait du shopping. On pourrait réutiliser nos bouteilles d'eau au lieu d'en acheter d'autres. Il faut faire quelque chose. Nos océans sont en train de mourir à cause de nos actions!

3. (Model answer)

    (a) Mon métier de rêve serait un métier intéressant où je pourrais aider les autres. Un gros salaire n'est pas important mais il faut gagner assez d'argent pour vivre.

    (b) À mon avis, c'est une bonne idée de prendre une année sabbatique si on ne sait pas ce qu'on veut faire plus tard. Sinon il vaut mieux commencer ses études ou trouver un emploi tout de suite.

    (c) Quand j'étais jeune, je rêvais d'être chanteur (chanteuse) car j'adore la musique. Cependant, ce n'est pas un métier facile et le succès n'est pas garanti.

Page 53 Using a picture stimulus
Questions:
1. (Model answer)

    • Sur la photo il y a deux filles qui boivent des boissons chaudes, peut-être du café. Elles bavardent et je pense qu'elles sont amies. La fille de gauche a les cheveux blonds et elle porte un tee-shirt blanc. La fille de droite a les cheveux noirs et elle porte une chemise bleue. Je pense que c'est l'été parce qu'elles sont assises dehors à la terrasse d'un café.

- Pour moi un(e) bon(ne) ami(e) est quelqu'un qui est toujours là pour nous. Il ou elle devrait être sympathique et avoir un bon sens de l'humour.
- Le week-end dernier deux de mes copains (copines) sont venu(e)s chez moi pour regarder un film à la télé. C'était un film d'action et il était vraiment passionnant. Après le film, nous avons commandé une pizza qui a été livrée une demi-heure plus tard.
- L'an prochain je vais partir en vacances avec mes ami(e)s à la campagne. Nous allons faire du camping parce que c'est moins cher que rester dans un hôtel. Nous voulons faire des randonnées pendant la journée et le soir nous allons préparer un repas ensemble. Je pense que ça va être génial, mais j'espère qu'il ne va pas pleuvoir.
- Mon / ma meilleur(e) ami(e) s'appelle […]. Je le / la connais depuis neuf ans car nous sommes allé(e)s à la même école primaire. On a les mêmes centres d'intérêts et je le / la trouve très sympa.

2. (Model answer)
- Sur la photo, il y a un groupe de filles qui sont assises sur des chaises vertes en plein air. On peut voir la tour Eiffel, alors elles sont à Paris et elles sont en train de consulter un plan de la ville. Je pense que c'est l'hiver parce qu'elles portent un manteau et que les arbres n'ont pas de feuilles.
- Je préfère des vacances actives à la campagne parce que j'adore la nature et faire des randonnées. Par contre, mon frère préfère des vacances au bord de la mer. Il adore les sports nautiques.
- Cette année je suis allé(e) en Espagne et nous avons fait du camping à la campagne dans le nord du pays. La plupart du temps, il faisait beau et nous avons fait des randonnées.
- L'an prochain j'irai en Nouvelle-Zélande en vacances parce que je voudrais voir le paysage extraordinaire où on a tourné beaucoup de films fantastiques. J'aime bien être actif (active), alors ce serait génial de faire des randonnées dans cet environnement. J'y voyagerai en avion bien sûr, ça sera un voyage très long!
- Mes vacances idéales seraient dans un endroit où je pourrais faire des activités intéressantes et culturelles, comme visiter des monuments et des musées, ainsi qu'un endroit pittoresque où on pourrait se détendre aussi.

Page 54 Role play (Foundation)
Questions:
1. (Model answer)
1. *Bonjour, où est-ce que vous voulez aller en vacances?*

   Je veux aller en Espagne.
2. *Où est-ce que vous voulez loger en vacances?*

   Je voudrais une chambre dans un hôtel au bord de la mer.
3. *Vous voulez passer combien de temps en vacances?*

   Je veux passer une semaine en vacances.
4. *D'accord. Qu'est-ce que vous aimez faire en vacances?*

   J'aime me bronzer et me baigner dans la mer.
5. *Bon je peux vous faire une réservation pour samedi prochain.*

   On part (Le vol est) à quelle heure?

   Le vol est à treize heures.

2. (Model answer)
1. *Qu'est-ce que tu fais avec ton portable?*

   J'utilise mon portable pour appeler ma famille et pour envoyer des textos / SMS.
2. *Moi aussi. Est-ce qu'Internet a des avantages?*

   Oui, on peut faire des recherches pour les projets scolaires (trouver des informations, faire des achats, communiquer avec ses amis).
3. *Combien de temps est-ce que tu passes en ligne chaque jour?*

   Je passe au moins deux heures en ligne chaque jour.
4. *Ah bon. Et les jeux vidéo? Qu'en penses-tu?*

   J'aime bien les jeux vidéo parce qu'ils sont divertissants.

   Oui, je suis d'accord avec toi.
5. *Quel est ton réseau social préféré? (Quels sont tes réseaux sociaux préférés?)*

   J'aime utiliser Instagram.

Page 55 Role play (Higher)
Questions:
1. (Model answer)
1. *Bonjour. Quand est-ce que vous voulez partir en vacances?*

   Je voudrais partir en vacances en juillet.
2. *Et comment est-ce que vous voulez voyager?*

   Je voudrais voyager en train parce que c'est confortable.
3. *D'accord. Il y a plusieurs possibilités. Quel pays avez-vous déjà visité?*

   Je ne suis jamais allé(e) à l'étranger.

   Alors, je recommande l'Italie ou la Grèce.
4. *Où est-ce qu'on peut loger?*

   Vous pouvez choisir. Il y a des hôtels et des campings.
5. *Qu'est-ce qu'on peut faire en Italie?*

   On peut faire toutes sortes de choses, visiter des monuments, se détendre, etc.

2. (Model answer)
1. *Combien de fois fais-tu du sport chaque semaine? / Tu fais du sport combien de fois par semaine?*

   Je joue au tennis trois fois par semaine.
2. *Qu'est-ce que tu aimes faire après le sport?*

   Après le sport j'aime manger parce que j'ai faim.
3. *Quelles autres activités sportives as-tu faites récemment?*

   La semaine dernière, j'ai fait de la natation avec ma mère.

   Moi aussi, j'aime la natation.
4. *Quand est-ce que tu fais du sport?*

   Normalement, je fais du sport le week-end.
5. *Qu'est-ce que tu penses du sport à la télé?*

   J'aime bien regarder les Jeux olympiques, c'est chouette.

Page 56 Listening strategies
Quick quiz:
Strike – travail / refuser / grève / manifestation

Drought – absence / eau / manquer / sécheresse

National Day – défilé / feu d'artifice / fête nationale / célébration

Road accident – collision / mort / blessé / véhicule

Bullying at school – harcèlement / intimidation / persécuter / menacer

Questions:
1. (a) C   **(b)** A
2. (a) she can study without being distracted
  (b) time of evening meal (1) / it's too early and she gets hungry (1)
  (c) there's a huge range of activities on site
  (d) lights have to be out by 10.30 pm

Page 57 Listening 1
Questions:
1. (a) read   **(b)** predict
2. (a) amies
  (b) ne savent pas
  (c) de drogues
  (d) responsabilités
  (e) financiers
3. (a) cher   **(b)** ouvert
  (c) intéressant   **(d)** ouvert
  (e) vieux

Page 58 Listening 2
Questions:
1. pollution of rivers – contrôler l'usage des pesticides; air pollution – réduire les gaz d'échappement; disappearance of species – arrêter le déboisement des forêts tropicales; pollution of the oceans (la pollution des océans) – réduire le plastique
2. (a) People who like languages.
  (b) He can choose when he does his work / what projects to take on.
  (c) He sometimes doesn't have much work / doesn't get enough money.
  (d) Find a cure for cancer (1) / solutions to environmental problems (1).

- **(e)** You have to work long hours / it can ruin your social life.
3. **(a)** He woke up late.
   - **(b)** His father's car had a flat battery / he had to take the bus.

Page 59 Reading strategies
Quick quiz:
1. **(a)** haste   **(b)** plaster
   - **(c)** honest   **(d)** interest
   - **(e)** spice   **(f)** strange
   - **(g)** stable   **(h)** hospital
2. **(a)** –ary   **(b)** –ty   **(c)** –ive

Questions:
1. During my work experience in France I had the opportunity to spend a day at the headquarters of a chain of bookshops situated on the coast. We went there by coach and the boss of the firm welcomed us when we arrived. I had thought that this visit wouldn't be interesting, but in fact I found it absolutely fascinating.
2. **(a)** They were disappointed.
   - **(b)** They had previously had a friendly (warm) welcome and attentive / efficient service.
   - **(c)** It was next to the toilets and they were disturbed by people all evening.
   - **(d)** The boss shouted at the waiters.

Page 60 Reading 1
Questions:
1. **(a)** He is jealous of her.
   - **(b)** His parents reward his sister for good exam results, but not him.
2. A, D
3. **(a)** They are a waste of time.
   - **(b)** They are fun. / They help him to relax. (1)
   - **(c)** His parents watch the news at a precise time on a TV. (1) He finds out about the news on social media on his tablet. (1)

Page 61 Reading 2
Questions:
1. 1–B; 2–D; 3–C; 4–A
2. **(a)** D   **(b)** A
3. **(a)** Marcel   **(b)** Didier
   - **(c)** Raoul   **(d)** Marcel

Page 62 Reading 3
Questions:
1. **(a)** He has neglected his appearance; he no longer shaves and his beard is unkempt.
   - **(b)** He has failed to take care of his appearance due to his drinking habits.
2. B; C; D

Page 63 Reading 4
Questions:
1. **(a)** in the Sahara desert (1) / he (*his plane*) had broken down (1)
   - **(b)** He only had enough drinking water for 8 days.
   - **(c)** completely isolated
   - **(d)** A voice (*le petit prince*) woke him (1) and asked him to draw a sheep (1).
2. **(a)** pour essayer de retouver Yvonne (Mlle) de Galais
   - **(b)** Les fenêtres étaient cachées par des arbres (1) / les rideaux étaient tirés (1).
   - **(c)** Il faisait nuit mais il n'y avait aucune lumière allumée.
   - **(d)** Il avait plu (1) / Il faisait froid (1).

Page 64 Translation into English
Questions:
1. **(a)** my brother's girlfriend
   - **(b)** at my grandparents'
   - **(c)** He has been working / has worked as a teacher for two years.
   - **(d)** I have just come back from France.
2. I have been going jogging regularly for two years. At the moment, I am training to take part in a ten kilometre race that will take place next weekend. Today, it was a bit cold but after running for half an hour I was hot. My sports / PE teacher has just told me that such conditions are good for a race.
3. Yesterday evening, some of my classmates came to my house to watch a film that I had downloaded. After watching the film, we were hungry and went into the kitchen to find a snack. My parents say I shouldn't snack between meals because they are afraid I will put on weight, but I don't care!

Page 65 Writing strategies
Quick quiz:
1. Ma sœur <u>est</u> gen<u>tille</u> mais pas très travailleu<u>se</u>. Elle ne <u>fait</u> rien <u>à</u> la maison.
2. Ils ont cher<u>ché</u> une chemise <u>blanche</u> au <u>grand</u> magasin.

Questions:
1. (Model answer) J'aime faire des achats parce que c'est amusant. Le week-end, je vais faire les magasins en ville avec mes amis. Normalement, nous achetons des magazines et des bonbons, mais la semaine dernière, j'ai acheté un pull qui n'était pas cher et des chaussettes noires.
2. (Model answer) Normalement, ma journée scolaire commence à huit heures et demie. Chaque matin, nous avons quatre cours suivis du déjeuner à la cantine. Après avoir mangé, je bavarde avec mes copains dans la cour avant la dernière leçon. Mon jour préféré, c'est le mercredi parce que j'ai deux heures de sciences. À mon avis, c'est la matière la plus fascinante de mon emploi du temps. Par contre, je déteste l'histoire car le prof est nul. Hier, après les cours, j'ai participé à un atelier cuisine où j'ai préparé un plat végétarien. L'année prochaine, j'irai au lycée pour continuer mes études.

Page 66 Translation into French (Foundation)
Questions:
1. **(a)** Ma mère est grande et elle a les yeux bleus.
   - **(b)** Nous habitons dans une petite maison à la campagne.
   - **(c)** Le week-end, je fais du cyclisme / vélo avec mon père.
   - **(d)** Je n'aime pas nager dans la mer.
   - **(e)** Le mois dernier, je suis allé(e) en France avec mes copains (copines / amis / amies).
2. **(a)** Ma sœur est timide mais travailleuse.
   - **(b)** Le dimanche, nous déjeunons (on déjeune) chez mes grands-parents.
   - **(c)** Il y a une piscine à côté du cinéma.
   - **(d)** J'aime faire de l'exercice le matin.
   - **(e)** Pendant l'été, j'ai joué au tennis.

Page 67 Translation into French (Higher)
Questions:
1. Je m'entends bien avec tout le monde dans ma famille à part ma sœur cadette (petite sœur) qui est paresseuse et qui n'aide jamais à la maison. Le week-end dernier, j'ai dû faire les courses et préparer le dîner. Nous avons mangé du poulet et des légumes et après, il y avait du fromage et des fruits. Je pense qu'il est important de manger sainement, mais les cochonneries ont quelquefois meilleur goût!
2. Mon frère aîné et moi faisons du travail bénévole pour une association caritative qui soutient des réfugiés. Je pense qu'il serait très difficile de quitter ma famille et mes amis et d'aller vivre dans un pays différent. Il y a beaucoup de réfugiés dans ma ville et certains vivent dans la rue. La semaine dernière, nous avons collecté des fonds en vendant des gâteaux.

Page 68 Writing (Foundation)
Questions:
1. (Model answer)

   Monsieur / Madame,

   Je vais arriver chez vous le trente juillet vers six heures du soir. Je voyage en train. Pour le petit déjeuner j'aime boire du thé et je voudrais des croissants avec du beurre et de la confiture. Je veux visiter votre région parce qu'elle est très pittoresque.

   Cordialement
2. (Model answer) Je pars en vacances. Me voici à l'aéroport et j'écoute de la musique. Mes bagages sont par terre. J'adore voyager en avion parce que c'est rapide.

Page 69 Writing (Higher)
Questions:
1. (Model answer)
   Monsieur,
   Je vous écris pour me plaindre de votre hôtel où j'ai passé trois nuits du 12 au 15 juillet. Quand je suis arrivé(e), la réceptionniste utilisait son portable et bavardait avec une amie, j'ai dû attendre au moins cinq minutes. Après avoir fini sa conversation, elle n'a pas été accueillante. Ensuite, je voulais aller à ma chambre au sixième étage mais l'ascenseur était

en panne et il n'y avait personne qui pouvait m'aider à monter mes bagages qui étaient très lourds. Les problèmes ont continué car j'avais réservé une chambre avec vue sur le lac, mais on m'en a donné une avec vue sur le parking. En plus, il n'y avait pas d'eau chaude et la télévision ne fonctionnait pas.

À mon avis, il faut offrir une meilleure formation à votre personnel parce que recevoir un accueil chaleureux est très important. Il faut aussi faire des réparations immédiatement. Si ce n'est pas possible, vous devriez proposer un remboursement aux clients mécontents afin de les encourager à revenir à votre hôtel.

Mes salutations distinguées,

[name]

2. (Model answer) En juin, j'ai participé à un échange scolaire. C'était ma première visite en France et c'était une expérience absolument super car je me suis bien entendu(e) avec mon (ma) correspondant(e) français(e) et sa famille. Au début, je trouvais difficile de les comprendre car ils parlaient vite mais ensuite, ils m'ont aidé(e) en parlant plus lentement. Je suis allé(e) au collège avec mon / ma correspondant(e) et j'ai assisté à ses cours. J'ai remarqué qu'on utilise moins de technologie en cours que chez nous. Pendant l'échange, nous avons fait plusieurs sorties. Le meilleur jour était quand nous sommes allé(e)s voir un vieux château à la campagne et le week-end, c'était tout à fait fascinant.

Je pense que les échanges sont très importants parce qu'on peut se faire de nouveaux amis et qu'on a l'occasion de découvrir une culture différente. Bien sûr, on développe aussi ses compétences linguistiques. Chaque élève devrait pouvoir profiter de cette expérience. L'année prochaine je reviendrai en France pour rendre visite à mon / ma correspondant(e).

Page 70 Articles
Quick quiz:
1. Le Portugal est plus petit que l'Espagne. – Portugal is smaller than Spain.

2. Il est journaliste. – He is a journalist.

3. J'apprends le français depuis trois ans. – I have been learning French for three years.

4. Elle habite une jolie maison dans un petit village. – She lives in a pretty house in a small village.

Questions:
1. (a) Le week-end, j'aime regarder le football à la télévision.

(b) Il y a une piscine et un centre sportif dans ma ville.

(c) La géographie, l'histoire et les arts plastiques / le dessin sont mes matières préférées.

(d) Il apprend l'allemand.

(e) La Suisse est un petit pays.

2. (a) Ma belle-mère est médecin.

(b) Elle a les cheveux blonds et les yeux marron (bruns).

(c) Elle a un bon emploi (travail) dans un grand hôpital.

(d) Le dimanche, on prend le déjeuner à treize heures / une heure de l'après-midi.

(e) J'adore les fruits mais je déteste les légumes.

Page 71 Prepositions
Quick quiz:
(a) après – after
dans – in
derrière – behind
entre – between
sous – under
sur – on

(b) malgré – in spite of
parmi – among
à travers – across
sauf – except
sous – under
selon – according to

Questions:
1. (a) En juin, nous allons en Italie en avion.

(b) Malgré la pluie, nous sommes sortis pour faire une promenade dans les champs.

(c) Mon frère a travaillé dans une colonie de vacances pendant deux mois.

(d) En été, nous irons en Espagne pour une semaine.

(e) Nous allons passer Noël chez mes grands-parents.

(f) J'ai laissé mon pull en coton en haut.

(g) J'apprends le français depuis quatre ans.

2. Je voudrais vivre (habiter) près de ma cousine qui habite (vit) en Écosse dans une vallée entre deux montagnes. Devant sa maison, il y a un lac où elle va nager avant le petit-déjeuner. Pendant la journée, d'habitude, elle fait une promenade avec son chien sauf quand il neige. En hiver, elle porte beaucoup de vêtements en laine et des bottes en cuir / bottes de cuir.

Page 72 The preposition à
Quick quiz:
1. (a) au   **(b)** aux; à

(c) à l'   **(d)** à la

2. (a) on the (first floor);

(b) at the (theatre);

(c) to (Marseilles)

Questions:
1. In spring, I spent my holidays in the south of France. I stayed in an apartment that was two hundred metres from the old port in Marseille. Every day, I went for a horse ride or I played boules with an old woman with grey hair. In the south, it's called playing *pétanque*. We used to meet at four o'clock at the port and spend two hours playing. But one day I had a bad back, so she invited me to a café. I ordered a cheese sandwich and a strawberry ice cream.

2. (a) Sur la photo, il y a quatre personnes qui sont **à la** maison.

(b) **À** gauche la fille sourit.

(c) Ils jouent **aux** cartes.

(d) La femme blonde **au** milieu a quatre cartes.

Page 73 Partitives and preposition *de*
Quick quiz:
1. des   **2.** du   **3.** de

4. de   **5.** de   **6.** du; des

Questions:
1. (a) Le parking est à gauche de l'hôtel et à côté du parc.

(b) Je dois emprunter le portable de mon ami(e) / mon copain (ma copine).

(c) Je voudrais de la soupe avec du pain et du beurre.

(d) Il y a de jolies maisons en face de la cathédrale.

(e) Il est rentré (revenu) du Japon et de Chine.

(f) Elle a un kilo de pommes de terre mais elle n'a pas d'oignons.

2. J'ai invité des ami(e)s de mes parents à dîner, mais je n'ai pas de provisions chez moi (à la maison). Je vais devoir aller au supermarché en face du musée pour acheter du poisson, des légumes et de la glace. Je n'ai pas besoin de café. J'ai déjà acheté de l'eau minérale au magasin à côté de la poste.

Page 74 Nouns
Quick quiz:
1–F; l'Asie (f), l'Europe (f), l'Amérique du Nord (f)

2–M; le lundi, le mois de janvier, le printemps

3–M; le kilo, le centimètre

4–F; l'Angleterre (f), la France, la Seine

5–F; la boulangerie, la boucherie

Questions:
1. (a) informaticien – M / informaticienne – F: IT technician

(b) infirmier – M / infirmière – F: nurse

(c) pharmacienne – F / pharmacien – M: pharmacist

(d) chanteur – M / chanteuse – F: singer

(e) chercheuse – F / chercheur – M: researcher

(f) ouvrier – M / ouvrière – F: worker

(g) directrice – F/ directeur – M: headteacher / manager / CEO

(h) employée – F / employé – M: employee

(i) étudiant – M / étudiante – F: student

(j) électricien – M / électricienne – F: electrician

2. (a) Il y a un groupe d'amis qui sont assis dehors sur des chaises autour d'une table.

(b) Ils sont dans un jardin et il y a beaucoup de soleil.

(c) Une des filles porte une robe rouge et une autre fille porte un chapeau.

(d) Ils mangent de la salade et ils boivent de la limonade.

(e) La fille qui porte la robe rouge a les cheveux longs.

Page 75 Adjectives
Quick quiz:
In French, an adjective changes its form so that it <u>agrees</u> with the word it is describing. It must match the <u>gender</u> (masculine or <u>feminine</u>) of the noun and whether it is <u>singular</u> or plural. Most adjectives add an <u>e</u> in the feminine form and an <u>s</u> in the plural and go <u>after</u> the noun. Adjectives such as **beau**, **gros**, **bon**, **joli**, **grand** and **petit** go <u>in front</u> of the noun.

Questions:
1. (a) Avez-vous les mains <u>propres</u>? – *Have you got clean hands?*

(b) Il porte un pantalon <u>bleu foncé</u> et une veste <u>gris clair</u>. – *He's wearing dark blue trousers and a light grey jacket.*

(c) On peut visiter les ruines de l'<u>ancien</u> château dans le <u>grand</u> parc. – *You can visit the ruins of the ancient / old castle in the big park.*

(d) Les réponses aux questions étaient <u>fausses</u>. – *The answers to the questions were wrong.*

(e) J'ai un portable <u>neuf</u>. Il était assez <u>cher</u>. – *I have a new mobile phone. It was quite expensive.*

(f) Nous habitons une <u>belle</u> maison dans une <u>vieille</u> ville. – *We live in a beautiful house in an old town.*

2. (a) Samedi dernier, j'ai fait une longue promenade dans un beau parc.

(b) Je visiterai / Je vais visiter un musée intéressant la semaine prochaine.

(c) Il y a beaucoup de belles assiettes et de vieux costumes.

(d) Où est la boulangerie italienne?

Page 76 Comparatives and superlatives
Quick quiz:
1. plus   **2.** moins   **3.** haut

4. plus   **5.** le plus grand

Questions:
1. Frédéric et Liliane are twins. Liliane is more intelligent than her brother and she always has the best marks. However, he is less shy than her and is happier to talk to people who he doesn't know. They both like watching TV, but Frédéric thinks that reality TV programmes are worse than game shows.

2. (a) La meilleure chanson a gagné le concours.

(b) C'est le pire hôtel.

(c) Elle est aussi active que sa mère.

(d) Il n'est pas aussi fort que son père.

(e) La Belgique est plus petite que la Suisse.

Page 77 Possessive and demonstrative adjectives
Quick quiz:
1. This hotel is near our house.

2. My cousins are spending their holidays at my home.

3. Pierre and his sister visited this / that museum.

4. I bought these / those vegetables in the market

5. Have you done your homework this week?

6. My sister is going out with her friends this evening.

Questions:
1. (a) sa   **(b)** vos / tes
(c) son   **(d)** leurs
(e) ma   **(f)** notre
(g) ce   **(h)** cet
(i) ces   **(j)** cette

2. Ce week-end, nous allons rendre visite à nos cousins. Leur père est le frère de ma mère, et sa femme est notre tante favorite. Cette fois, mon cousin Robert veut me montrer son vélo neuf, et sa sœur Susanne, ma cousine, a l'intention d'essayer cette nouvelle recette de biscuits.

Page 78 Indefinite and interrogative adjectives
Quick quiz:
1. masculine singular: tout

feminine singular: toute

masculine plural: tous

feminine plural: toutes

2. masculine singular: quel

feminine singular: quelle

masculine plural: quels

feminine plural: quelles

Questions:
1. (a) <u>Toutes</u> mes amies – *all my friends*

(b) <u>Quel</u> fromage voulez-vous? – *Which / what cheese do you want?*

(c) <u>Quelle</u> horreur! – *How dreadful!*

(d) <u>Tous</u> les professeurs – *all the teachers*

(e) <u>Toute</u> l'année – *all year*

(f) <u>Quelle</u> est ta chanson préférée? – *What is your favourite song?*

2. (a) Quel film veux-tu (voulez-vous) voir?

(b) Chaque mois (tous les mois), j'achète quelques magazines.

(c) Quelle couleur est-ce que tu préfères (préfères-tu) / vous préférez (préférez-vous)?

(d) Tous les billets / tickets sont chers.

(e) J'ai perdu tout mon argent.

(f) J'ai mis toutes mes affaires dans la valise.

(g) Chaque personne doit acheter un billet.

(h) Il y a quelques mois, je suis allé(e) en France.

Page 79 Adverbs
Quick quiz:
1. exactement   **2.** absolument
3. clairement   **4.** entièrement
5. généralement   **6.** récemment
7. courageusement **8.** totalement
9. parfaitement   **10.** précisément
11. doucement   **12.** abondamment

Questions:
1. (a) <u>Hier</u>, je suis allé au théâtre.

(b) Quand je suis en France, je peux communiquer <u>facilement</u> car je parle français <u>couramment</u>.

(c) Je joue du piano <u>régulièrement</u>, c'est-à-dire quatre fois par semaine.

(d) Mon ami français a parlé très <u>rapidement</u>, alors je n'ai rien compris.

(e) Les enfants bavardaient <u>constamment</u>, sans arrêt!

(f) Il a joué <u>vraiment</u> <u>bien</u> car il a marqué trois buts.

(g) L'autre équipe a gagné car elle a <u>mieux</u> joué que nous.

(h) <u>Demain</u>, nous irons voir un film.

2. De temps en temps, je fais du bénévolat dans un musée, en général le samedi, mais quelquefois le dimanche. Récemment, j'ai dû parler poliment avec des visiteurs qui se comportaient mal et qui parlaient trop fort (bruyamment). Normalement, je ne dois jamais parler sévèrement aux visiteurs, mais je suis constamment surpris(e) que les parents ne surveillent pas toujours leurs enfants.

Page 80 Quantifiers and intensifiers
Quick quiz:
(a) beaucoup de – a lot of
très – very
assez – quite
trop – too
un peu – a little
tout à fait – utterly

(b) vraiment – really
tellement – so
tant de – so much
plein de – lots of
de plus en plus – more and more
de moins en moins – fewer and fewer

Questions:
1. (a) <u>Tant</u> de pays en Afrique sont très pauvres. – *So many countries in Africa are very poor.*

(b) Il y avait <u>trop de</u> soleil sur la terrasse. – *There was too much sun on the terrace.*

(c) Il avait <u>juste assez</u> d'argent pour acheter <u>une tranche de</u> pain. – *He had just enough money to buy a slice of bread.*

(d) L'examen était <u>incroyablement</u> dur! – *The exam was incredibly hard!*

(e) Après avoir couru un marathon, elle était <u>complètement</u> épuisée. – *After having run a marathon, she was completely exhausted.*

2. (a) Le film était trop long et tout à fait ennuyeux.

(b) Il y a de moins en moins de gens qui n'ont pas accès à Internet.

(c) Je ne suis pas du tout sûr(e).

(d) J'ai lu pas mal / plusieurs de ses livres.

(e) Après tant d'efforts, il a gagné la course relativement facilement.

(f) Il a commencé à courir de plus en plus vite.

Page 81 Subject and object pronouns
Quick quiz:
1–F **2**–T **3**–T **4**–F **5**–T

Questions:
1. (a) <u>Ils</u> <u>lui</u> donnent un vélo.

(b) <u>Il</u> <u>leur</u> a parlé.

(c) <u>Elle</u> est en train de <u>le</u> lire.

(d) <u>Nous</u> voulons <u>le</u> voir.

(e) Je ne <u>les</u> ai pas achetés.

(f) <u>Il</u> <u>les</u> <u>leur</u> a montrées.

2. (a) Je vais l'acheter la semaine prochaine.

(b) Le serveur lui a donné l'addition.

(c) Le professeur nous a parlé.

(d) Je la lui ai donnée.

(e) Je les ai téléchargées.

Page 82 Stressed and possessive pronouns
Quick quiz:
1. pour lui   **2.** derrière moi

3. avec elles   **4.** c'est à toi

5. sans nous   **6.** chez vous

7. pas eux   **8.** c'est elle

Questions:
1. (a) Leur maison est plus petite que <u>la nôtre</u>. – *Their house is smaller than ours.*

(b) J'ai mon passeport, mais mon frère ne trouve pas <u>le sien</u>. – *I've got my passport but my brother can't find his.*

(c) Elle avait oublié son parapluie, alors elle a emprunté <u>le mien</u>. – *She had forgotten her umbrella so she borrowed mine.*

(d) Mes parents sont gentils. Comment sont <u>les vôtres</u>? – *My parents are kind. What are yours like?*

(e) Ma sœur a de bonnes notes, elles sont meilleures que <u>les miennes</u>. – *My sister has got good marks, they are better than mine.*

2. (a) Il est moins patient que moi.

(b) Ils / Elles sont plus riches que nous.

(c) Mes clés sont ici, mais les leurs sont là-bas.

Page 83 Relative and demonstrative pronouns
Quick quiz:
1. celui

2. ceux

3. celle

4. Celles-ci

Questions:
1. (a) Voici l'église <u>où</u> mes parents se sont mariés. – *Here is the church where my parents were / got married.*

(b) Où est la fille <u>qui</u> a gagné? – *Where is the girl who won?*

(c) C'est le magasin <u>qu'</u>on peut voir à côté de la poste. – *It's the shop you can see next to the post office.*

(d) Le cadeau <u>que</u> j'ai acheté n'était pas trop cher. – *The present I bought was not too expensive.*

(e) Je suis allé voir le film <u>dont</u> il a parlé. – *I went to see the film he talked about.*

(f) L'homme <u>dont</u> la femme travaille dans mon collège est malade. – *The man whose wife works at my school is ill.*

(g) Je ne trouve pas les documents <u>dont</u> j'ai besoin. – *I can't find the documents I need.*

2. (a) C'est l'homme que j'ai vu à la gare.

(b) Le livre dont j'ai besoin n'est pas à la bibliothèque.

(c) C'est la femme qui m'a aidé(e).

(d) L'hôtel où nous avons logé était petit.

Page 84 Pronouns *y* and *en*
Quick quiz:
1. some   **2.** of them   **3.** any

4. of it   **5.** it

Questions:
1. (a) J'y vais en bus.

(b) Je m'en souviens.

(c) Je vais en acheter.

(d) Nous y passons une semaine.

(e) Il y a participé.

(f) Je n'y ai pas pensé.

2. (a) Voici le fromage. Tu en veux (Vous en voulez) encore?

(b) Est-ce que tu es (vous êtes) allé(e) en France? – Oui, j'y suis allé(e) la semaine dernière.

(c) Est-ce qu'il participe aux activités extrascolaires? – Oui, il y participe le lundi.

(d) Est-ce qu'elle a répondu à son e-mail? – Oui, elle y a répondu hier.

(e) Voudriez-vous (Voudrais-tu) du lait avec votre (ton) thé? – Oui, j'en voudrais beaucoup.

Page 85 Conjunctions and connectives
Quick quiz:
(a) ensuite – then
et – and
ou – or
si – if
lorsque – when

(b) à cause de – because of
afin de – in order to
pourtant – however
sinon – otherwise
y compris – including

Questions:
1. (a) *ou* – Do you want to go to the cinema this evening or stay at home?

(b) *pendant que* – I listened to music while I was doing my homework.

(c) *donc* – I was ill so I didn't go to school.

(d) *mais* – We wanted to go for a walk but it was raining.

(e) *même si* – I absolutely want to go to this show, even though it is very expensive.

2. (a) Je fais toujours mes devoirs avant de regarder la télé.

(b) Quand nous sommes allé(e)s en France, nous avons visité beaucoup de musées.

(c) Comme je me suis réveillé(e) en retard, je ne suis pas arrivé(e) au collège / à l'école à l'heure.

(d) À mon avis, les émissions de télé-réalité sont amusantes. Cependant, mes parents ne sont pas d'accord.

(e) Je pense que le problème le plus grave est le réchauffement de la Terre tandis que mon ami(e) pense que c'est le déboisement.

Page 86 The present tense
Quick quiz:
1. visitez   **2.** mangeons

3. envoie   **4.** jettent

5. achète   **6.** commençons

7. lève   **8.** emploies

Questions:
1. (a) Ils <u>réagissent</u> très vite. – *They react very quickly.*

(b) On <u>vend</u> des magazines au kiosque. – *They sell magazines at the kiosk.*

(c) Le train <u>ralentit</u>. – *The train is slowing down / slows down.*

(d) Nous <u>choisissons</u> des cadeaux. – *We are choosing some gifts / presents.*

(e) Je ne <u>dors</u> pas bien. – *I don't sleep well.*

(f) Mon frère <u>écrit</u> tous les jours à sa copine. – *My brother writes to his girlfriend every day.*

(g) Ils <u>lisent</u> le journal. – *They read / are reading the (news) paper.*

(h) Normalement, je <u>prends</u> un café. – *Normally I have a coffee.*

2. (a) J'envoie des textos / SMS à mes amis tous les jours.

(b) Normalement, nous faisons une promenade (randonnée) le matin.

(c) Je ne le connais pas très bien.

(d) Qu'est-ce que vous buvez?

(e) J'apprends le français depuis cinq ans.

(f) Nous allons au cinéma aujourd'hui.

Page 87 Key verbs
Quick quiz:
1. to be afraid
2. to be right
3. to need
4. to want
5. to be thirsty
6. to be hungry
7. to agree
8. to be in the process (of doing)

Questions:
1. (a) Cet été, nous (voulons) aller en Espagne. – *We want to go to Spain in the summer.*

(b) Je (pourrais) améliorer mon français. – *I could improve my French.*

(c) On (doit) respecter le règlement scolaire. – *We / you must obey the school rules.*

(d) Nous (devons) partir quand il fait jour. – *We must (have to) leave when it is light.*

(e) Ils (veulent) faire grève la semaine prochaine. – *They want to go on strike next week.*

(f) Je ne (dois) pas faire de bêtises. *I must not do anything stupid.*

(g) Ils (peuvent) venir avec nous. *They can come with us.*

2. (a) Il veut faire une fête ce week-end.

(b) Je ne peux pas venir demain.

(c) Il n'est pas d'accord avec moi.

(d) On peut voir beaucoup de sites touristiques à Paris.

(e) Pouvez-vous (Peux-tu) m'aider?

(f) Hier soir, j'ai dû faire mes bagages.

(g) Mes parents veulent aller en Italie.

(h) Je voulais rester chez moi (à la maison).

Page 88 The perfect tense
Quick quiz:
1. a
2. avons
3. êtes
4. ai
5. as
6. sont
7. est
8. est
9. a
10. sommes
11. ont
12. ai

Questions:
1. (a) avons mangé
(b) j'ai choisi
(c) avons fait
(d) j'ai mis
(e) a bu
(f) a écrit
(g) sont allés
(h) je suis venu(e)
(i) sommes arrivé(e)s
(j) as lu
(k) as perdu
(l) ont vu
(m) est tombée

2. Hier, j'ai fait beaucoup de choses. Le matin, je suis allé(e) en ville et j'ai acheté

des magazines. J'ai déjeuné dans un petit café avec mes ami(e)s et ensuite (après ça), nous avons (on a) joué au foot. Un(e) de mes ami(e)s est tombé(e) et nous avons dû appeler une ambulance. On l'a emmené(e) à l'hôpital et il / elle y a passé la nuit.

Page 89 The imperfect tense
Quick quiz:
1. (préparait)
2. (étais) (voulais)
3. (attendions)
4. (avait) (faisait)

Questions:
1. (a) habitais – *I used to live in a small house.*

(b) mangeait – *She didn't use to eat fish.*

(c) finissaient – *Lessons used to finish early.*

(d) apprenions – *We had been learning French for four years.*

(e) venait – *He had just arrived.*

2. (a) Ma sœur n'aimait pas les bananes.

(b) Je venais de finir mes devoirs quand le téléphone a sonné.

(c) Nous faisions une promenade dans le parc quand il a commencé (s'est mis) à neiger.

(d) Ils / Elles préparaient le dîner pendant que je mettais la table.

(e) Il travaillait à la banque depuis deux ans.

(f) Il faisait beau quand nous étions en vacances.

Page 90 The pluperfect tense
Quick quiz:
1. j'avais pensé
2. elle était allée
3. ils avaient vu
4. nous avions dit
5. vous aviez mangé
6. ils étaient partis

Questions:
1. Un jour mon frère est arrivé à l'école en retard parce qu'il ne s'était pas réveillé à l'heure. Puis, il avait raté le bus et il avait dû aller au collège à pied. Le directeur s'était fâché et l'avait puni. Mon frère ne pouvait pas sortir à la récré et il était resté dans la salle de classe. Avant ce jour-là, il n'avait jamais eu de problèmes à l'école.

One day, my brother arrived late to school because he hadn't woken up on time. Then, he had missed the bus and had had to walk. The headteacher had got angry and had punished him. My brother couldn't go out at break time and had stayed in the classroom. Before that day he had never had any problems at school.

2. (a) Avant de visiter Paris, je n'étais jamais allé(e) en France.

(b) Nous n'avions pas pu boire de thé parce que ma mère avait oublié d'acheter du lait.

(c) Elle ne pouvait pas bien marcher parce qu'elle s'était cassé la jambe.

(d) Je voulais faire du shopping mais j'avais perdu mon portefeuille.

(e) Il m'a dit qu'il n'avait pas lu le texto / SMS que j'avais envoyé.

Page 91 The immediate future tense
Quick quiz:
1. demain soir
2. cet après-midi
3. mardi prochain
4. dans dix jours

Questions:
1. (a) Je vais voir mes cousins. – *I am going to see my cousins.*

(b) Il va pleuvoir. – *It is going to rain.*

(c) Il va faire chaud. – *It is going to be hot.*

(d) Nous allons nous réveiller tôt. – *We are going to wake up early.*

(e) Ils vont choisir le menu pour la fête. – *They are going to choose the menu for the party.*

(f) Est-ce que tu vas acheter des souvenirs? – *Are you going to buy souvenirs?*

2. (a) Qu'est-ce que tu vas faire la semaine prochaine?

(b) Je pense qu'il va faire froid ce week-end.

(c) Où est-ce que vous allez passer vos vacances cette année?

(d) Ils / Elles vont s'amuser sur la plage.

(e) Ma sœur va partir de bonne heure demain matin.

(f) Nous allons regarder un film vendredi.

Page 92 The future tense
Quick quiz:
1. avoir
2. être
3. recevoir
4. faire
5. envoyer
6. pouvoir
7. devenir
8. aller
9. voir
10. savoir

Questions:
1. (a) vous ferez
(b) elle aura
(c) tu prendras
(d) nous choisirons
(e) vous irez
(f) mes amis seront
(g) Mathieu achètera
(h) je jetterai
(i) ils reviendront
(j) j'emploierai

2. (a) Est-ce que tu le verras demain?

(b) Si j'ai de la chance, je gagnerai au loto.

(c) Il n'achètera rien.

(d) Nous devrons prendre le bus.

(e) Ils / Elles iront au théâtre ce soir.

(f) Est-ce que vous ferez du vélo ce week-end?

(g) S'il fait beau demain, nous irons faire un pique-nique.

Page 93 The conditional
Quick quiz:
1. (ferais)
2. (pourrais)
3. (aurait)
4. (parlerions)

Questions:

1. **(a)** voudrais – *I would like to visit the museum.*

   (b) pourriez – *Could you help me?*

   (c) devrait – *One ought to go to bed early.*

   (d) irions – *We would go to Italy.*

   (e) achèterais – *I would buy some souvenirs.*

   (f) seraient – *They would be happy.*

   (g) voudrais – *What would you like to do?*

   (h) conseillerais – *I would advise you to phone (ring).*

   (i) dirais – *I would say he is wrong.*

   (j) aurait – *One / we wouldn't have the time.*

2. Si j'étais très riche, j'aimerais (je voudrais) habiter dans une grande maison. Il y aurait dix chambres et une piscine énorme. Mes ami(e)s (copains / copines) viendraient me voir et nous nous détendrions (on se détendrait) dans le jardin ou nous ferions (on ferait) de l'équitation. S'il faisait beau, nous pourrions (on pourrait) faire des randonnées (promenades).

Page 94 Negative forms
Quick quiz:
1. never
2. no longer / not anymore
3. neither ... nor
4. no one / not anyone / nobody
5. only / nothing but
6. hardly / scarcely

Questions:
1. **(a)** Le chinois n'est pas difficile.

   (b) Il ne parle pas clairement.

   (c) Nous ne le comprenons pas très bien.

   (d) Je n'achète pas de provisions.

   (e) Nous n'avons pas mangé de bonne heure.

   (f) On ne va pas faire de courses demain.

2. **(a)** Je n'ai plus de lait.

   (b) Je n'ai qu'une bouteille d'eau.

   (c) Nous ne faisons rien ce soir. / On ne fait rien ce soir.

   (d) Ils / Elles n'ont jamais gagné au loto.

   (e) Personne n'est venu à la fête.

   (f) Je n'aime ni les pommes ni les poires.

   (g) Mon père ne travaille plus.

   (h) Nous ne sommes pas allé(e)s au musée. / On n'est pas allé(e)s au musée.

   (i) Il n'y est pas resté.

   (j) Je ne veux pas sortir ce soir.

Page 95 Reflexive verbs
Quick quiz:
1. je me lève
2. ils se disputent
3. nous nous reposons
4. tu t'ennuies

5. vous vous inquiétez
6. mes amies s'entendent

Questions:
1. **(a)** Je me suis excusé(e) pour le retard.

   (b) Ma sœur s'est assise près de la fenêtre.

   (c) Ils se sont bien entendus avec leurs amis.

   (d) Nous nous sommes disputé(e)s de temps en temps avec nos parents.

   (e) Mes copines se sont fâchées avec lui.

   (f) Luc et David ne se sont pas amusés au parc d'attractions.

   (g) Elle s'est brossé les dents.

2. Il fait très beau et très chaud, et la mer est bleue! Il y a beaucoup de gens sur la plage, et ils ont des serviettes et des parasols de toutes les couleurs / multicolores. La plupart des gens se bronzent et se relaxent sur la plage mais quelques-uns nagent et s'amusent dans l'eau.

   Normalement, nous allons dans le sud de la France. L'année dernière, je me suis baigné(e) dans la mer mais cette année, je voudrais faire de la voile avec mes parents. On ne se dispute jamais quand on est en vacances.

Page 96 The imperative
Quick quiz:
1. fais
2. travaille
3. va
4. mangeons
5. soyez
6. réveillez-vous

Questions:
(a) Sors de la gare et tourne à gauche.

(b) Allons au théâtre.

(c) Ne m'attendez pas.

(d) Lève-toi de bonne heure / tôt demain matin.

(e) Mangeons maintenant.

(f) Ne soyez pas en retard.

(g) Choisissez un plat et un dessert.

2. To protect the environment, buy products without packaging. Separate rubbish and recycle it as much as possible. Switch off the lights when you leave a room, and if no one is at home turn down the central heating. Go on foot or by bike for short journeys. Don't forget to encourage others to take the same measures.

Page 97 Impersonal verbs
Quick quiz:
1. it's freezing
2. it is cold
3. there will be
4. you only have to
5. it's about
6. it seems

Questions:
1. **(a)** il fera beau – *I think it will be fine tomorrow.*

   (b) Il n'est pas facile d' – *It's not easy to learn this language.*

   (c) il faut – *In my opinion, we must find solutions to this problem.*

   (d) il vaut mieux – *We / you can go there by bus, but it's best to take the train.*

   (e) Il s'agit de – *It's about the First World War.*

   (f) Il suffit de – *You only have to follow the recipe.*

2. **(a)** Il a neigé pendant les vacances.

   (b) Il n'y avait plus de lait.

   (c) Il faut partir de bonne heure.

   (d) Il s'agissait de son enfance passée en Espagne.

   (e) Il y avait une centaine de participants.

   (f) Il est important de faire de l'exercice régulièrement.

Page 98 The infinitive
Quick quiz:
1. de	**2.** à	**3.** de
4. à	**5.** à / de	**6.** de
7. à	**8.** de	**9.** à
10. à	**11.** à	**12.** de

Questions:
1. **(a)** pleuvoir – *It's beginning to rain.*

   (b) apprendre – *I have just learnt some new words.*

   (c) voir – *We will go to the museum to see the new exhibition.*

   (d) acheter – *I tried to buy some souvenirs for my family.*

   (e) avoir joué – *After having played (After playing) tennis, they were very tired.*

   (f) être arrivés – *Having arrived at school, we went to our classroom.*

2. **(a)** D'habitude, mon frère fait ses devoirs avant de regarder la télé.

   (b) Il a décidé de jouer au tennis au lieu de faire de la natation.

   (c) Je vais en Espagne pour perfectionner / améliorer mon espagnol.

   (d) Nous préférerions passer nos vacances au bord de la mer.

   (e) Après être sorties en retard, les filles ont raté le bus.

   (f) Après avoir fini de manger, il a quitté la salle (pièce) sans dire au revoir.

   (g) J'aimais jouer au foot.

   (h) Mon petit frère adore lire.

   (i) Il a oublié d'envoyer une carte d'anniversaire à sa grand-mère.

Page 99 The present participle
Quick quiz:
1. finissant	**2.** travaillant	**3.** étant
4. écrivant	**5.** buvant	**6.** ayant
7. disant	**8.** faisant	**9.** sachant

Questions:
1. **(a)** En cherchant dans sa chambre, il a trouvé ses clés.

   (b) Il a fait ses devoirs en mangeant un sandwich.

   (c) En voyant l'accident, nous nous sommes arrêtés immédiatement.

   (d) Elle s'est cassé la jambe en tombant sur le trottoir.

(e) N'ayant pas beaucoup d'argent, je ne suis pas allé(e) en ville avec mes ami(e)s.

2. My friend got into shape by eating fewer carbohydrates and less fat, by drinking eight glasses of water a day and by doing a lot of exercise. On the other hand, I did it by going jogging every morning, by having smaller portions at dinner and by avoiding chocolate.

Page 100 The passive voice
Quick quiz:
1 ✓; 3 ✓; 4 ✓
Questions:
1. (a) a été construit – *The Grand Palais hotel was constructed / built in 1900.*

(b) a été détruit – *It was destroyed by a fire in 2012.*

(c) no passive

(d) est servi – *In the new hotel, breakfast is served from 7 o'clock.*

(e) doivent être libérées – *The rooms must be vacated before midday.*

(f) seront nettoyées – *The rooms will be cleaned by the staff during the day.*

(g) no passive

2. Martinique was discovered by Christopher Columbus in 1502. In 1635, the island was occupied by some French people and a colony was established. Now, it is administered as an overseas department and is inhabited by nearly four hundred thousand people. The former capital of Saint Pierre was destroyed by a volcanic eruption in 1902 and the capital was moved to Fort-de-France.

Page 101 The subjunctive mood
Quick quiz:
il faut que – it is necessary that

afin que – in order that

bien que – although

jusqu'à ce que – until

Questions:
1. bien que la maison ne nous <u>appartienne</u> plus – *although the house doesn't belong to us any more*

Mais il faut que ce <u>soit</u> tout de suite. – *But it has to be straight away.*

Il faut que je le <u>voie</u>, que je lui <u>parle</u>, qu'il me <u>pardonne</u> et que je <u>répare</u> tout… – *I have to see him, to talk to him, he has to forgive me and I have to make up with him.*

2. (a) I want you to come and see me tomorrow.

(b) I must write to him and do it immediately.

(c) I will wait until you are ready.

(d) Although he is afraid of heights, he will go up the tower.

(e) It seems that he knows the truth.

Page 102 Practice paper: Listening (Foundation)
1. Safia – F; Guy – E; Djamila – D

2. (i) B   **(ii)** D   **(iii)** B

3. B; G; A

4. (a) She likes the huge choice of things to buy online.

(b) Disadvantage is that it takes time to find the best prices.

(c) He thinks online shopping is practical for people living in rural areas.

(d) He had to send jeans back that were too small.

5. C; E; F

6. (a) deuxième   **(b)** devenue

(c) vélo   **(d)** ambitieuse

(e) souffrir

Page 104 Practice paper: Speaking (Foundation)
Role play (Model answer)

1. *Bonjour. Je peux vous aider?*

Je voudrais une chambre pour deux personnes.

2. *Très bien, et vous désirez quelle sorte de chambre?*

Je voudrais une chambre avec balcon et vue sur le parc.

3. *D'accord. Vous voulez rester combien de temps?*

Je voudrais rester deux nuits.

4. *Pas de problème. Qu'est-ce que vous aimez faire en ville?*

J'aime visiter les musées parce que c'est intéressant.

Il y a beaucoup de musées dans notre ville.

5. *À quelle heure est-ce que le restaurant est ouvert le soir?*

De sept heures à dix heures et demie.

Picture-based task (Model answer)

Décris-moi la photo.

● Sur la photo il y a des ados qui regardent leurs portables. Je pense qu'ils envoient des textos ou surfent sur Internet. Je pense qu'il fait beau temps parce qu'ils portent tous un jean et un tee-shirt ou une chemise.

Que penses-tu des réseaux sociaux?

● À mon avis les réseaux sociaux sont super parce qu'on peut rester en contact avec ses amis. Mon réseau social préféré est Instagram parce que j'aime prendre et partager des photos.

Comment est-ce que tu as utilisé ton portable hier?

● Hier j'ai utilisé mon portable pour envoyer des textos à mes copains et pour écouter de la musique.

Que fais-tu d'habitude sur Internet?

● Normalement j'utilise Internet pour faire mes devoirs car je dois quelquefois faire des recherches. J'aime aussi télécharger des films et de la musique.

Quel est ton site internet préféré? Pourquoi?

● Je n'ai pas de site préféré mais en général j'aime tous les réseaux sociaux parce que j'adore tchatter avec mes amis. Je pense

que Wikipédia est très utile pour les devoirs mais mes profs ne l'aiment pas!

Conversation (Possible questions and answers)

Theme: Future aspirations, study and work; **Topic:** School

Quelle est ta matière préférée?

● J'adore la chimie parce que je la trouve facile et intéressante. En fait j'aime toutes les sciences parce que les profs sont vraiment géniaux.

Et la matière que tu détestes le plus?

● Je déteste l'histoire parce que le prof est nul et je pense que c'est une matière ennuyeuse.

Qu'est-ce que tu as fait au collège hier?

● Hier j'ai eu cours en maths, anglais et sciences le matin. Pendant la récré j'ai bavardé avec mes copains et on a mangé à la cantine.

Qu'est-ce que tu vas étudier l'an prochain?

● L'an prochain je vais étudier les sciences parce que je veux être médecin. On doit étudier ces matières pour avoir une place à l'université.

Que penses-tu des langues?

● Je pense que les langues comme le français, l'espagnol et l'allemand sont importantes, mais je suis faible en langues alors je ne les aime pas tellement. Et vous? Est-ce que les langues sont importantes à votre avis?

Theme: Local area, holiday and travel; **Topic:** Town, region and country

Parle-moi de ta maison et ton quartier?

● J'habite une assez grande maison dans un quartier très tranquille. J'aime bien y habiter parce qu'il y a beaucoup d'arbres et d'espaces vertes.

Comment es-tu venu(e) au collège aujourd'hui?

● Aujourd'hui je suis venu(e) en voiture avec mon père parce qu'on était en retard, mais normalement je viens à pied.

Qu'est-ce qu'il y a pour les jeunes dans ta ville?

● Il y a un centre sportif et un cinéma dans ma ville mais les magasins ne sont pas tellement bons.

Qu'est-ce que tu feras dans ta région le week-end prochain?

● Le week-end prochain je ferai une sortie avec ma famille à la campagne. Elle est très pittoresque et on va faire un promenade.

Que penses-tu des transports dans ta ville?

● À mon avis les transports en commun sont assez bons car il y a des bus et trains fréquents. Cependant les billets sont chers!

Page 105 Practice paper: Reading (Foundation)
1. (a) Fabrice   **(b)** Jérôme

(c) Sandrine   **(d)** Fabrice

2. (a) Easter   **(b)** supermarket

(c) online   **(d)** rabbit

(e) 19%

3. (a) She doesn't think much of TV reality shows. / They are a waste of time. / She has no interest in them.

(b) She watches catch-up TV. / She doesn't have time to watch programmes when they are broadcast. / She watches on her tablet. (any 2)

4. (a) (last) Wednesday (1) at 8.45 pm / at a quarter to nine in the evening (1)

(b) around the world

(c) 80 days

(d) he only met Phileas Fogg on the day they left London (1) / which is when he started working for him (1)

5. (i) C   **(ii)** A   **(iii)** B

6. In my school there is a large / big swimming pool (1). I like to swim / go swimming after school (1). Last Saturday (1) I took part in a competition (1). It was exciting (1). During / In the holidays (1), I'm going to revise for my exams (1).

Page 108 Practice paper: Writing (Foundation)

1. (Model answer) C'est le mariage de ma sœur. Elle porte une robe blanche et elle a un bouquet de fleurs. Il y a des gens dans le jardin. J'aime les fêtes en famille parce que tout le monde est heureux.

2. (Model answer)

Monsieur,

Je vais venir en avion de Londres et arriver à Brest dimanche prochain vers 18 heures. Je vais travailler chez vous pendant deux semaines. En général, quand je ne travaille pas, j'aime faire de la natation et du shopping. Le soir, j'aime regarder la télé. Je voudrais travailler en France pour améliorer mon français.

3. (a) (Model answer) C'est bientôt les vacances et moi, j'adore partir à l'étranger parce que j'aime utiliser mes connaissances en langues. Normalement, je pars avec ma famille et nous restons souvent dans un camping parce que c'est moins cher qu'une chambre d'hôtel; on organise des activités comme l'équitation et le canoë-kayak. En hiver, j'aime faire du ski et cette année, je suis parti(e) en voyage scolaire en Italie pendant une semaine. La neige était super et le soir, nous sommes allés manger dans un restaurant typiquement italien. Je voudrais bien passer des vacances en Asie et l'été prochain, je passerai deux semaines en Inde. Je pense que ça sera génial.

(b) (Model answer) Dans mon collège, il y a un choix énorme d'activités culturelles et sportives extrascolaires. Par exemple, les élèves qui aiment la musique peuvent jouer dans l'orchestre ou chanter dans la chorale. Ces activités sont très importantes parce qu'on apprend à travailler en équipe et on développe de nouvelles compétences. Récemment, on a

organisé une journée pour collecter des fonds pour les personnes qui ont été victimes de catastrophes naturelles. On a fait des gâteaux et on a vendu ces gâteaux pendant la récré. Le trimestre prochain, je vais participer à la production théâtrale du collège; on va jouer une pièce de Shakespeare!

4. (a) Ma mère est petite.

(b) J'aime faire la cuisine.

(c) En été, je travaille dans le jardin.

(d) Il y a beaucoup d'arbres dans le parc près de ma maison.

(e) Hier soir, j'ai fait une promenade à la campagne.

Page 109 Practice paper: Listening (Higher)

1. (a) bruyant   **(b)** cher

(c) démodé   **(d)** cher

(e) grand

2. (i) A, D   **(ii)** B, D

(iii) C, A

3. (a) Her parents will take away her phone.

(b) She's glad it's only one day.

(c) You can have real conversations with friends (1). It's good not to be distracted by your phone (1).

4. Alésia – C; Jérôme – E; Charlotte – B

5. (a) There is not enough emergency (temporary) accommodation (1). Winter is approaching and life is hard on the streets (1).

(b) To arrange the meeting point (1). To say what you are going to bring, such as warm clothes or a hot meal (1).

(c) religious beliefs (1)

(d) Must think of others who are less fortunate than yourself (1).

6. (i) B   **(ii)** B

7. (a) There might be fewer tourists (1) because hotels will be too expensive (1).

(b) Those looking for work (1) opportunities in the construction or hospitality sectors (1).

(c) More people will take part in sport.

(d) There will be a lot of noise / disruption during construction.

Page 111 Practice paper: Speaking (Higher)

Role play (Model answer)

1. *Salut, tu fais souvent du shopping?*

Je fais des achats le week-end en ville.

2. *Moi aussi. Que penses-tu des achats en ligne?*

J'aime bien faire des achats en ligne parce que c'est très pratique.

3. *Qu'est-ce que tu as acheté récemment?*

Récemment j'ai acheté un pull bleu en laine.

C'est chouette ça.

4. Qu'est-ce que tu aimes acheter?

Des vêtements et des magazines.

5. Quel est ton magasin préféré?

J'aime bien les grands magasins.

Picture-based task (Model answer)

Décris-moi la photo.

- Sur la photo il y a cinq filles qui sont au collège. Elles portent leur uniforme scolaire, une jupe à carreaux bleus et noirs, une veste bleu foncé et une chemise bleu clair. Je pense qu'elles sont en train d'aller à un cours, car elles portent leurs sacs et dossiers. Elles bavardent et elles ont l'air heureuses.

Que penses-tu du règlement scolaire?

- À mon avis le règlement scolaire est important pour maintenir l'ordre et la discipline. Nous ne devons pas courir dans les couloirs par exemple; ça c'est une règle tout à fait raisonnable car il pourrait être dangereux si tout le monde courait d'un endroit à un autre. Cependant, je ne comprends pas pourquoi la couleur de nos gants en hiver est important, c'est bête!

Qu'est-ce que tu as fait comme activités extrascolaires récemment?

- Je n'ai pas le temps de participer à beaucoup d'activités extrascolaires parce je suis très occupé(e) avec les préparations pour mes examens. Cependant, je suis membre de la chorale et hier nous avons eu une répétition pour un concert la semaine prochaine.

Qu'est-ce que tu feras au collège l'année prochaine?

- L'année prochaine je participerai dans la chorale parce que j'aime bien chanter. Je ferai aussi des visites scolaires au théâtre et aux musées.

Qu'est-ce que tu changerais dans ton collège si tu étais directeur / directrice?

- Si j'étais directeur / directrice je changerais l'uniforme parce que je déteste la couleur de notre uniforme actuel. En plus, je permettrais aux filles de se maquiller et de porter des boucles d'oreille.

Conversation (Possible questions and answers)

Theme: Identity and culture; **Topic:** Cultural life

Comment est-ce que tu aimes passer ton temps libre?

- Pendant mon temps libre j'aime me détendre en écoutant de la musique sur mon portable. J'aime toutes sortes de musique, mais celle que je préfère est le pop parce que je trouve les rythmes très accrocheurs. Parfois j'utilise des services de streaming, mais aussi je télécharge des chansons de mes groupes et chanteurs préférés.

Quel genre de film est-ce que tu aimes regarder?

- J'adore les comédies romantiques parce que je les trouve divertissantes. Cependant, j'aime aussi les adaptations cinématographiques des livres car elles m'encouragent à lire le livre. D'autre part je déteste les films d'horreur parce qu'ils me font peur.

Parle-moi d'un livre que tu as lu récemment.

● Récemment j'ai lu un roman historique que j'ai trouvé très captivant. L'action a eu lieu en France pendant la Première Guerre mondiale et il s'agissait d'un soldat blessé sur le champ de bataille qui est tombé amoureux de la femme qui le soignait. C'est un livre que je recommanderais.

Qu'est-ce que tu feras ce week-end?

● Ce week-end j'irai en ville pour voir la nouvelle exposition sur l'histoire de notre ville au musée. Je pense que ça sera très intéressant. L'après-midi je rencontrerai mes amis au café et ensuite nous irons au parc parce qu'il y aura un feu d'artifice le soir. J'adore les feux d'artifice parce qu'ils sont pleins de couleurs.

Theme: Local area, holiday and travel; **Topic:** Town, region and country

Décris la ville/le village où tu habites.

● J'habite dans une ville de cent-mille habitants non loin de Londres. Dans ma ville, il y a beaucoup de choses à faire et à voir comme le musée, les ruines de la ville ancienne et la cathédrale. Si on veut sortir le soir, il y a un cinéma et un théâtre ainsi que beaucoup de restaurants où on peut déguster la cuisine de toutes les régions du monde.

Que penses-tu des transports dans ta région?

● À mon avis, les transports en commun sont excellents dans ma ville parce qu'on peut aller facilement à Londres en train, un trajet d'une vingtaine de minutes. En plus, on n'est pas loin des autoroutes et des aéroports.

Quels sont les avantages de vivre en ville?

● Je pense que c'est bien de vivre en ville parce que c'est plus facile de faire des achats et il y a toujours beaucoup de choses à faire. Cependant, la ville peut être plus bruyante et polluée que la campagne où la vie est plus calme et lente. Où est-ce que vous voudriez vivre?

Moi, je voudrais vivre à la campagne parce que c'est plus tranquille. Qu'est-ce que tu as fait dans ta ville/ton village le week-end dernier?

● Le week-end dernier, j'ai rencontré mes copains/copines en ville. Après avoir bu un café, nous sommes allé(e)s voir une nouvelle exposition au musée. Ensuite, nous sommes allés au cinéma voir un film qui était vraiment amusant. On a ri tout le temps!

Qu'est-ce tu voudrais changer dans ta ville/ton village? Pourquoi?

● Ce que je voudrais faire pour changer ma ville, c'est créer un skate-park pour les jeunes parce qu'en ce moment, il n'y a rien pour ceux qui aiment faire du skate. Ça serait génial d'avoir aussi un meilleur marché de Noël en décembre. Celui qui a lieu chaque année est trop petit. Je pense

que l'année prochaine, il faudra plus de chalets avec une plus grande variété de marchandises.

Page 112 Practice paper: Reading (Higher)

1. **(a)** Solange **(b)** Malik
   (c) Ria **(d)** André
   (e) use as an alarm clock
   (f) being able to take and share photos

2. **(a)** She has to prepare the breakfast for her brothers.
   (b) eats / rests / goes home / helps her mother (in the kitchen).
   (c) Classes of 50 / no books / not enough tables / pupils squashed together on benches (any 2).
   (d) She thinks it's important.
   (e) You improve your chances in life.
   (f) They have to work in the fields / get married.

3. **(a)** She is homeless.
   (b) Some teachers might be aware of her situation.
   (c) She is very tired / she sometimes falls asleep in class.
   (d) Her mother lost her job.
   (e) Being ignored by passers-by.

4. B; C; G

5. **(i)** C **(ii)** D **(iii)** A

6. **(a)** Elle s'est probablement sentie malheureuse / triste / déprimée.
   (b) Des insultes racistes.
   (c) Elle a pu voyager en Afrique pour voir sa famille. / On fête deux traditions religieuses chez elle.
   (d) Elle est tolérante. / Elle n'a pas de préjugés.

7. I am looking forward to your visit to us in a fortnight / two weeks (1). My parents and I have thought about what we could / what activities we could do (1) during the week of your stay (1). If the weather is fine on the Sunday (1) it would be great to go to the theme park (1) near here (1). If not, it would be better to go roller skating (1). Before you arrive / your arrival (1) I have to finish a project for school (1).

Page 115 Practice paper: Writing (Higher)

1. **(a)** (Model answer) Salut! Pendant mon temps libre, j'adore écouter toutes sortes de musiques mais mon genre préféré est la musique classique parce que ça m'aide à me concentrer quand je travaille. Le samedi après-midi, après avoir fait les courses et les tâches ménagères, nous faisons souvent une promenade à la campagne en famille. Samedi dernier, il pleuvait et le soir je suis allé(e) voir un film d'action au cinéma. C'était vraiment passionnant et je le recommanderais à mes copains. Pendant les vacances scolaires, je vais

faire un stage de peinture au club de jeunes. J'apprendrai de nouvelles techniques et nous visiterons aussi des musées d'art.
Bisous…

(b) (Model answer) Salut! En ce moment, je suis en vacances avec ma famille au bord de la mer. Nous avons loué une belle maison avec vue sur la plage. Devant la maison, il y a une petite terrasse où nous pouvons déjeuner. Pendant notre séjour, j'ai fait un stage de voile et l'après-midi, j'ai nagé dans la mer après m'être bronzé sur la plage. J'aime bien les vacances où on peut faire des activités différentes chaque jour. L'année prochaine, j'irai en vacances avec mes copains. Nous avons choisi un centre de loisirs où nous pourrons faire des sports un peu extrêmes comme l'escalade et le rafting. Je crois que ce sera formidable!
Bisous…

2. **(a)** (Model answer) Tout le monde aime les fêtes, que ce soit les fêtes de famille ou les fêtes religieuses, locales ou nationales. Récemment, nous avons fêté le cinquantième anniversaire de mariage de mes grands-parents. Mes parents avaient réservé une salle dans un bon restaurant qui se trouve dans un endroit très pittoresque à la campagne. À notre arrivée vers midi et demi, on nous a offert un verre de champagne et on a parlé avec les autres invités. Mon père a fait un petit discours et ensuite, on s'est mis à table pour un déjeuner délicieux. Après avoir mangé, nous sommes sortis dans le joli parc pour faire une petite promenade. C'était une journée tout à fait géniale.

À mon avis, les fêtes sont très importantes car c'est une chance pour les gens de se réunir et de s'amuser. En décembre mes grands-parents viendront chez nous pour fêter Noël. J'achèterai des cadeaux pour mes proches et on aura des spécialités à manger et à boire. Noël est vraiment ma fête préférée de l'année.

(b) (Model answer) Suite au récent tremblement de terre en Asie, notre collège a organisé une journée pour collecter des fonds au profit des personnes touchées par cet événement. On nous a encouragés à venir au collège avec nos propres vêtements au lieu de porter notre uniforme scolaire. Nous pouvions le faire après avoir donné de l'argent pour aider les victimes de cette catastrophe; la plupart des élèves ont participé à cette initiative. Pendant la récré, plusieurs élèves ont vendu des biscuits et des petits gâteaux qu'ils avaient faits en cours de cuisine. La semaine prochaine d'autres élèves donneront un concert qui aura lieu pendant la pause-déjeuner.

Je pense que les actions caritatives sont vraiment importantes dans notre société parce qu'il existe plein de bonnes causes et que de nombreuses personnes ont besoin d'aide. En effet, il faut penser à ceux qui n'ont pas les mêmes chances que nous dans la vie. On peut aider en collectant des fonds ou de manière pratique, par exemple en servant un repas chaud aux sans-abri.

3. Beaucoup de gens aiment vivre (habiter) dans ma ville (1) parce qu'on peut faire (1) de longues promenades dans le grand parc (1). J'habitais dans le centre-ville (1) mais l'an dernier (1), nous avons (on a) déménagé (1) en banlieue (1). Le mois prochain (1), mon oncle va venir nous voir (nous rendre visite) (1) et nous irons au théâtre (1). Je préférerais (1) voir une comédie (1).

Published by BBC Active, an imprint of Educational Publishers LLP, part of the Pearson Education Group, 80 Strand, London, WC2R 0RL.

www.pearsonschools.com/BBCBitesize
© Educational Publishers LLP 2019
BBC logo © BBC 1996. BBC and BBC Active are trademarks of the British Broadcasting Corporation.

Typeset by Newgen KnowledgeWorks Pvt. Ltd., Chennai, India
Produced and illustrated by Newgen Publishing UK
Cover design by Andrew Magee & Pearson Education Limited 2019
Cover illustration by Darren Lingard / Oxford Designers & Illustrators

The right of Liz Fotheringham to be identified as author of this work has been asserted by her in accordance with the Copyright, Designs and Patents Act 1988.

First published 2019

22 21 20 19
10 9 8 7 6 5 4 3 2 1

British Library Cataloguing in Publication Data
A catalogue record for this book is available from the British Library.

ISBN 978 1 406 68590 9

Printed and bound in Slovakia by Neografia.

The Publisher's policy is to use paper manufactured from sustainable forests.

Notes from the publisher
1. While the publishers have made every attempt to ensure that advice on the qualification and its assessment is accurate, the official specification and associated assessment guidance materials are the only authoritative source of information and should always be referred to for definitive guidance.
Pearson examiners have not contributed to any sections in this resource relevant to examination papers for which they have responsibility.

2. Pearson has robust editorial processes, including answer and fact checks, to ensure the accuracy of the content in this publication, and every effort is made to ensure this publication is free of errors. We are, however, only human, and occasionally errors do occur. Pearson is not liable for any misunderstandings that arise as a result of errors in this publication, but it is our priority to ensure that the content is accurate. If you spot an error, please do contact us at resourcescorrections@pearson.com so we can make sure it is corrected.

Acknowledgements
The author and publisher would like to thank the following individuals and organisations for their kind permission to reproduce copyright material.

Text Credit(s):
BBC: 1-6, 8-10, 12-18, 20-22, 24-28, 30, 32-38, 41-44, 47-48, 51, 59, 70-99 © 2019; **France Bleu:** Le Guen, V 'Les Français préfèrent Noël au Nouvel an', © France Bleu, 2016, 17. Estate of Antoine de Saint-Exupery *Le Petit Prince* © 1943, 63.

Photographs
(Key: t-top; b-bottom; c-centre; l-left; r-right)
123RF: Sergey Novikov 24, Sarah Nicholl 95; **Alamy Stock Photo:** Leclercq Olivier/ Hemis 18; **Shutterstock:** Misha Beliy 08, PlusONE 27, Pressmaster 30, Feel good studio 31, Africa Studio 33, Shutterstock 44, Halfpoint 45, Joseph Sohm 49, Wavebreakmedia 53t, Ekaterina Pokrovsky 53b, Bellena 68, Shutterstock 72, Syda Productions 74, Oneinchpunch 104, Halfpoint 108, DGLimages 111.

All other images © Pearson Education

Websites
Pearson Education Limited is not responsible for the content of third-party websites.